K-pop
Live

K-pop Live

FANS, IDOLS, AND MULTIMEDIA PERFORMANCE

Suk-Young Kim

STANFORD UNIVERSITY PRESS • STANFORD, CALIFORNIA

Stanford University Press
Stanford, California

Printed in the United States of America on acid-free, archival-quality paper

Library of Congress Cataloging-in-Publication Data
Names: Kim, Suk-Young, 1970– author.
Title: K-pop live : fans, idols, and multimedia performance / Suk-Young Kim.
Description: Stanford, California : Stanford University Press, 2018. |
   Includes bibliographical references and index.
Identifiers: LCCN 2017050970 | ISBN 9781503605039 (cloth : alk. paper) |
   ISBN 9781503605992 (pbk. : alk. paper) | ISBN 9781503606005 (epub)
Subjects: LCSH: Popular music—Korea (South)—History and criticism. |
   Popular music—Performances—Korea (South) | Concerts—Korea (South) |
   Music and technology—Korea (South)
Classification: LCC ML3502.K6 K577 2018 | DDC 781.63095195—dc23
LC record available at https://lccn.loc.gov/2017050970

Typeset by Bruce Lundquist in 10/14 Minion Pro

For Miles, the Rising Star

CONTENTS

NOTES ON THE TEXT

1. For transliteration of Korean words, I will consistently use the official Korean-language romanization system released by South Korea's Ministry of Culture and Tourism in 2000, also referred to as Revised Romanization of Korean. Exceptions are made for proper names well known in the English-speaking world by alternate romanizations (e.g., Park Chung-hee rather than Bak Jeong-hui); for authors who have published their names in alternate romanizations (e.g., Kim Suk-Young rather than Gim Suk-yeong); and for performers who deliberately use alternate romanizations for their names (e.g., Lee Hi rather than Yi Ha-i). In the case of these exceptions, the Official Romanization of Korean appears in parentheses after the first occurrence of the term.

2. For East Asian names, surnames precede given names according to the convention of the home country; hence East Asian names appear with the surname first (e.g., Lee Su-man, not Su-man Lee; Ueno Toshiya, not Toshiya Ueno).

3. For the combination of Anglicized first names and Korean last names, the first and the second rules do not apply (e.g., Edward Kang rather than Gang Edward).

4. K-pop band names like BIGBANG or SHINee are mostly left in their own Anglicized spellings, since the groups deliberately use idiosyncratic spellings for professional purposes and are known as such in both Korean and international media.

5. All translations not otherwise credited are my own.

6. When quoting others' work, I use the transliteration system originally chosen by other authors.

K-pop
Live

INTRODUCTION

I know everything is called live now, which really just
means we were all alive when we taped it.
Bill Maher, "Bill Maher Reflects on Humor, Politics in Wild Election"

LOS ANGELES is a city with a thousand faces, a mirage of fragmented impressions, chromatic shades, and sound bites. A major hub where multicultural flows converge, it is a must-stop destination for touring bands from the other side of the Pacific.

EXO, the "it" band of today's K-pop world, is no exception. They performed at the Los Angeles Sports Arena on February 14, 2016, to a nearly sold-out crowd. The arena, with roughly sixteen thousand seats, was overheated with zealous fans hours before the concert began, to the point that at least two audience members in the standing area were carried out on stretchers even before the band appeared on stage. The body heat emanating from sweltering fans and the screams of excitement from the audience provided undeniable proof that I was indeed at a live event, breathing the same air with pop stars whose natural habitat nowadays happens to be two-dimensional pixel screens of TVs, laptops, and cell phones.

K-pop as a cultural phenomenon started to gain momentum around the turn of the millennium, a time when physical album sales were rapidly collapsing while the online music market was still evolving and maturing. The growth of the digital online music market around this time was impeded by prevalent practices of piracy and illegal downloading, which presented serious challenges to artists who had been sustaining their careers through traditional revenue sources, such as CD sales. That model was vanishing for them, while the market for live shows and multicity tours in Korea and overseas was almost nonexistent.

Ironically, such challenging circumstances were the biggest reason for companies to aggressively push K-pop's global reach and expand into foreign markets. But K-pop's global expansion came, not via live world tours, but via music videos, recorded TV music chart shows, and other media promotions that became wildly popular on YouTube and solidified K-pop's reputation as a form of entertainment that thrived predominantly online. The paradigm shift in music consumption also brought about a change in understanding K-pop not just as a sonic genre but as a multimedia performance with a heavy emphasis on visuals.[1] With this process came the reinvention of K-pop artists, who transformed themselves from mere singers to all-around entertainers whose primary career goal was to gain popularity by excelling in all aspects of media performance, such as singing, dancing, being a charming guest on variety shows, and always presenting an attractive public persona, all under the constant scrutiny of the mediatized world.

So if K-pop's ecosystem is the digital media environment, why does this book begin with a scene from a live concert? Why does the main title place "live" after "K-pop," suggesting that the concept of "live" and its abstraction, "liveness," will be the main critical focus?

To be sure, there is evidence that the K-pop industry nowadays is witnessing steady growth in live performances, which could potentially challenge the assumption that K-pop's natural habitat is online. For instance, the highly successful K-pop band BIGBANG's Made tour in 2015–16 ranked as one of the top-ten-grossing tours in the United States in 2015; during the first half of the 2016, BIGBANG became the band to attract the most live concert attendees in Japan, the second-largest music market in the world.[2] Along with BIGBANG, more and more K-pop bands are expanding their tours beyond L.A. and New York City to include a wider range of North American cities, such as Atlanta, Austin, Chicago, Dallas, Honolulu, Houston, Las Vegas, Orlando, Seattle, Toronto, and Vancouver.[3] On other continents, tour and fan meeting stops for K-pop bands include not only such obvious choices as Beijing, London, Paris, and Tokyo but also Auckland, Dusseldorf, Milan, Moscow, and Santiago. No wonder *Billboard* magazine on May 3, 2016, featured an article significantly titled "K-pop Concerts Continue to Grow outside Asia," signaling a growing trend in live K-pop concerts.[4] The article notes how "areas like North America, South America and Europe have all had three consistent years of K-pop concert growth since 2013."[5] Given that Asia has been K-pop's main market for live concerts and online fandom for most of its history, the growing number of live concerts outside Asia could justify this book's focus on live performances as a means of capturing a major change in K-pop's global circulation.[6]

But the book's primary inquiry into K-pop's liveness is not driven merely by the data showing an increasing number of live K-pop concerts. The book is mainly concerned with a more theoretical investigation of "liveness" as a technological, ideological, and affective mode in which human subjects interact with other human and nonhuman subjects in the digital age. We live in an era where it is extremely difficult to be engaged in a social relationship unmediated by digital technology, whether texting, video chat, or immersion in virtual reality; in this heavily mediatized environment, the question of what is live becomes a question of how we live our lives as increasingly mediated subjects—fragmented and isolated by technological wonders while also yearning for a sense of belonging and aliveness through an interactive mode of exchange that we often call "live." Predominantly conceived as digital music but constantly courting the idea of live performance, K-pop is a prime medium to unfold this paradox.

I had eagerly anticipated the EXO live concert, but as it progressed, my sense of the immediacy of "being there" gradually turned into frustration. I had to squint in order to discern through the dense crowd the minuscule bodies of eight performers on stage, all of whom appeared no larger than Tinker Bell from the loge where I was seated (figure 1). My frustration stemmed not only from a middle-aged person's declining vision but also from the betrayed

FIGURE 1. EXO performs in the Los Angeles Memorial Sports Arena on February 14, 2016. Note that the screen projects the image of a crimson curtain to enhance the feeling of a live stage despite poor visibility of the live performers. Photo by Kim Suk-Young.

promise of a live event that was supposed to guarantee the experience of intimacy and copresence. But just as my frustration began to mount, the stage curtain was transformed into a large screen surface for digital projection; as the live performers were taking a break from their strenuous dance routine, magnified faces of the stars started to appear on the screen as if to compensate for the spectatorial limitations of audience members seated far away from the stage. One by one, each member of the band directed his amorous gaze at the camera, looking directly into the eyes of the viewers, whose point of view had became entirely conflated with that of the person behind the camera. Each band member reached out his hand to hold the hand of the cinematographer-cum-audience, transforming a 2-D video screen into an affective interface where thousands of anonymous concert attendees suddenly became positioned as intimate subjects who could touch and interact with these stars.

The eye-level camera angle, often referred to as a point-of-view shot, is quite illustrative of how vision—and the intimate feelings of live interaction with others—are produced in today's YouTube videos. Regardless of the genre, whether amateur review videos of children's toys or professionally produced music videos, this angle is widely used.[7] It produces a sense of touch and interaction despite the two-dimensionality of the images presented on screen. As a way of breaking the fourth wall—the computer screen in this case—the technique assumes a gazing viewer outside the screen whose hands are already featured inside the lower left and right corners of the screen.

The way prefilmed clips of EXO members were transmitted for the consumption of live concert attendees collapses multiple registers of time and space: the filmed subjects from the past literally reach out to viewers of the present, while the filmed space becomes a portal for viewing subjects to escape through as they reach out to grab EXO's hands. Though illusory pixels, the hands touch with an intimate magic that makes viewers' hearts beat faster.

Such haptic illusion, intentionally produced to gesture tactile intimacy, resides within what Eve Kosofsky Sedgwick referred to as texture that is "*liminally registered on the border of properties of touch and vision.*"[8] Much as Sedgwick turns our attention to the crossroads of the senses, art historian Ina Blom, in discussing the work of video artist Paik Nam June (Baek Nam-jun), proposes that technology produces a new kind of tactility and sensibility that can be realized only by means of "haptical and telephatical transmitters."[9] I see K-pop as one of those powerful transmitters of complex sensory entanglement that produces the semblance and verisimilitude of live interaction, and the pursuit of liveness in K-pop performance across media as a way to realize an impression of such synesthetic ideals.[10] Under this premise, this book proposes K-pop as a multimedia performance, since combining multiple sensations to see sound, hear vision, and touch feelings across various times and spaces is a foundational way multimedia performance works.[11] The complexity of such a marriage is enabled by the mediation of technology, and it is especially evidenced in the way multimedia technology produces feelings of intimacy while also producing a sense of fragmentation.

The pervasive use of technology in the K-pop industry conflates seemingly intertwined processes—digitized events actively pursue the aura of live events, while live performances rely heavily on digital technology and are eventually digitized for online consumption—to the point that genuine intimacy and the illusion of intimacy are not always clearly distinguishable. But more significantly, and perhaps more disturbingly, technology not only is a means to visualize, make, and even fake a sense of belonging but often becomes the end of it—the very embodiment of it. Like the Deleuzian characterization of desire as "purely virtual movement whose moving is itself its destination," the use of technology in K-pop productions and consumption is not always subordinate to the instrumental aspect and can become its own autotelic performance—its ultimate intention.[12]

Hence, the mediatization of the live event is not only a phantom-like surplus from the past but also a catalyst for shaping the impressions of a live interaction in the here and now. As we see in the staging of haptic illusion at the EXO live concert, it works along the interface created by the dual forces of what Antonin Artaud saw as "*the virtuality of the possible* and what already exists in materialized nature."[13] Straddling multiple layers of imbrications—community and commerce, the virtual and the material, the local and the global—this book teases out the historical, social, and cultural reasons for K-pop's pursuit of liveness as a specific mode of human contact brought about by a particular media environment that has enabled global connectivity.[14]

In the process, I hope to illuminate how the various manifestations of liveness—including liveliness—present a spectrum of how we experience contacts with other humans as a necessary condition for life. Like the air we breathe, which we do not think of consciously but constantly depend upon, the sensations of liveness emanating from social contact are a significant way of evidencing that one is alive. In this regard, this book is a technologically inflected extension of Daniel Sack's proposal to reach beyond the permutations of copresent performers and spectators that have been a foundational aspect in the conventional discussions on liveness:

> How might live performance intervene as an expansion and troubling of what we mean by living in this new millennium, and who or what gets considered temporally and vitally live? This requires that we open our understanding of liveness to include some of its other connotations, to accentuate its sense of "aliveness" or "liveness."[15]

The easily established affinities between *live* and *alive*—with *live* signifying the mode of copresence as well as durational patterns in everyday life (hence extending *live* to include *living*), and *alive* being the affective manifestations of existence—are more based on deeply ontological affinities that are established by technology than they are linguistic derivatives for each other. K-pop becomes a critical medium to trigger the important question of human existence in the digital age, where the promotion of technology is increasingly becoming its own teleological destination.

What Is K-pop?

More virtual than real in their undeniable resemblance to wide-eyed animation characters, the close-up projection of EXO members' faces sets us free from the limits of natural eyesight; nearly invisible live bodies on stage are transformed into tangible love objects magnified on screen. But as soon as concertgoers start to feel used to the projection, the digital splendor vanishes to commence another set of live performance by EXO—this time featuring heavily choreographed, broad sweeping motions. Although I still cannot see the details of their faces, the vivacious impacts of their bodily movements traverse the vast arena. In this multiethnic crowd, many are in tears and almost everyone screams at each and every gesture, feeling the performers' presence on a kinesthetic level. After all, this is a live event.

As the dramatic choreography continues on stage, I cannot stop thinking about how K-pop is an animal that thrives on excess.[16] The rich tone of the singers' voices harmonizes with the dense texture of their choruses. Its mesmerizing young stars flaunt the celebration of heightened beauty. The oval faces of girls and boys with candy-colored lips and heavy eyelashes glisten under the scorching stage lights. Their impeccably toned bodies sport flashy costumes beaded with sequins and tassels while incessantly showcasing a complex dance routine as the electrifying shriek of a solo vocalist smoothly transitions into the rugged offbeat jamming of rappers.

> K-Pop is scary! . . . If I was an artist in Korea, I'd be nervous. The pace of the popularity of the music is quick. You got one song that can last for a week, and that's it. . . . That's really scary. You put so much work into one song, but yet it's going to get old quick. Korean people want something new every week, and I think that's the hardest pressure, probably. To come up with something catchy all the time, a hit all the time, and you've got tons of artists and the lifespan of one song is so short. It's pretty hard.[17]

As can be seen in this interview with Ellen Kim, a dancer and choreographer based in Los Angeles who has worked with the K-pop industry, K-pop is a fast-evolving machine, producing products that, like Kleenex, are used once and thrown away. In a highly competitive industry like K-pop, little is left to chance. What could come across as spontaneous improvisation on stage is a result of years and years of hard, formulaic practice.

Those who want to make it in the world of K-pop should make dramatic changes in their lifestyle at the dawn of their adolescence.[18] If they are scouted by a talent management agency, which usually doubles as a K-pop training school and at times triples as a record label in the Korean entertainment world, these youngsters voluntarily suspend their private lives and submit themselves to the rules of the company; from smaller sacrifices such as giving up cell phones to bigger ones such as being uprooted from their families to live and train with their potential teammates under the watchful eyes of managers and trainers, they willingly forfeit personal freedom to focus single-mindedly on vocal and dance lessons, learn foreign languages and impeccable stage manners, and prepare themselves for a successful debut. They go on, practicing in obscurity, day after day, night after night, usually sleeping only four to six hours or at times even forgoing sleep altogether, hoping that the hard work and sacrifice will transform them from nameless trainees into megastars.[19] They are prepared to storm the stages of all Asia and steal the hearts of many more beyond the continent. Their songs may be heard in the public squares of Paris, London, Buenos Aires, and Lima, where diehard fans may stage flash mobs to petition their stars to visit their cities.[20]

K-pop fans, especially Korean fans, are also known for their deep involvement in making and breaking K-pop stars' careers. *Idols*, as the performers are often called, is a fitting term to capture the religious fervor that fans display in pursuing their heavily guarded favorites. Many support their stars via phone-in voting where charges apply, which allows them to debut or raise their rank on the music charts.[21] Many purchase multiple copies of their stars' albums to increase sales revenue and gain access to promotional events where their idols make appearances. Some go on to become diehard (*sasaeng*) fans, or the ones who invade stars' lives to get their attention. Some will hire a bullet taxi to chase their stars' vehicles; others will install hidden cameras to monitor stars' lives in their private residences. Even more devious fans will go so far as to send toxic drinks to their stars or send love letters written in menstrual blood, just to be remembered. Even with an understanding that there is a tendency in the Western media to exoticize the relatively lesser-known fandom of a still marginal music scene, K-pop fans are arguably one of the most enthusiastic fan bases in today's popular cultural landscape.[22]

In the broadest sense of the word, *K-pop*, as an abbreviation for Korean popular music, includes all genres of popular music that emerge out of South Korea. The word was first used in 1995 by the Hong Kong media network Channel V to label the Korean music videos that they featured. Obviously, the term was fashioned after *J-pop*, already in wide circulation to designate Japanese pop music that was enjoying its heyday. The V Channel used the term *K-pop* to reference Korean music that was generally popular in Korea rather than idol music, which then was in a nascent state. But in the late 2000s, when the term entered a wide circulation, it came to designate a much smaller fraction of South Korean music. According to pop music critic Choe Ji-seon, it references "music dominated by idols' dance music which strives to gain a competitive edge in the international market. In this respect, indie music or rock, or anything that does not belong to dominant idol music, usually is not characterized as K-pop."[23]

At the same time, as the etymology attests, K-pop is a music scene whose Korean origin and global destination constantly vie to define its identity. Ethnomusicologist Michael Fuhr aptly noted that K-pop emerges "as a result of a relationship, namely, of the inherent tension between the global imaginary it depicts and issues of national identity that were underlying, intersecting, and conflicting with it."[24] In this book, I use the term *K-pop* with Choe's and Fuhr's definitions in mind—as a way of referencing idol multimedia performance, which became globally popular at the turn of the millennium while constantly being expected to carry the banner of "Made in Korea."

As a way of embracing these multiple aspects of the term generatively, I consider the "K" in "K-pop" as an abbreviation of the following "K" words, which collectively uphold the diverse makeup of K-pop:[25] "kaleidoscopic" pop, embracing a wide range of multimedia performance, not just music; "keyboard" or "keypad" pop, which consumers can access digitally rather than through live performance; "Kleenex" pop, highly disposable in nature;[26] "ketchup" pop, which is premade and has a predictable taste; "korporate" pop (I am now using "K" like the Kardashians), a highly polished commercial product whose sole aim is to generate profit in global marketplaces;[27] and, quite obviously, "Korean" pop as the nation's hottest export item, closely—and often problematically—bound up with South Korean national pride.[28]

While the main body of this book will unfold the signification of each abbreviation, it most consistently references aspects of "kaleidoscopic" pop and "keyboard/keypad" pop. Kaleidoscopic pop leads to the crucial concept of multimedia, which, in this book, is articulated on two fronts: first as multiple forms of performance, combining acting, singing, dancing, and talk shows to create a complex array of multimedia performances rather than just a music genre;[29] second, as the kaleidoscopic convergence of various media platforms (TV, YouTube, live performance, virtual reality) that collectively make K-pop a transmedia phenomenon. The term *keyboard/keypad pop* underlines the dominance of digital media, but it also is a way to highlight how, despite the overwhelming predominance of digital music production and consumption, K-pop still staunchly adheres to the idea of live music. Why should there be an emphasis on live music performance when a much better view of the performance is guaranteed on your computer screen? But before we get to the bottom of that question, what do we even mean by "live" and "liveness"? And what do these have to do with the characteristics of K-pop I have broadly sketched out in this section?

Why Liveness Matters

K-pop as a genre specifically cultured for digital media has a direct impact on the K-pop idols' training process, as testified by Neil Hannigan, who attended SM Entertainment's global audition in the New York City area and ended up spending some time as a trainee of the largest K-pop entertainment company, SM Entertainment:

> There are weekly evaluations where how you act on a camera decides how you will feel on a stage. There are three judges and all the other trainees sitting there watching how you do the video. That's basically an audience for yourself, and there are multiple cameras from different angles. It feels like a stage because

all of the trainees are there and you're higher than them. If you feel confident there, that means you're ready for a stage; if you don't feel confident there and you mess up in front of your trainees and judges and coaches, it means you're not ready yet.[30]

In testimony similar to Hannigan's, another former trainee of a large K-pop entertainment company, Edward Kang, recalls an extensive camera training session where advanced trainees who were close to debut were expected to work on their facial expressions.[31] Numerous other examples, such as reality TV shows like *Who Is Next* and *Mix and Match* that center on the YG Entertainment trainees' survival process, illustrate how their progress in singing and dancing is monitored by video camera.

As can be gleaned from these testimonies, the recording of trainees' rehearsals provides more than a practical means for them to monitor and improve their own performance; more significantly, these testimonies evidence how priority is given to the way performers' bodies look on screen rather than on a live stage. Vocal training is also more tuned in to recorded music than to live singing. As Hannigan notes, the SM producers "basically teach you how to sing for a recording, because when you sing for a recording it has to be a lot more controlled."[32]

The K-pop industry's focus on digital performance, however, is complicated by the fact that it is not easy to define the boundary between what is live music and what is not.[33] Peggy Phelan, the most prominent defender of the purist ontology of live performance, has proclaimed that "performance cannot be saved, recorded, documented, or otherwise participate in the circulation of representations of representations."[34] Her resistance to the "recorded" and the "documented" as an antithetical force to a live performance is, in large part, a reaction to a digital culture that increasingly impinges on the live—a point that has been reiterated by Jennifer Parker-Starbuck, who sees *live* as referencing "a bodily presence capable of resisting the onslaught of commercial capitalism."[35]

Phelan's perspective has been countered by performance studies scholar Philip Auslander, who sees no ontological fissures between the live and the mediatized. He suggests that "the relationship between live and mediatized forms and the meaning of liveness be understood as historical and contingent rather than determined by immutable differences."[36] Auslander's proposition that "what counts culturally as live experience changes over time in relation to technological change" has been seconded by many scholars working on the theoretical and empirical ramifications of liveness.[37] Shannon Jackson and

Marianne Weems, for instance, confirm the mutability of what is often imagined as a binary opposition: "Once we remember the history of technology that is embedded in the history of theater, it becomes impossible to polarize the live purity of performance with the mediatized impurity of technology. They have been in each other's pockets from the start."[38] For instance, television scholar Nick Couldry's term *group liveness*, which stands for real-time communication among mobile phone users dispersed across physical space, illustrates how certain modes of liveness cannot even exist without digital mediation.[39]

K-pop production embodies the complex entanglement of the live and the digital described by the aforementioned scholars, for it makes ongoing efforts to stage a semblance of live performance as a way to craft the genre's musical authenticity. The conspicuous tension between liveness and mediatization emerges from the inevitably increasing usage of portable electronic gadgets as a primary mode of production and consumption of K-pop. For instance, the vast majority of people attending an exciting live event nowadays tend to bypass the opportunity to experience that given moment with their naked eyes; at any live K-pop concert, most attendees opt to "mediatize" their natural gaze by placing the phone screen or the camera lens in front of their eyes, constantly pressing camera shutters and video recording buttons; they thereby bring media intervention into the unfolding live event, making it difficult to categorically separate live from mediatized.

If recording a live event in real time is a prevalent practice in K-pop concerts, so is creating a live event out of what began as a TV show. The past few years have seen a rise in a K-pop production trend of having reality TV shows, such as *Boys24* or *Produce 101*, which function as audition programs for idol hopefuls, incorporate live concerts as a part of their programming (figure 2). With the enormous popularity that *Produce 101* has garnered, the idol groups formed as a result of the program—I.O.I. and Wanna One—have staged multiple live concerts since their debut. *Boys24* in particular has set a new K-pop trend: TV shows (aired from June 18 to August 6, 2016) became a launching pad for live concerts to take place over a much longer duration (open run since September 22, 2016), with performers marketed as "idols for live performance" (*gong-yeon-hyeong aidol*).[40] These instances evidence that consumption of the mediatized and of the live presentation of K-pop are becoming increasingly complementary to—or even dependent upon—each other.

Moreover, the recent surge in the use of virtual reality in K-pop performance further renders meaningless the binary between what is live and what

FIGURE 2. Groomed for live performance, BOYS24 members greet fans on stage after their daily performance. Photo by Kim Suk-Young.

is not. As explained by Gabriella Giannachi, virtual theater "has moved beyond concerns of liveness . . . allowing the audience to be present in both the real and the virtual environments."[41] While Giannachi's stance can be useful for an analysis of K-pop hologram performance, I propose that the complex dimensions of liveness in the K-pop industry are not equated with the real alone, as Giannachi assumes; rather, both real and virtual actors can conjure up impressions of liveness, copresence, and immediacy. In this regard, K-pop performances approximate what performance studies terms "mixed-reality performance," or "mixing of the real and virtual as well as their combination of live performance and interactivity"—a concept that extends the debate on liveness into the digital age.[42]

K-pop Live ultimately is an attempt to contemplate how "live" becomes a force across various media platforms to make, fake, or break a community forged around K-pop performances. As will be explored throughout the book, the pursuit of liveness embraces two paradoxical forces: a yearning for a sense of belonging in a fragmented world and complicity with the rules of the neoliberal marketplace that commodify liveness. The case studies assembled here stage various forms and degrees of liveness as they create a spectrum book-ended by these two forces: an embodied desire for living together that is also subject to commercial reproduction and fabrication.

On the level of history, the collapsing boundary between live and media-tized performance has to do with the fact that music and theater performance have different genealogies. Before the invention of music recording devices like gramophones, music production was equal to music performance, with a full view of artists producing music on the spot. But music was reduced to the sonic sphere with the advent of recording technology, which made it possible to re-produce sound infinitely without the continuing labor of live performers. The tide turned back with the arrival of multimedia technology, which enabled full coordination of audiovisual effects; music was once again expressed in the vi-sual dimension, with much emphasis on music videos and stage performances. Of all genres, pop music in particular became a synesthetic sphere where audio and visuals are forever married. In my view, the live and the mediatized have become similarly intertwined.

The key term under scrutiny here is *live* and its derivative noun *liveness*. These are wide-ranging terms that can be used to reference modes of performance, media platforms, processes of pop music production and consumption, ephem-erality, and even value judgment systems. So versatile and mobile is their seman-tic range that it is probably wiser to approach the notion of "live" by exploring what the concept stands against: "digital," "mediatized," "recorded," "second-hand," "rehearsed," and "inauthentic" are all concepts that have been considered antithetical to the notion of "live." These oppositions carry value to the extent that they function as a useful starting point for conceptual discussion, but they do not hold up well in actual practice, as the opposite poles tend to converge.[43]

The first oppositional concept, "digital," references a mode of audiovisual performance, given the frequently used opposition between digital and live performance; the concern is whether the performers and audience are copre-sent in the same time and space. Often interchangeable with "digital" is "media-tized," which pertains to the media platform used for audiovisual presentation; the underlying assumption is that what we see on stage is a live event, whereas what we see on screen are mediatized objects. The third oppositional term, "re-corded," concerns the matter of production; this view postulates that in order for music or a music video to be recorded, there has to be a live performance that took place in the studio or on stage in the past; this binary is most con-cerned with temporal flow in the sense that live music and dance can exist only in the present, whereas recorded music or music videos revive live music of the past. Conversant with the notion of "recorded" is the concept of "secondhand," which often refers to the process of consumption; it is based on the premise that infinitely reproducible recorded music or music videos are not the original in the sense of being played in the studio or live on stage by live performers; hence the listeners and spectators are getting something that has been consumed already. By the same token, its implications are fluidly interchangeable with those of "rehearsed"—the premise is that improvisational freshness is an essential part of what constitutes "live"—or even "inauthentic," which is relevant to the view that treats the performance of live music as something more valuable and genuine than its counterpart. Live performances are seen as more authentic because they cannot be redone or edited and hence accentuate the risk-taking nature of liveness.

The equation of live with authentic in the K-pop industry has already been proposed by John Lie, who points out that K-pop lacks authenticity in the context of Eurocentric ideals of a romantic artist:

> Modern authenticity, tied to the notions of sincerity, of staying true to oneself, is understood as the outward expression of an inwardly experienced correspondence between the true self and the self in the world—a unity between the two that is uncompromising with respect to the movement of time and to external contingencies. To put this another way, K-pop is a mercenary pursuit, does not stay true to its art (such as its arts may be). In this sense, K-pop flatly contradicts the European Romantic ideal of the artist as a seeker after Beauty and Truth.. . . . Nearly every aspect of K-pop is functional, intended to satisfy the market rather than fulfill some deep artistic or political urge.[44]

Lie sees K-pop artists' urge to resist lip-syncing as analogous to a concert pianist's desire to satisfy the audience's wish to see the performer play from memory, as a way of staging musical authenticity. He concludes that "the only reason for a K-pop performer to resist lip-syncing is to fulfill the audience's expectations for the performer to sound authentic, and thus to fulfill the commercial imperative of pleasing the audience."[45]

While it is difficult to dispute that K-pop industry is a hypercommercialized enterprise operating according to the logic of the marketplace and therefore is hardly a seeker after "Truth," what is missing from Lie's concluding remarks about the live stage being a testing ground of authenticity is the notion that K-pop is not just music but a total performance (figure 3). K-pop (read "kaleidoscopic" pop) is a multimedia performance privileging well-choreographed dancing as much as, if not more than, singing itself. In other words, Lie might be right if we were to look at K-pop in the narrowest possible way—only as a music genre. For concert attendees, one of the main attractions is to see the living bodies of K-pop stars—their faces, makeup, costumes, and movements—and this can be done only in live concerts. One can lip-sync to music, but one cannot "body-sync" dance—or we are not there yet technologically, as the holographic rendition of human bodies has a long way to go to appear more like its biological originals.

Hence the attraction for fans to go to live concerts is to see K-pop idols "sing live" as much as "dance live" and "talk live," while fulfilling their desire to verify whether the beauty (not "Beauty" as in John Lie's criticism of K-pop, but still very strongly pronounced physical beauty) of idols on screen holds up when seen in reality with the naked eye. Since spectacular visuality, which includes good looks, a unique fashion statement, and dance moves, is at the center of the K-pop frenzy, live concertgoers want to confirm whether the visual pleasure they find on the two-dimensional pixel screens still holds when their idols are present in flesh and blood.

FIGURE 3. Wanna One stages a "human piano" with their Pilobolus-like choreography for KCON LA 2017. K-pop performance emphasizes intricate choreography as much as expert singing. Photo by Kim Suk-Young.

So to go back to the basic premise of this book, which looks into K-pop as a multimedia performance, lip-syncing, despite its replacement of a live human voice with digitally recorded singing, does not betray the notion of live performance as authentic performance so long as the idols do not fake their dance on stage in front of a live audience. EXO's exquisite choreography on stage confirmed this point, as their perfectly recorded voices were at times accompanied by whimsical improvisations of their dance moves, which can happen only during fleeting moments of a live event.

Thus what makes an event live is either a real-time connection or a shared sense of immediacy and authenticity stemming from participants who congregate either online or offline. More than the media platform or the simple mingling of performers and spectators, what matters for liveness is not ontology but perception. Media and arts scholar Steve Dixon elaborates by illustrating how liveness for the spectator is not just about being physically present at the moment when the event unfolds; it's about the phenomenological experience, which tends to differ depending on the degree of attention paid to the event rather than on the presence of live corporeal bodies per se:

> Presence is about interest and command of attention, not space or liveness. In considering the presence of live bodies versus media image, the now common presence of televisions in bars and other public places provides a convenient example. When the company and conversation is stimulating, the presence of the TV seems distant or unnoticed, when it is not, the TV may gain attention and command the sense of presence over the live bodies in the space. . . . In this sense, presence in relation to audience engagement and attention is dependent on the compulsion of the audiovisual activity, not on liveness or corporeal three-dimensionality.[46]

Here Dixon's example of a TV in a bar is mostly concerned with the presence of spectators' attention to the event being broadcast on TV, but what about, for lack of a better word, the performer's perception? In other words, whose eyes are seeing the performance as live and whose ears are not sensing the music as live? What can be said about the intense rapport between the performer and the spectator as a defining factor of liveness, whether or not they are copresent temporally and physically? And more significantly, can there be a unique Korean variant to liveness, founded on the fluid interchangeability between the performer and the spectator?

Liveness, the Korean Version?

One of the reasons K-pop is constantly morphing is that the positionality of the agents involved in the making of the K-pop scene constantly changes. Fans often double as consumers, but they are not always equated with consumers, nor are they oppositional to bystanders. Because stars are made, not born in the K-pop industry, idols start out as amateur admirers, much like their future fans, as in the case of IU (Aiyu) and Ailee (Eilli), who started out as amateurs promoting themselves by posting videos of themselves performing K-pop cover songs. Moreover, stars constantly have to stage their affection for their supporters—becoming fans of their fans—since their careers depend on the affective connection they make with the fans, especially in South Korea.[47] In this respect, the parasociality that conventionally defines the one-sided relationship between fans and stars—that fans profess one-way love for the stars while stars are unaware of the multitude of fans—does not hold well in K-pop analysis. Or at least, stars do their best to give an impression that their fans are engaged in a two-way love affair by deploying various media platforms, where affection travels in multiple directions. I take this point further to claim that the malleable interchangeability of positions between various agents of K-pop and the communal sensibility forged in the process (visited more closely in the next chapter) are what gives an inimitable coloration to K-pop as a cultural scene—and characterizes the Korean variation of the notion of liveness.

As a scholar who has been researching liveness in the multimedia environment for some time, I have been asked why the discussion of liveness is mostly produced by Western academics with Western performances in mind. This question nagged me for some time, and at the risk of entertaining the spirit of cultural essentialism I am proposing the following answer: although K-pop is far from being just Korean, if we were to suppose for a moment that K-pop was "Korean" pop, the live spirit that brings participant and observer, producer, and consumer into a dynamic dance would very much resonate with what Koreans refer to as *heung*. Closely aligning with the discussion of liveness, this uniquely Korean concept has no exact English counterpart, but it can be roughly translated as spontaneous energy stemming from excitation, inspiration, play, and frolicking. Neither a single definition nor a clear translation exists, but there is a shared understanding among native speakers of Korean that *heung* refers to the innate energy in every human being that is reserved for the spontaneous joy of playing that shines through despite counterforces. To elaborate its nuances further, it springs, not simply from fun, but from a communal rapport despite difficulties and hardship.

In its most immediate sense, *heung* is a word frequently used to illustrate extraordinary emotional registers related to a wide range of fun and excitement. It manifests itself in exhilarating physical movements, usually accompanied by an arousing musical quality that makes passive observers rise from their seats and join the unfolding performance by rhythmically shrugging their shoulders (what Koreans call *eo-kkae-chum*, literally translated as "shoulder dance"); additionally, the physical expression of *heung* is often accompanied by enthusiastic verbal responses to the performers' narrative (which are often referred to as *chuimsae* in the genre of *pansori*).[48] *Heung* frequently is associated with instances of arousing rhythm in traditional Korean music (*gugak*).[49] One instance is presented by a Korean newspaper article about three foreigners who experienced Korean *heung* by learning to play Korean traditional percussion music;[50] the internationally renowned Korean filmmaker Im Kwon-taek (Im Gwon-taek) likewise associated traditional music with *heung* when he spoke of his representative film, *Seopyeonje* (1993), as an attempt to capture the "*mat* [taste], *meot* [style], and *heung*" of *pansori*.[51] Im's films, such as *Seopyoenje* and *Chunhyang* (2000), depict how masterful singing in *pansori* performance—set skills learned through extreme hardship and struggle—can arouse *heung* (*heung-eul dot-u-da*) to make the audience members fuse with the performance in a communal spirit.

In addition to *pansori*, *heung* is frequently tied to the discussion of *pungmul*, or a "Korean folk music tradition that includes drumming, dancing, and singing" and that is "rooted in the dure [collective labor] of farming culture."[52] The idea of working together, often in challenging conditions, is essential for the rapport and interchangeability of performers and spectators, which I see as a defining ideological and affective dimension of liveness in this book. In pursuing this thesis, I am indebted to ethnomusicologist Nathan Hesselink, who linked the notion of *heung* to "liveness and joy" and saw "neighborhood spirit" and "a sense of collective responsibility" as a passage between the two.[53]

Many contemporary culture makers and critics alike have attributed the widespread success of Korean pop culture to Korea's ability to freely express its *heung*; most notably, K-pop artists themselves see *heung* as an affective mediator between the self and the other, the local and the global, the past and the present, in fueling K-pop's liveness (as in "liveliness"). For instance, IU claimed: "When I think of *samulnori* or *madangnori* I first think of shoulder dance.[54] Elderly people gathered together and lifting their shoulders up and down rhythmically [to the traditional music]. Perhaps K-pop's popularity lies in its excitement, which communicates well across the board."[55] *Heung*, as IU interprets it, is not only associated with music and dance but also deeply ingrained in the communal gathering of people—the social aspect of liveness. Other prominent K-pop artists' careers also embody the resilient relationship between K-pop and the lively spirit of *heung* through their training and work. Himchan (member of boy band B.A.P.) and G-Dragon (member of boy band BIGBANG) attended traditional Korean music schools before becoming K-pop stars; not surprisingly, G-Dragon titled his solo song "Niliria" after a well-known folk song from Gyeonggi Province in South Korea, and G-Dragon's teammate Taeyang employs *samulnori* as a significant motif in his music video "Ringa Linga," which features a vivacious multiracial crowd dancing to the rhythmic performance of traditional Korean music and dance. The last example in particular attempts to show how *heung* is a mode of sharing what is seen as uniquely Korean with the global audience of today.

The Korean government also cultivates this trend, branding the nation by promoting a lively image of it through the affective register of *heung*. Take, for instance, the website of the 2018 Pyeongchang Winter Olympics Committee, which provides its version of *heung* as representative of the national psyche under the subsection titled "Friendly Koreans":

> Korea's unique culture is not yet widely known overseas. Korean culture is marked not only by the dynamics and diligence often found in various business and industrial sectors but also by friendliness and passion that stem from the pursuit of diversification. The Korean soul is replete with "*heung*," which treasures friendship and passion for life.[56]

Friendship and passion, in this case, are other names for communal experience, which captures the core of *heung*: celebration of the openness of a community, optimism, inclusiveness, and improvisational liveness.

As far-fetched as the connection between the folk music of premodern Korea and the K-pop of the globalized twenty-first century may appear, the sense of community emerging from the collective endeavor to coordinate labor may be what links these disparate Korean music scenes of the past and the present: it literally takes a farming village to produce *pungmul*, and it takes a global village to produce the many moving parts of K-pop and make it one of the liveliest cultural scenes today. *Heung* is a notion that far precedes the advent of the mass media that incubated the K-pop industry, but the playful spirit of the community still persists—over the pixel screens as well as face to face in a live concert—to explain one significant aspect of K-pop's liveness. Indeed, I very much agree with Sohn Jie-Ae (Son Ji-ae), the former CEO of Arirang TV, which produces numerous K-pop programs, who saw *heung* as one of the defining features of K-pop, together with other quintessential Korean characteristics such as *kki* (talent for entertaining) and *kkang* (staunch endurance and bravery to overcome hardship).[57] *Heung* in the premodern era might have stemmed from live interactions among community members, but it prevails in the digital age because of real-time information sharing that fosters—and at times fabricates—intimacy via K-pop's participatory culture. I propose that the Korean people's innate love for singing and hanging out together as an expression of *heung* is what cuts across *pungmul* and K-pop—not to champion cultural essentialism but to try to understand the historical and local dimensions of K-pop's liveness.

Notes on Ethnography

The spontaneous spirit embedded in the notion of *heung* has informed me throughout the book-writing process. Much of my time has been spent as a scholar stiffly sitting at a desk, watching and listening to K-pop while writing notes that turned into this book, but I've spent equal time as a participant observer visiting live concerts, K-pop conventions, and exhibitions; interviewing various actors in the K-pop industry; and eavesdropping on fans' casual conversations both online and offline. As a result, I've paid equal attention to the printed archive of books, journal and newspaper articles, and narrative data gathered through in-depth interviews and interpretation of existing interviews. This is not only a nod to oral transcripts, which have been overshadowed by the conventional authority of written texts,[58] but also an attempt to let my positionality flexibly adapt to the realm I am studying. In the spirit of capturing the vibrant pulse of K-pop, whose defining feature is its "inherent mutability," I plunged myself into the research process through a wide range of roles along the fluid spectrum between participant and observer, producer and consumer.[59]

Mutability is constant change, and change is best documented as a living process. As Tom Boellstroff et al. proposed, ideal ethnographic research should resiliently adapt to the ever-changing research environment,[60] whether that takes place online or offline. Given K-pop's dominance in the virtual world, online ethnography is becoming an increasingly important methodology; In this book I flexibly use visual, audial, and narrative data gathered online, such as e-mail interviews and social media postings by entertainment companies, fans, and idols. In doing so, I have tried to remind myself that social media can present "a distorted view of events, such that we only get the perspective of the people who are already in our social network."[61] I have kept close the lessons of what performance studies scholar D. Soyini Madison has termed "positive naiveness," or "acknowledging that you do not know and that you must rely with humility on others and trust upon the knowledge of knowers." Madison states that "the idea of the knower and the known is provocative in its implications of identifying who knows and who is striving to know. As ethnographers, our knowing is always leveraged by a level of unknowing that we struggle to fill by asking the knowers."[62] In the fast-moving world of K-pop, where new knowledge is created every second by so many moving parts, assuming positive naiveness to keep the field of vision open becomes even more pertinent.

It is in this context that I consciously assume a wide spectrum of roles, being at once a producer and a consumer of K-pop-related content in the physical and virtual worlds. More on the producing end of the spectrum, I actively took part in the making of the BuzzFeed five-part video series on K-pop as an expert interviewee, served as a panelist at KCON LA 2015 and 2017, worked as a journalist covering KCON Paris 2016 and KCON LA 2017, and was a featured guest in NPR's Radiolab coverage on Korean paparazzi, which touched upon the world of K-pop idols. Although these activities might not be immediately related to the production of K-pop music per se, they create the corollary network of K-pop content that helps sustain the boom as a living process. On the observing end of the spectrum, I was a media analyst when dissecting music videos, a historian when lecturing on K-pop's evolution in classrooms, a fan when attending live concerts of my favorite K-pop acts, an anthropologist of tourism when visiting K-pop shrines, and a bystander when mandatorily watching K-pop-related TV shows for the sake of research.

Similarly, when interviewing human subjects, I tried to understand them as an intersection of multiple agencies rather than casting them in a singular mold, whether that of trainee, producer, songwriter, or journalist. I stand by my definition of K-pop as a multimedia performance, and the multitude embedded in the notion penetrates all aspects of the encounters that took place during this book's research.

Chapters

All the chapters of this book offer empirical case studies demonstrating how indispensable the notion of "live" is to the highly mediatized form of K-pop. The chapters are laid out as a step-by-step guide through the K-pop industry's efforts to diversify media platforms to access a wider global network of music consumers while adhering to the idea of live music. Two premises organize the chapters: First, liveness is shaped according to the specificity of the media environment; hence, each chapter will focus on distinctive media platforms, such as terrestrial and cable TV, YouTube, hologram shows, and live concerts. Second, although each chapter is organized around a distinctive medium, the attempt to demarcate the boundaries so clearly ends up being futile. Various media shaping the mode of live performance are permutable and increasingly converging, making it difficult to draw definitive boundaries between media platforms. Therefore, while each chapter has a main focus on one media plat-form, it also features other forms of encroaching media platforms that are in-separable from the main platform.

Chapter 1, "Historicizing K-pop," portrays K-pop as an ideological and technological playing field where forces of a rapidly changing media environ-ment, a neoliberal marketplace, and the ensuing desires to make and break var-ious social networks interact. As K-pop has become increasingly visible around the globe in the past ten years or so, the South Korean government has been trying to forge a meaningful partnership with the K-pop industry. By situating such a move in its historical trajectory, this chapter shows K-pop as a dynamic force that has been shaped equally by top-down movements, such as industry-led paradigm shifts in media technology, and bottom-up movements, such as users' creative ways of employing that technology.

Chapter 2, "K-pop from Live Television to Social Media," presents the unique production and consumption modes of K-pop as they pertain to the specific medium of television. The history of television reveals that this plat-form is inherently linked to the format of live theater, with much emphasis placed on a live broadcasting model. Two specific examples of K-pop-related TV shows explored in this chapter—the top-of-the-chart show *Music Core* (*Eumak jungsim*) and an English-language live chat show, *After School Club*—encourage real-time participation by viewers that opens a new dimension of TV liveness in the digital era. Defining this dimension as simultaneous pro-duction and consumption of music rather than improvised and nonrehearsed performance, this chapter poses challenges to the purist notion of "live." The two case studies present contrapuntal visions of how domestic and foreign fans exercise ownership over K-pop by using various digital platforms and show how TV channels optimize their visibility by transposing TV media content onto social networks.

Chapter 3, "Simulating Liveness in K-pop Music Videos," looks into K-pop music videos as a central medium for articulating the dynamics between liveness and mediatization. Music videos' primary platforms, such as YouTube and Vevo, are based on the replaying of recorded performances, so they are not conceived as primary venues for live performances. At most, music videos can only simulate the vestiges of live performances that have already happened. A comparative analysis of two examples of K-pop music videos—"Twinkle" by TaeTiSeo, a subunit of the representative K-pop girl group Girls' Generation, and "Who You?" by G-Dragon, leader of the boy band BIGBANG—shows that there is still a tremendous investment in the notion of live performance in K-pop as a way of forging artistic authenticity for the genre. Also illuminated in the process is the significance of invoking various performing-arts traditions, such as revues, Broadway-style musicals, Hollywood musicals, and performance art, to make K-pop music videos more approachable to a global audience.

Chapter 4, "Hologram Stars Greet Live Audiences," explores the emerging interface between digital technology and live performances. Two key players of the K-pop industry, YG Entertainment and SM Entertainment, have invested heavily in creating infinitely reproducible and exportable K-pop shows featuring their top stars in holographic form. With a subsidy from and in partnership with the South Korean Ministry of Science, ICT (Information and Communications Technology), and Future Planning (*Mirae changjo gwahakbu*), a government unit deeply committed to the national branding campaign, both companies have actively sought opportunities to present their hologram works in foreign markets that the actual stars have difficulty reaching through traditional live tours. By comparing YG Entertainment's hologram concert with SM Entertainment's hologram musical, the chapter investigates how live performance can be realized without live performers but only with live spectators.

Chapter 5, "Live K-pop Concerts and Their Digital Doubles," looks into live K-pop tours overseas, an increasingly prominent mode of the genre's global circulation. While the case studies in this chapter exhibit the most conventional and purest notion of liveness, defined as copresence of performer and spectator, they nonetheless provide multiple examples of how live concerts simply cannot exist without any interventions of digitally augmented audiovisual effects. The chapter also explores how live K-pop tours are promoted by digital campaigns carried out on social media and in online music stores, making it impossible to separate the live event from its digital counterpart. By comparing and contrasting BIGBANG's Made tour (2014–15), which took place in seventy cities across four continents, with CJ Entertainment and Music (CJ E&M)'s KCON, a multiday K-pop festival and convention hosted in Europe, Japan, the Middle East, and the United States, I analyze different strategies these events deploy in their efforts to attract Korean and global audiences while they incidentally participate in a campaign to enhance the nation's soft power.

Chapters 2 and 3 address obviously mediatized K-pop platforms where the congregation of live audiences does not take place. Most viewers see music videos and TV shows onscreen in private settings. In Korea, music videos were consumed on cable TV channels in the mid-1990s, but in the new millennium, especially since the emergence of YouTube in 2006, they have migrated to computer screens, tablets, and cell phones. The K-pop-related shows are originally produced for network TV but end up leading enormously prolific second lives online on YouTube.

Chapters 4 and 5 address the synchronous gathering of a live audience in actual physical space, whether the performers are living human beings or digitally rendered holograms. The difference between performers is a precarious one, not definitive, since even in traditional live concerts, performers on stage reach audiences through multiple degrees of digitization (their voices are amplified via music recording and their facial expressions are augmented via camera close-ups projected on a large screen in the concert arena). Holograms sometimes present more vivid performances, with perfectly angled placement on stage and gravity-defying motions that physical bodies cannot achieve.

Although the chapters are organized according to media platforms—a concept akin to genres—the book ultimately unpacks the futility of trying to differentiate music videos from TV music shows, or live concerts from hologram shows, since each version of performance is increasingly designed to be adaptable and amenable to other platforms. In the end, there is nothing more important for the industry than to enable transmedial diffusion of image-oriented performances staged by K-pop idols. As authors of *Spreadable Media* claim, "If it doesn't spread, it's dead." This book adds an additional line—à la Dr. Seuss—to this rhyming wisdom: "If it doesn't hop, it's not K-pop."

1

HISTORICIZING K-POP

K-Pop in some ways feels like a move forward among the new generation, who, for better or worse, won't harbor the painful memories (of the 1950–1953 Korean War) that so many older Koreans have. It's all about moving forward and incredibly optimistic in its presentation and lyrics and point of view.

Janice Min, interview by Kim Ji-soo, 2014

THIS EPIGRAPH is the evaluation of K-pop provided by Janice Min, the CEO of *Billboard Magazine* and *Hollywood Reporter*, during her keynote speech at the music industry convention MU:CON in Seoul in 2014. At first, her statement appears to be true for most K-pop fans, who are young, trendy, media savvy, and future oriented. If they happen to be Koreans, they are also capable of wiping the slate clean to move on from their parents and grandparents, whose lives were directly affected by the turbulent forces of war, division, the democracy movement, and economic upheavals. For most fans, K-pop is not at all about political or historical burdens. It is about here and now, and the creation of unprecedented connections with the rest of the world.

But there is another side to K-pop—history specific to Korea that has given rise to this distinctive form of popular culture. Although this book was initially inspired by the exponentially growing popularity of K-pop in the new millennium, and although the case studies mostly stem from the past decade when K-pop started to enjoy worldwide circulation, every moment in the present is rooted in the past. Sometimes clearly remembered and at other times accidentally erased, the past continues to exist, casting shadows that define the contours of K-pop's face today. So this chapter takes into consideration various transformations that shaped the ideological and technological foundations of K-pop by exploring a broader social, political, and cultural context, namely the formation of *hallyu* (the Korean cultural wave), of which K-pop is a prominent aspect.[1]

Hallyu (韓流) is a compound word, which literally stands for "Korea" (韓) and "stream" or "flow" (流). Embedded in the second character, "stream" or "flow," is the notion of something difficult to contain and stabilize. Like a fast-changing trend, it flows away without congealing, thereby signifying temporality and ephemerality. The term is broadly known to have been coined in the Chinese-speaking world in the late 1990s, but more specifically starting with the 1997 airing of the Korean TV drama *What Is Love* on CCTV to a popular acclaim.[2] The widely accepted version of *hallyu* history posits the K-pop idol band H.O.T.'s highly publicized Beijing concert (2000) as the official opening of the age of *hallyu* in the new millennium.[3]

But contrary to this commonly held knowledge, Jang Gyu-su, a historian of the Korean entertainment industry, proposes that it was the Korean Ministry of Culture and Tourism, not Chinese media, that first officially coined the term *hallyu* to promote Korea's popular songs in the Chinese-speaking world.[4] It is no surprise that any given nation-state would use its culture to advance its soft power, but what was problematic about this move, according to Jang, was that those South Korean officials were not aware of the term's Japanese roots and appropriated a Japanese phrasing to refer to a cultural boom that the Korean government saw as the epitome of its own national pride. Drawing on a meticulous investigation of the original sources in which the term *hallyu* appeared in China, Japan, and Korea at the end of the last millennium, Jang shows that the term was based on the pattern in the Japanese language that was used to address a national culture enjoying popularity across Asia: phrases like *Hong Kong wave* (香流) in the 1980s, *Japanese wave* (日流) in the 1990s, and *Chinese wave* (華流) in the 2010s provide the context in which the term *Korean wave* (韓流) emerged.[5] Thus the Korean cultural wave, despite its embedded ethnocentric pride and local traits, is entangled in transnational cultural politics, as the etymology itself shows. Whether intentional or not, the use of foreign terms to promote Korean culture and vice versa is an indispensable dimension of global cultural politics nowadays.

In an age where cultural flows and influences are multidirectional, transnational, and tangled together, the nation-state's will alone cannot entirely account for the global emergence of the Korean culture boom, regardless of the Korean government's persistent series of campaigns to advance its cultural influence.[6] According to Jang, many factors contributed to the rise of Korean wave: the increasing production and sales costs of Hong Kong films, which were enormously popular throughout Asia in the 1980s, created a need for alternative content that was more affordable; the exponential growth of Japanese satellite TV stations and Taiwanese cable TV stations created a need for more content to fill their slots; and the devaluation of Korean currency in the aftermath of the International Monetary Fund (IMF) crisis (1997–2001) made Korean media content affordable in the international marketplace.[7] These entangled factors collectively produced the conditions for Korea to have its turn in the limelight.

Hallyu, for the most part, is post-IMF aesthetics,[8] a neoliberal lifestyle, an affective mode, social relations, ethno-national pride, the statist project, and transnational cultural politics—all caught up in the dizzying pace of South Korean popular cultural development. These complex and often contradictory forces of history have made many scholars of Korean culture consider hallyu's many facets: Choi JungBong (Choe Jeong-bong) characterized it as "a national campaign" or a "corporate-state project," much as John Lie saw South Korea's export-driven statist culture as the main force behind the K-pop machinery.[9] Michael Fuhr, Jin Dal Yong, Lee Sangjoon (Yi Sang-jun), and Abé Mark Nornes, on the other hand, have paid attention to the converging trends of hallyu—globalization, hybridity, dynamic inter-Asian cultural flow, and the rise of social media[10]—and Joseph Nye and Kim Youna have considered the nationalistic bent of the hallyu trend as having a potential to "develop into another form of hegemonic cultural imperialism in the [Asian] region."[11] As these scholars have admirably sketched out the historical dimensions and sociocultural factors that have created and sustained hallyu, I intend in this chapter not to repeat the general overview but to selectively highlight particularly notable ideological and technological changes that demarcate constantly morphing liveness in the K-pop industry.

The Ideological Workings of K-pop:
The *Teletubbies Generation*, Generation Like,
and Media Tribalism

Where to pinpoint the historical origins of K-pop? Some scholars go all the way back to the premodern era,[12] whereas others focus on the Japanese colonial and post–Korean War period.[13] This book begins with more immediate history, the 1990s—a crucial juncture in Korea, as many events shifted the dynamics between the authoritarian state and free individual subjects. The 1990s was marked by dramatic, monumental changes—the advent of the civilian government, economic bust, the rise of civil society, cultural diversification, and the dismantling of the conventional social order—all of which set the stage for a cultural paradigm shift to take place.

These changes in many ways were the results of the "globalization policy" (*segyehwa*) touted by Korea's fourteenth president, Kim Young-sam (Gim Yeong-sam). A civilian who assumed the office in 1993 by democratic election after more than three decades of military dictatorship, Kim announced on November 17, 1994, that Korea would pursue globalization in all aspects of life, particularly "extensive structural reforms across six major areas: education, the legal system and economy, politics and mass media, national and local administrations, environment, and culture."[14] All of these areas eventually became deeply involved in fueling the K-pop industry and marked a turning point for the Korean government to approach "cultural industries from an economic perspective instead of a cultural perspective."[15]

Economic historians see this turn in an overwhelmingly negative light, certainly with the benefit of hindsight, for Korea's globalization boom, fueled by many irresponsible fiscal decisions made by the government, ended with the disastrous 1997 financial meltdown.[16] But cultural historians remember the decade in a rosier light, as a time when Korean society became invigorated by more diverse, discursive, and outward-looking energy.

Economically speaking, Kim Young-sam's globalization policy was disastrous. In the spirit of joining the world market, the government opened Korea to a massive influx of foreign capital without proper preparation to help the domestic economy adjust to these major changes. Korean companies also joined the globalization boom and made excessive investments in foreign markets. As a result, South Korea's foreign debt quadrupled in the four years from 1992 to 1996, and a moratorium on foreign investments was declared in 1997.

Concurrent with the catastrophic economic bust, significant changes on a sociocultural level brought about foundational changes in Korea's long-standing social order. First, because of the colossal financial crisis, much conventional wisdom of South Korean society—an androcentric worldview stemming from men being traditional breadwinners, the myth of lifetime employment, and unconditional respect for elders—was dismantled as the rapid disappearance of jobs disempowered many elderly male workers. Consequently, the traditional social hierarchy broke down as more women joined the workforce and younger people had advantages in getting hired because they provided cheaper labor. The rise of youth culture and the idea of a disposable workforce and self-promotion championed by K-pop (read "Kleenex pop") had their origins in this social shift.

Despite or perhaps because of the harsh logic of economic globalization that was sweeping the country in the worst form of neoliberal predatory capitalism, South Korea started to look toward the world as an extension of its globalization dream. This began with the increased mobility of South Koreans venturing beyond national boundaries. Before 1989, citizens had to receive a permit from the government to travel overseas; when foreign travel became deregulated, increasing numbers of middle-class people joined the travel boom in the mid-1990s. Between deregulation in 1989 and the financial crisis in 1997, South Koreans collectively spent $8 billion on foreign travel alone, testifying both to the people's thirst for exploring foreign land and culture, and to the financial scale of the globalization boom that went bust in 1997.

Another prominent event of the 1990s that led to cultural globalization was Korea's lifting of the ban on Japanese culture, which introduced many Japanese pop cultural products while propelling Korean artists into the Japanese market.[17] A new taste for world culture and trends, especially among the younger generation, had an enormous impact on the globalization of K-pop in the long run—and significantly for the discussion of liveness, consuming global culture along with the global community without a significant time lag became a standard consumptive pattern.

Civil society was concurrently on the rise with these developments, which had already started to emerge toward the end of the military dictatorship. Shin Gi-wook (Sin Gi-uk) and Choi Joon Nak (Choe Jun-nak) point to how "Korea's cultural industries (e.g., music, TV programs, movies) experienced a renaissance after Korea's 1987 democratization, exploring topics previously prohibited or frowned upon under authoritarian rule."[18] If college students constituted the critical mass of South Korea's turbulent democracy movement in the 1980s, then the students in the 1990s came to constitute a substantial core of pop culture consumerism, which touted the neoliberal sensibilities of individualism and self-promotion, or what the anthropologist Song Jesook (Song Je-suk) expressed as "neoliberal ideals of employability, flexibility, and self-sufficiency."[19]

The leading figures of the K-pop industry, such as Yang Hyun Suk (Yang Hyeon-seok) and Park Jin-young (Bak Jin-yeong), embodied the desire of their generation in the 1990s "that had grown up consuming a wide range of cultural items from the United States and was associated with individual choice, considerable spending money, and overseas travel."[20] Likewise, the parents of today's K-pop fans were at the heart of Korea's latest trends in the 1990s, bursting with a sense of freedom from political oppression, desire for diverse cultural expressions, and cravings for newness.

Such a shifting cultural paradigm is well captured by the ethnomusicologist Roald Maliangkay, who saw the youth of the 1990s as qualitatively different from the previous generation:

> Since many young people dreamed of breaking free from the turgid mold that saw teenagers and college students subjected to unequal and unnecessary pressure in education and in the job market, respectively, the "individualism" they were accused of was, in fact, a shared longing for structural social change. When they spoke of individualism and the pursuit of Western products and values, critics took this as a sign of faltering respect for the traditional social values and pointed at their overall affluence and the fact that unlike their predecessors of the so-called 386 Generation they comprise the century's first generation not to have directly experienced any of the hardships so many had suffered during and prior to the violent democratic movement of the 1980s.[21]

Amid many iconic figures of this generation, Seo Tae-ji and Boys (1992–96) stand out for their lasting impact on today's K-pop industry. True game changers, they burst into popularity as the icons of the youth of the 1990s, who, although not a powerful political collective, shared the desire of the new generation (*sinsaedae*) for a less regimented and oppressed life.[22] But unlike the previous generation of youth, who were at the heart of the democracy movement when collective protest was a prerequisite for social change, for the new generation "the expression of social criticism, so it seems, sometimes entails little more than keeping up with the latest trends."[23]

Of many foundational shifts that Seo Tae-ji and Boys brought about—such as introducing hip-hop to mainstream Koreans and blending it with the unique sensibilities of Korean folk music and *heung*—one notable aspect in terms of K-pop genealogy was that their teenage fandom prioritized the visual performance of music and dance over lyrics and melodies.[24] This was part of a broader trend stoked by the rising popularity of music videos in Korea. But because of the considerable impact of Seo Tae-ji and Boys in shaping cultural trends of the 1990s, the centrality of the visual dimension to their performance helped open the era of music videos in Korea. Maliangkay sees this emphasis on visuality as symptomatic of the teenage idols' rise to stardom:

> Record companies would create many acts that were less musically innovative, but combined deeply romantic ballads with upbeat dance tracks and good

looks. With the use of elaborate, often narrative music videos that highlighted the latter, the industry was able to compete with the many foreign acts that now appeared on music TV stations and on the large screens of the popular rock cafes. They were the first ripples of the Korean Wave.[25]

Having spent my formative years in early 1990s Korea, I remember that transitional time, which witnessed the "first ripples of the Korean wave," and indeed it was characterized by the emerging screen culture. Foreign music channels such as Hong Kong V Channel and MTV in newly opened bars in the Gangnam District would play in an endless loop the sultry dance grooves of Madonna followed by Michael Jackson's pelvic thrusting, and the large screens in record shops were dominated by the blinding platinum-blond hair of the members of the Danish band Michael Learns to Rock against an azure backdrop, cultivating an addiction to visual allure that had yet to fully exist in Korea. Those seductive images of multimedia musicians came across as a glimmering vision from the outside world when Korea was beginning to ride on the global cultural tides. But the formation of visually oriented consumers in the '90s, which laid the foundation for K-pop and *hallyu* at large to thrive in coming years, was related, not solely to cultural circumstances in Korea, but also to much broader pop cultural trends of the 1990s around the world.

In the history of the pop culture industry, the 1990s will indisputably be marked as the era dominated by MTV, which was undergoing significant changes in its programming. Originally established as "Music Television" in 1981, MTV's primary goal in the initial stages was to play music videos by pop musicians. Nowadays, its airtime is taken up mostly by reality shows, drama, and comedy with occasional forays into music videos. This crucial shift took place in the 1990s when MTV started to reduce music video slots and filled them with a broader range of contents. As a result, the "M" in "MTV" no longer stood for music alone, but also for "multimedia" and "multientertainment" TV. The ethnomusicologist Timothy Taylor commented that this shift in contents eliminated pop musician's "sell-out stigma."[26] Quoting the music industry insider Peter Nicholson, Taylor emphasized that "the old cliché that the artist 'sold out' doesn't apply in this situation, because it is a harmonious relationship that is built on the truth of popular culture's perception of the music and the brand."[27] The confluence of music and brand into a hyperconsumerist cultural practice is not pertinent to the United States alone: it is equally relevant to other consumerist societies like South Korea in the 1990s, where the nation was about to brand itself, corporation-style, through pop music.

Teletubbies and the Ways of Watching

Another coterminous factor to consider: the primary K-pop fandom of the new millennium, from teenagers to those in their midtwenties, is composed of what I call the *Teletubbies Generation*,[28] born and raised in the mid-1990s and thereafter. In my attempt to explain the importance of visuality in K-pop genealogy, I coin this term to designate particular media-viewing patterns that were pervasive around the globe. Not only South Koreans but also fans worldwide who are the main consumers of the K-pop boom in the new millennium share memories of *Teletubbies* due to globalized media products in the 1990s that circulated almost simultaneously, without too much time lag between production and consumption.[29] The simultaneous consumption of *Teletubbies* globally created a sense of live contact among the global audience, who built a quasi-community on a shared cultural reference, much as K-pop communities are built online nowadays.

Of the numerous pop figures and cultural icons that enjoyed worldwide popularity among children of the 1990s, why single out *Teletubbies*? How did this TV series acquire an iconic status for understanding K-pop consumption? To be clear, I am using the term *Teletubbies Generation* not only as a literal marker of the show's influence on generations of children but also as a metaphor for the training of certain generations to look at the world and to be looked at in a highly specific way. *Teletubbies*, in this regard, is not just a TV program but a figurative way vision is constructed.

During the late 1990s, I myself received a heavy dose of *Teletubbies* in Korea when I occasionally babysat my two toddler nieces, who showed endless fascination with these anthropomorphic media receptacles.[30] A children's television series targeted at preschool viewers, *Teletubbies* was produced by the British Broadcasting Corporation (BBC) from March 31, 1997, to February 16, 2001. The program emerged when the heightened visual culture of the 1990s, epitomized by MTV, had fully articulated itself as the dominant mode of social interaction mediated by viewing. Because *Teletubbies* is children's programming, it encompassed several generations of viewership in the late 1990s, namely young parents and toddlers. In Korea, these two generations present bookends of K-pop fandom: young adults of the 1990s constituted the fans of first-generation K-pop bands, such as Seo Tae-ji and Boys and Sechs Kies, and the toddlers of the 1990s have grown up to constitute the demographic majority of today's K-pop fandom.

Recently, *Teletubbies* resurfaced again in my life when my own kids started showing a fascination, as my nieces had some twenty years ago. What intrigued the little viewers under age five was not only the jovial, rainbow-colored Teletubbies but also the viewing pattern structured and presented by the show. As I see it, the *Teletubbies* characters represent the ideal body of the current TGIF (Twitter, Google, iPhone, Facebook) generation. On their round tummies is an embedded screen featuring mediatized images of children in a faraway location. Their heads have built-in antennae in order to receive clear images of the world outside the viewers' immediate environment. Teletubbies' bodies acquire an entirely new purpose because they can display distant images. Wouldn't many of the current TGIF Generation, constantly glued to their cell phones, tablets, and smart watches, love to implant portable screens in their bodies and never again risk losing their treasured electronic gadgets?

Another significant feature of *Teletubbies* programming is the intentional and consecutive repetition of the same video clips. When one video clip—usually five to six minutes long and featuring preschool children engaged in various activities such as painting or playing—is over, the Teletubbies unanimously request "again, again" in their cute infantile voices. Then the same video clip immediately repeats itself for the second time. This encouragement of digital regurgitation has much to do with features that have become familiar in today's digital consumption, such as instant replay and binge watching. K-pop visual materials, especially music videos and their previews, are designed in a way that encourages multiple viewing; with their dense structure and fast-moving jump cuts, so much visual information is packaged into every second that viewers have to watch any given video multiple times just to make basic sense out of it. In fact, I am ready to argue that music video producers create the video in a way that mandates multiple viewing experiences, since in the digital economy the traceable number of views each clip displays constitutes a cultural currency of its own (more on this later).

At the same time, the young viewers of the program are watching not only the featured videos as projected on one of the Teletubbies' tummies but also Teletubbies reacting to the videos. This scenario contains basic elements of reaction videos, which are so enormously popular as to constitute a distinctive subgenre in K-pop consumption. The joy and surprise that the Teletubbies display at repeated viewings are as much a focal point as the actual content featured on their screen. As media critic Sam Anderson has noted, the element of discovery constitutes the core attraction of watching reaction videos:

> Reaction videos are designed to capture, above all, surprise—that moment when the world breaks, when it violates or exceeds its basic duties and forces someone

to undergo some kind of dramatic shift. This is another source of the genre's appeal: in a culture defined by knowingness and ironic distance, genuine surprise is increasingly rare—a spiritual luxury that brings us close to something ancient. Watching a reaction video is a way of vicariously recapturing primary experience.[31]

The last sentence here needs further elaboration: "primary experience," as Anderson calls it, stands for discovering something for the first time. It is a gestural sign of live consumption (*live* here as "unrehearsed"). The embedded elements of liveness as a prized commodity in digital media consumption, as illustrated by *Teletubbies*, very much define a K-pop viewing experience.

The three major aspects of the *Teletubbies Generation*—a portable screen as an organic part of the ideal body, a repetitive viewing pattern, and the element of watching others react to visual materials—profoundly define K-pop fandom. These traits condition and are in turn conditioned by the ever-increasing global digital network, which provides an ideal ground for an industry like K-pop to thrive. As K-pop critic Cha U-jin notes, the rise of digital media consumption is an indispensable part of K-pop's publicity campaign:

> Although K-pop looks like a big thing, Korean pop has no business basis when they go out to the world. Even the large Korean entertainment companies such as SM, YG, and JYP appear as small venture companies in the face of the global music industry. To make it in the U.S., K-pop artists have to be discovered by EMI or other global networks. In order to make it in Japan, they have to work with companies like Avex, Universal Japan, or Sony Japan. This is why resorting to exponentially growing Internet media for global outreach is very important for Korea's entertainment companies, since they provide the companies with opportunities to promote themselves autonomously. JYP was the first one to have changed its YouTube channel to a global channel using all English in 2007. Six months later, YG and SM followed suit. This is why technology matters for these companies who have got to attract attention. For that matter, YG even has its own Social Network Services (SNS) department.[32]

Indeed, all three major companies run their own YouTube channel with a substantial number of followers. As of September 11, 2017, the number of YouTube channel subscribers for SM entertainment is 11.6 million; for YG Entertainment, 3 million; and for JYP Entertainment, 4.9 million. Facebook SM has garnered 5.4 million total likes, YG 3.3 million likes, and JYP 2.1 million likes. On Twitter, SM is followed by 4.8 million, YG by 5.3 million, and JYP by 1.8 million.

However, these numbers can be deceptive in that they do not reflect the global presence of particular stars whose prominence far exceeds that of their companies; for example, as of September 11, 2017, YG's boy band BIGBANG alone has 7.9 million YouTube subscribers, more than double the number of those who follow their company, and Choi Siwon (Choe Si-won) of SM's boy band Super Junior has 5.8 million followers on Twitter, again significantly more than the number of the company's followers. Although Choi is known to have the largest number of followers among Korean Twitter users, compared to the number of followers for global pop stars, such as 101 million for Justin Bieber and 70.2 million for Lady Gaga, the number is paltry. But when compared to the absence of the Japanese powerhouse entertainment group Johnnys, which produced numerous J-pop idols from SMAP to Arashi, from social media online traffic in the English language, Korean companies' presence is rather prominent, reflecting K-pop industry's more pressing need to explore the global market.[33]

Another digital media pool is China, a rapidly growing market for pop cultural consumption. China uses its own system of social media, where the number of followers for Korean pop stars often exceeds that of global stars. For instance, on Sina Weibo, the Chinese social media platform built on a hybrid model between Facebook and Twitter, boy band Super Junior's member Choi Siwon has sixteen million followers as of September 11, 2017. The number is staggering when compared to Justin Bieber's 304,066 followers,[34] again, reflecting the very different social media environment run by American as opposed to Chinese media companies. On Weibo, BIGBANG has at least 9.2 million followers (on a combination of various BIGBANG-related accounts, such as Big Bang_Asia, BIGBANGNEWS, and the BIGBANG Chinese site), with its member G-Dragon on a separate account having 14.4 million followers. This shows the equal importance of the Chinese and American markets for these K-pop artists.

But K-pop's digital media pool exceeds any national territories. Of more recent K-pop artists, BTS has made a noticeable presence on social media, boasting 11.5 million Twitter followers as of December 28, 2017, and generating huge numbers of retweets with their tweets. The band even entered the 2017 Guinness World Records for having the most Twitter engagements for a music act.

I do not dispute that counting the numbers of likes and followers on social media is a superficial practice that does not necessarily lead to qualitative discussions. However, it is also indisputable that these numbers are the signs of our time, when there is no such thing as bad publicity. According to the PBS-produced documentary "Generation Like," such numbers are huge marketing assets, literally translatable into dollar figures, social influence, and symbolic capital.[35] The quantifiable numbers of "likes" on Facebook and YouTube and "follows" on Twitter have come to be commodities that can literally be bought and sold for a certain price. The K-pop industry is not free from such rules of the digital age and will do everything possible to generate substantial followers, who will voluntarily spend their time to generate a constant stream of online publicity.

Media Tribalism: The Making and Breaking of Sociality

Such are the needs of "korporate" pop, mandating a large online fandom with coordinated action among content users dispersed across space. Although a systematic study of K-pop fandom lies beyond the scope of this book, the sociality of the community is pertinent to the understanding of K-pop as a bottom-up movement.

K-pop fans active within Korea are known for their group action and activism, both online and offline. They use their ability to mobilize groups via online communication to support their stars, for instance by voting for their idols in a music chart show in a manner typical for Generation Like. Their offline activities range from simple actions to complex activism: many K-pop fans coordinate to fill up the concert arena of their idol band and wave light sticks demonstrating their band's unique color to create an oceanlike effect, such as yellow ocean for BIGBANG concerts, red ocean for TVXQ concerts, and blue ocean for Super Junior concerts.[36] More complex activism has included influencing public opinion and court decisions to protect their idols' interests. For example, in 2009, when the trio JYJ broke away from SM Entertainment's popular quintet TVXQ in protest of unfair contract terms, their long-term battle with SM Entertainment was sustained by fans who successfully mobilized to introduce a fair entertainment practice known as the JYJ Law.[37] But the flip side of supportive fandom, which approximates ideal civil society, is an antifandom zealous to use its group identity and collective voice to haunt and persecute the objects of their dislike. The most notorious cases include the rappers Tablo (Tabeullo) and Jay Park, who were subject to menacing witch hunts by Korean Web users that resulted in a damaging hiatus in their careers.[38]

Such instances can be seen as very much in line with Couldry's notion of group liveness, a new kind of liveness that connects spatially disconnected participants when users of mobile technology participate in a simultaneous interaction. But what is unique about group liveness in K-pop is that the online connections that fans generate do not end in cyberspace but often materialize in tangible offline actions. The reverse is also true, where collective offline fan actions spill online. The most pertinent case of this online-offline continuum concerns the "black ocean" treatment given to the K-pop group Girls' Generation.[39] An undisputed leader in today's K-pop scene, Girls' Generation in 2008 was a rookie group, just one year into their debut, when they performed in Dream Concert—an annual event hosted at the Jamsil Olympic Stadium, which can potentially accommodate an audience of one hundred thousand. Prior to the live concert, the group's antifans coordinated their action plans online to antagonize Girls' Generation offline during the concert by turning off light sticks and thereby creating a "black ocean" that lasted for ten minutes. During that time, the members of Girls' Generation had to stage a couple of upbeat songs from their jolly debut album *Into the New World* to a dark and silent arena. These antifans' sabotage of Girls' Generation continued online long after the conclusion of the Dream Concert.

In contemplating K-pop fans' extraordinary online and offline coordination, as in the aforementioned black ocean or witch-hunt incidents, the concepts of Generation Like or the *Teletubbies Generation* fail to fully capture the complex implications of social interaction among fans. If "Generation Like" stands mostly for the affirming gestures of affection for idols carried out by fans and followers online, the live coordination that characterizes K-pop fandom offline points to the destructive possibilities of collective action. As one South Korean teenage fan girl declared in an interview, "Going to a live K-pop concert is like going to a war with other fandoms."[40] If the *Teletubbies Generation* illustrates the importance of unique viewing patterns in K-pop fandom, then the caustic collective behaviors of K-pop fandom illustrate that the act of watching K-pop performance is never neutral. In addressing the subversive side of group liveness, it is worth looking into the concept of "media tribalism" as a way to explore the darker side of Generation Like or the *Teletubbies Generation*.

Coined by the Japanese cultural studies scholar Ueno Toshiya, the term *media tribalism* derives from *urban tribalism*, which refers to "the small social groups based on urban (youth) subculture. Urban tribes formalize the relationship between people out of styles, tastes, and fashion choices within popular cultures and subcultures, as a mediatory moment."[41] Ueno expands the notion of urbanity not only as a physical place of a cityscape but also as a mediatized space that is intricately linked to its physical counterpart. In doing so, Ueno goes further to claim that no subculture can exist without relying on some sort of media: "Urban tribes are always already presented, articulated, and constituted by and through various types of media, which, in contemporary cities, are based on the artificial tribal sense and affiliative solidarity constituted in the accumulation of commodities."[42] Although the article, written in 1999, predates the arrival of mass online communication platforms such as TGIF, it touches upon the crucial stage in media development that started to blur the boundaries between online connectivity and offline connection.

Expanding on Ueno's use of the term as a way of mediating the online and offline social collective, I would add that *tribalism*, with its primitive connotations, emphasizes a strict boundary between who is a member and who is not. Therefore, the term is useful for understanding the darker side of the collective behavior of K-pop fans who assert their identity on the basis of tribal rivalry and exclusion: much like commodity accumulation, it points to the possessive behavioral traits that K-pop communities display in their desire to enjoy exclusive ownership of K-pop-related knowledge and access to K-pop acts.[43] This is very much the antithesis of the joyful and optimistic spirit of *heung* emerging from sincere rapport among communal participants, who have overcome conflict and struggle together. In the darker aspects of K-pop's sociality, this type of tribalism based on cloistered online and offline communities can "dispel *heung*" (*heung-eul kkaeda*) with its destructive obsession.

Ueno suggests that the reason media tribes are popular in a seemingly homogeneous society like Japan is that they are "supplements or surrogates for class, ethnicity and other agencies."[44] Although Ueno is primarily concerned with the myth of ethnic and cultural homogeneity that has helped define the facade of Japanese society, we can also extend the notion of homogeneity to encompass the alarming degree of uniformity that has come to characterize global pop culture, or the force that political scientist Benjamin Barber has described as pressing "nations into one homogenous global theme park, one McWorld tied together by communications, information, entertainment, and commerce."[45] If Ueno saw tribalism as a surrogate model to fracture both the myth and practice of social homogeneity, I propose that the notion of tribalism as seen in South Korean fandom focuses more on identity formation on the basis of exclusion. Rather than creating diversity, the fans conform to the fabricated tribal identity and cannot counter the homogenizing commercial forces of the marketplace. More often than not, media tribalism is complicit with the rules of the corporate world, or "McWorld" (hence "korporate" pop), which dictates its action plan, such as having to purchase merchandise to join a fan club and gaining more power within the fandom hierarchy via one's purchasing power.

To sum up, the sociality fostered by the live interactions of the K-pop community is deeply entangled in notions of Generation Like, the *Teletubbies Generation*, and the ambivalent politics of media tribalism. If the *Teletubbies Generation* marked the emergence of a new cohort whose sociality was conditioned by certain ways of seeing, then Generation Like took that social identity further by engaging in online group action that produced the classic sense of group liveness. While these two concepts are highly pertinent to the understanding of K-pop fans as a social collective, the concept of media tribalism potentially draws our attention to the darker implications of live collective action, making us see a more complete spectrum of K-pop's chiaroscuro. After all, *generation* and *tribe* imply two very different modes of social collective that are calibrated by varying ideological stances.

The Technological Makings of Liveness: Digital Economy, Digital Imagineering

The previous section on the ideological makings of liveness began with the 1990s, a transformative era when diverse forces collided to create seismic shifts in cultural paradigms. This section begins with the 1990s for a similar reason: this was also a crucial period for noticeable technological changes relevant to understanding today's K-pop industry. If the previous section pondered the "Korean" and "korporate" nature of K-pop, then this section turns to K-pop as "keyboard" or "keypad" pop by focusing on the rapidly shifting use of media and technology. This section will be devoted to three streams of thought that together lay out the technological conditions to explain K-pop's history: the shift from a broadcasting to microcasting model in TV and other media platforms; the shift from compact disks to digital files in music production and consumption; and finally the emergence of the Internet and the creation of digital imagineering.

The 1990s witnessed diversifying modes of media consumption, which often aligned with what media scholars call a transition from "broadcasting" to "narrowcasting." According to media studies scholar John Caldwell, the term *broadcasting* refers to "the overdetermined way that the networks themselves made television out to be one thing."[46] A clear example of broadcasting would be large-scale terrestrial networks' determination of how and what should be shown on TV, giving viewers very little control over their TV consumption patterns. *Narrowcasting*, on the other hand, refers to processes in the late 1980s and 1990s that "industrially produced [diversity] in an overdetermined way in a multicultural era."[47] Bringing this shift closer to the discussions of liveness, the broadcasting model featured the embedded notions of group liveness, since what viewers could watch at a certain time was predetermined by TV stations. But such top-down imposition of what is to be simultaneously consumed no longer holds in the narrowcasting model, and holds even less under the microcasting model, since the very premise of narrowcasting and microcasting was based on the fracturing of a sizable viewership engaged in the simultaneous consumption of shared content. In this respect, real-time liveness embedded in the broadcasting model became fragmented in the narrowcasting and microcasting models.

The "narrowcasting" of the 1990s by and large took the form of proliferating cable channels in South Korea; they were first introduced in 1995 and diversified the monopoly of three major terrestrial TV stations (KBS, MBC, SBS), which were regarded as the big three in the broadcasting era. But the narrowcasting model that emerged in the 1990s rapidly evolved into "microcasting" in the new millennium, when high-speed Internet and mobile gadgets allowed for even more varied experiences of media consumption. In line with the growing trend in microcasting, increased use of online stores and social media networks accessed via smartphones—Facebook, Twitter, and Google Hangouts in particular—transformed the idea of individual mobility. Both physical mobility and upward social mobility became indispensable to the purposes of mobile technology and media, which provided constant streams of new information, products, and services globally networked outside the framework of any single broadcasting station or state. With this shift came transforming notions of liveness: if the unilateral broadcasting model enabled group liveness based on the producer's control over the consumers' viewing patterns, then the microcasting model generated fragmented liveness based on consumers' choice to access a broader range of programs at the time they desired.

This process, which affects both the production and the consumption of media content, can be well explained through what Henry Jenkins has termed media convergence:

> Media convergence is more than simply the digital revolution; it involves the introduction of a much broader array of new media technologies that enable consumers to archive, annotate, transform, and recirculate media content. Media convergence is more than simply a technological shift; it alters the relationship between existing technologies, industries, markets, genres, and audiences.[48]

As the forms of media convergence became diversified, so did the cultural dynamics between Korea and Japan, especially with regard to how changing technology in music consumption became imbricated in the national branding of pop music.

Contrary to the hopes of many South Korean officials, who would like to promote K-pop as the dynamic strength of contemporary Korea, *K-pop* as a term was forged in relation to *J-pop*. According to Japan scholar Michael Bourdaghs, the term *J-pop* was "coined in 1988 as the name for domestic music segments on the popular Tokyo FM radio station J-WAVE" and "achieved wide currency in 1992 to 1994,"[49] the exact time when Korea was ambitiously launching its globalization policy. One significant aspect of the term is that "J-pop seems to presume the existence of counterparts: K-pop, C-pop, and so forth,"[50] implying that the primary market of J-pop was Asia and beyond, where the term would be more intuitively understood in relation to other nations' pop music scenes, much as the term *Korean wave* came into existence on the basis of preexisting terms like *Hong Kong wave*, *Japanese wave*, and *Chinese wave*, which are widely used in Japan.

Needless to say, if one country's pop music is to circulate only within its national boundary, there is no need to explicitly state the country of origin as a way of identifying the national brand. The branding is most necessary when pop music and culture circulate broadly outside national boundaries. As Michael Bourdaghs noted about J-pop, "Originally the term was a branding strategy that seemed to situate Japanese popular music, regardless of genre, on the world stage. After all, both the J and the pop were from English, as if the word had been coined abroad instead of by the Japanese marketing executives who were its actual inventors."[51]

Unlike the term *J-pop*, which was strategically chosen to imply the aura of a foreign genre by the Japanese, the term *K-pop* was coined outside Korea at

the end of the 2000s as a term distinguished from its widely known predecessor. One notable aspect that marked the wide circulation of the two terms—
J-pop in the early 1990s and *K-pop* in the late 2000s—was a significant shift
in what Jeffrey Funk terms a "technology paradigm,"[52] which had a profound
impact on the way we consume music. According to Funk, a "technology paradigm can be defined at any level in a nested hierarchy of subsystems, where
we are primarily interested in large changes in technologies, or what many call
technological discontinuities."[53] To bring this paradigm shift closer to our case
study, the first decade of J-pop's popularity, from 1988 to 1998, saw a transition in the music consumption format from long-play (LP) records to compact disks (CDs). This was when J-pop CD sales boomed, "doubling the size
of prerecorded music sales in Japan."[54] It would not be too much of a stretch to
claim that the soaring popularity of J-pop was inherently related to the popularity of the new medium of compact disks. Since each medium not only provided content (J-pop music in this case) but also served as a platform (a CD
in this case), the merging of the two opened a way for new patterns of music
consumption to thrive. As Bourdaghs noted, vinyl records are played on a
shared stereo system, but compact disks are played individually: "As members
of the family increasingly listened to music on individual playback devices
rather than a shared stereo system, and as new digital-recording and distribution technologies reduced the cost of producing and marketing recordings,
the mass market splintered."[55] The shift from LP to CD was analogous to the
aforementioned shift from broadcasting to narrowcasting and then again to
microcasting.

Similarly, K-pop boomed precisely when the transition from CDs to digital
music files took place and traditional CD sales were suffering—in part because
of the financial crisis, in part because of an inevitably shifting media platform.
Music producers had little choice but to explore various possibilities for the industry to survive in the new millennium, so rather than producing a complete
CD album they took advantage of minialbums or single releases as a way to
encourage more frequent, albeit sporadic, music consumption. South Korean
music critic Shin Hyun-joon (Sin Hyeon-jun) noted that "the collapse of album
sales and the still maturing online music market" was the biggest reason to
push K-pop's global reach.[56] K-pop was quick to adopt the emerging trend of
à la carte music consumption as the industry devised effective means to sell
single songs that stood alone and, for the most part, were consumed by an individual wearing headphones on a mobile gadget.

But the mobile gadgets alone could not have propelled this shift: this change in hardware used for music consumption had to be supported by the broader availability of high-speed Internet access as well as the development of hardware that would allow for multimedia music consumption to take place: if MP3s enabled the mobile consumption of sound, then smartphones, large online streaming capacity for sound and images, and ubiquitously available high-speed Internet connectivity had to enable the mobile and facile consumption of multimedia K-pop. Catalysts that made the transition from broadcasting to microcasting, from LPs to digital music files, included both hardware and software.

The Internet: Imagining through the Digital

Q: What are your thoughts about the fact that there are these massive stars in other countries that we don't even know about?

Paint: Well, I am from YouTube. I know all about their lives.

"From YouTubers React to K-pop #2," Fine Brothers Entertainment

Prominent YouTube personality Paint supposes that YouTube is a land of its own, comparable to countries and regions in a geopolitical sense. This place is transnational and borderless, allowing new digital networks to emerge and thrive as never before. The ties of this imagined community that encompasses multinational users of YouTube, Facebook, Twitter, Google, and more have enabled intimate global connectivity, thanks to the increasing technical capability for data computation and transmission. As of 2015, current technology can handle massive data equivalent to listening to "31,773 hours of music," sharing "3.3 million pieces of content on Facebook," or watching "138,889 hours of videos on YouTube" in just one minute.[57]

The rise of global connectivity raises questions about the formation of the digital economy and how K-pop not only survives but also thrives in it. According to a Bloomberg article, in 2016 alone, K-pop music videos collectively "were watched about 24 billion times, with 80% of views coming from outside Korea."[58] But how did Korea as a specific geographic location become one of the epicenters of the new pop music trend? What conditions, especially concerning the accessibility of the Internet and information sharing, have enabled this place to be associated with a major cultural hub in the digital age?

According to urban geographers Edward Lamecki and Bruno Moriset, the "digital economy is based on three interlinked, converging technological trends: first the commoditization of fast, cheap computing capacity and data storage; second, the domination of standardized software platforms which allow digital connectivity—notably the Internet; and third, the building of a worldwide, integrated digital network."[59] These three trends concern a broad spectrum of issues, but I will focus on those relevant to the generation and circulation of K-pop content.

Computing Capacity and Data

In terms of computing capacity and data storage, the most relevant aspect for the K-pop industry is the prevalence of MP3s and smartphones in music consumption, as these are becoming increasingly adaptable to rapid data processing and compact storage. The invention of the MP3, which was made possible by eliminating "irrelevant information, most of which was ignored by human ear," in CDs' "maximalist repository" made music files even more portable than compact disks by entirely eliminating the physicality of music files.[60] Fascinatingly documented by Stephen Witt's book *How Music Got Free*, the invention of the MP3 triggered music piracy and illegal downloads on an unprecedentedly large scale. With the invention of the MP3, music—not just mainstream music but also music regarded as peripheral—was suddenly traveling much more broadly across the globe as a free commodity via the Internet, ready to be played at a mouse click. Additionally, as mentioned in the introduction, piracy and illegal downloads drove small-scale music industries such as Korean pop music to the edge of bankruptcy, forcing them to become viable in foreign markets.

Bringing the issue closer to Korea and K-pop, Samsung Electronics enjoyed a worldwide reputation as the major producer of semiconductors as early as the 1980s, positioning Korea as a harbinger of computing technology. As the production of portable electronic gadgets grew exponentially and became more and more competitive in the mid-1990s, Samsung invested heavily in developing new mobile phones, such as the Anycall series (1993–2010) and the Galaxy series (2009–present), with a brand image that promoted multitasking, flexibility, novelty, and mobility. As smart phones were capable of playing MP3 files, the nexus between the hardware (smartphone) and the software (music files) became more dense.

It is not surprising to find an enduring and ever-expanding relationship between the two hottest export items manufactured in South Korea nowadays—Samsung smartphones and K-pop music. Sam Grobart, a journalist who visited Samsung Electronics' major manufacturing base in Gumi, South Korea, significantly observed:

> The first thing you notice about Gumi is the K-pop. Korean pop music seems to be everywhere outside, usually coming from outdoor speakers disguised as rocks.

The music has an easy, mid-tempo style, as if you were listening to a mellow Swing Out Sister track in 1988. The music, a Samsung spokeswoman explains, is selected by a team of psychologists to help reduce stress among employees.[61]

Though the connection between the Samsung factory and K-pop music seems to have been predicated on the simple practicality of enhancing labor efficiency, there is a more enduring engagement between the two, with deeper roots in the culture of rapid transformation and disposability.

The enduring connection between cell phones and K-pop idols is fascinating, particularly in terms of the increasing assimilation of what used to be distinctive sectors of communication, media, and entertainment. The trend was most palpable in the promotion campaign for Anycall, Samsung's cell phone series, which were the first to enjoy global success. With the launching of new Anycall models, Samsung sponsored iconic talents across Korean pop culture to organize promotional bands that collaborated on albums, music videos, and special ringtones to be downloaded at a set fee. Taking a cue from the cell phone name, in 2005, the first promotional video, "Anymotion," was released, featuring two K-pop fixtures: dance diva Lee Hyori (Yi Hyo-ri) and Eric, a member of the popular boy band Sinhwa. This nine-minute video featured a story of an aspiring singer and dancer (played by Lee Hyori) who eventually realizes her dream of stardom with the help of her friend (played by Eric). Although not strictly a commercial film, "Anymotion" nevertheless featured sleek models of the latest Anycall line at crucial moments of communication between the protagonists.

Known as "entertainment marketing," which taps into music, dance, video, and other elements to stimulate consumers' sensibility, videos such as "Anymotion" are distinct from other commercial films in that they do not bluntly promote the product but rather give an impression that their primary mission is to provide visual pleasure for viewers while subtly embedding the advertised product in the seductive story line. According to a Samsung spokesperson, "The refreshing aspect of entertainment marketing is that it promotes products as a seamless part of cultural events."[62] With the success of the first campaign, which attracted "younger consumers in their teens and twenties who are known to update their cell phones more frequently than consumers in their thirties and beyond," Samsung launched four sequels over the next four years: "Anyclub," "Anystar," "Anyband," and the final installment of a song/music video titled "AMOLED," an acronym for active-matrix organic light-emitting diodes, of which Samsung is known to be the world's leading producer.[63]

A smaller-scale Korean manufacturer of smartphones, LG, has also been trying to catch up with the entertainment marketing capitalizing on K-pop's global visibility: in 2011, when LG was debuting its cell phone model Optimus, it partnered with KARA, a K-pop girl group popular in Japan, and when the company attempted to break into the South American market, it hosted a K-pop contest called "K-pop by LG" in Colombia.

Smartphones, in this sense, are no longer just hardware for mobile computing devices and data storage; rather, they have become part of an inherent flow of the K-pop trend—the nation's source of soft power. As such, they have become active participants in a campaign for national branding taking place simultaneously on industrial and cultural fronts. They are foundational means for promoting national cool at the intersections of the creative and digital economies while creating an impression that they enable neoliberal ideas of individuals' social mobility.

Software Platforms That Allow Digital Connectivity
It is not my goal to delve into how technological inventions, such as laser diodes or optical fibers, were crucial in laying the foundation for the commercialization of the Internet. What concerns me the most here is how globally adopted software platforms enabled two-way connectivity between the K-pop industry and worldwide fandom, particularly in terms of forging a different notion of liveness in the digital age. Although online music consumption such as streaming or watching music views does not foster the traditional sense of liveness based on the physical copresence of listeners, easy accessibility to the online music of their choice at the time of their choice gave listeners a new brand of liveness based on ongoing consumption patterns in everyday life.

Software platforms, according to economists David Evans, Andrei Hagiu, and Richard Schmalensee, are "invisible engines based on written computer code" and power "many modern industries, including digital music, mobile phones, on-line auction, personal computers, video games, Web-based advertising, and online searches."[64] These platforms, which have created a whole new ecosystem of media and hardware convergence, tend to be most successful when they are fueled by users' feedback.[65] As Evans, Hagiu, and Schmalensee argue: "Software platforms are inherently multisided. They usually serve distinct groups of customers, who benefit from having each other on the same platform."[66] Precisely such a multidirectional flow of information exchange along software platforms through Application Programing Interfaces (APIs) has spurred exponential growth of the digital economy in the past two decades.

The ubiquitous presence of globally shared platforms enabled the real-time sharing of applications, such as Google Hangouts, YouTube, and Twitter, thereby creating near-live interaction between K-pop's producers and consumers. Major applications that K-pop consumers use became established around the globe almost simultaneously without too much time lag: YouTube launched Korean-language service on January 23, 2008, just two years after the site was acquired by Google. But more significantly, K-pop channels, run by major Korean entertainment companies such as SM, YG, and JYP, were made available in English in 2007. Facebook Korea registered as a limited corporation in October 2010, and Twitter opened its Korean branch in September 2012.[67] Google Hangouts, the latest software to be scrutinized in this book, was launched almost concurrently worldwide in March 2013. The close time proximity of these events, propelled by the multisided nature of software platforms, illustrates how meaningless it is to separate centripetal flows of information (from the world to Korea) from centrifugal flows (from Korea to the world), since the entire goal of a common software platform is to enable free-flowing, multidirectional connectivity.

The highly reliable connection enables a semblance of live (real-time) communication that is powerful enough to transcend traditional language barriers; perhaps this is one of the reasons highly circulated content on the Internet places so much emphasis on translingual content, featuring visual images and emotive sounds that are not bound by specific languages. What better material than K-pop music videos and performances? Just think of "Gangnam Style," the most viewed video clip in the history of the Internet. Although most of its three billion viewers do not understand the Korean lyrics, the sense of live communication comes from the universal language of bodily humor as well as the fact that the whole world is simultaneously participating in its reproduction.[68]

A Worldwide, Integrated Digital Network

Korea occupies an advanced position in the global race to create a broadband network, since a fast and affordable network "shapes the ubiquity of the digital economy across time and space."[69] An alternative to dial-up, broadband enables "access to internet provided at speeds significantly higher than those used by the traditional method."[70]

In Korea consumers can find one of the most affordable, high-quality broadband services in the world. Chung Inho (Jeong In-ho) explains how free-market price competition is one of the major factors allowing for Korea's low-cost service: "Broadband belonged to the advanced services, distinguished

from the basic services such as telephone services according to legal classifica-
tion system of the Korean telecommunications business law, and therefore did
not require much intervention or regulation by the government."[71]

Chung further points out additional factors in Korea's broadband success,
such as the "hurry hurry" (*ppalli ppalli*) mentality and geographical specificities. Describing the former, he advances the notion that the uniquely Korean
national character places a "high value not only on how well it was done but
also on how fast it was done."[72]

The latter points to the geographic specificities in Korea, where "more than
50% of households live in apartment complexes, and population density is very
high, which enables carriers to realize economy of density and lower their costs
for building and operating networks."[73] Whatever the reason behind Korea's
rapid and wide-ranging adoption of a 3G network, it opened an era of video
calls and mobile TV technologies where multimedia stars came to dominate
the music industry and were seen everywhere—on TV, computer, tablets, and
mobile phones. The K-pop industry's quick adaptability to changing technology was noted by a US tech blogger:

> The US's music industry was built for the 20th century—a world of scarcity, lim-
> ited distribution channels, hyperfocus on music and a strong reliance on copy-
> right—but the Korean pop music landscape is focused on a much more 21st
> century strategy. They focus on "industrializing" the production of music, with
> hit factories and star making academies. They focus on a multimedia experi-
> ence. Korean pop music is released on TV. New debuts are released on TV with
> a video . . . and, of course, via YouTube. And that's the third point: Korea is in-
> credibly wired. It was the first country with 3G networks in place and one of the
> first to have super high bandwidth broadband widely available. The end result?
> The industry, mostly built up in the past two decades, is built for the modern
> digital world, while the US industry still pines for the way things used to be.[74]

As flattering as the assessment might appear for those working in the K-pop
industry, this piece also raises questions about the rest of the world. If Korea
is indeed a leader in mobile technology fueled by cheap and fast broadband,
then how does K-pop content cross the national border to the rest of the world,
where high-quality Internet connections are not necessarily in place? Needless
to say, the primary destinations of K-pop as korporate pop are advanced countries with a well-established digital infrastructure to circulate its content: that
is, places wealthy enough to generate revenue.

But even within Organisation for Economic Co-operation and Development (OECD) countries, there is a wide disparity in terms of access to high-speed Internet and data circulation. According to the OECD Communications Outlook released in 2013, "Mobile television has not seen wide adoption outside Japan and Korea,"[75] testifying to the fact that the convergence of traditional means of communication and Internet communication happens at different paces in different places, even within the developed world. The point is that fashionable content such as K-pop, with its focus on visual clips, might be brokering the propagation of speedier Internet networks outside Korea. In a way, Korea's rapid adoption of broadband is setting an example for other countries and cities to adopt its digital urbanism, "which endeavors to generate systemic development effects by leveraging IT applications—especially those provided by local enterprises—in the whole range of urban functions, making the city a living laboratory of the digital economy."[76] When K-pop music videos crisscross the world through fiber-optic cables in real time, what travels with them is the idea of a utopian digital economy, urban space that still proudly carries a national banner. In this regard, I make a small digression here to provide a qualitative interpretation of *ppalli ppalli* with Korean national characteristics in mind: speed is not just about technology but also about a mode of social interaction where expedited connection among people could potentially give rise to *heung*, a uniquely Korean mode of affect that emerges from interactions among community members.

Imagination as the Fourth Element in the Digital Economy
The previous three intermingled components of the digital economy as categorized by Malecki and Moriset are relevant to K-pop's global circulation, but I believe a foundational aspect is missing in their discussion—namely, imagination. For the digital economy to be at the heart of the creative economy, there has to be a substantial discussion of imagination stemming from human talent, especially with regard to a labor-intensive industry like K-pop.[77]

The discussion that addresses the intersections of the digital economy and the imagination is often dominated by unbounded optimism about the unlimited potential of human imagination ("The sky's the limit"). Take, for instance, business consultant Alf Chattell's uplifting vision of the future in a tone typical of a motivational speaker: "Perhaps the only limits in the emerging digital economy will be the limits of imagination. Fuelling the imagination will perhaps be the greatest source of value. And the tools to fuel the imagination are developing fast. Powerful, easy-to-use tools—tools which might be called imagineering tools—will soon be available to us all."[78] Optimistic as well as prophetic, Chattell's belief in "imagineering" nonetheless provides an occasion to critically examine the intersections of media infrastructure and human resources. As the hybrid term *imagineering* itself proposes, the implication is that creativity, or a creative economy for that matter, is rooted in the flexibly aligned nexus between art and technology, hardware and software. But behind the celebratory tone hailing this partnership lies a precarious collusion between the institutional commodification of imagination and neoliberal subjects' complicit desire to advance their economic interests. The cultural studies scholar Andrew Ross aptly points to this complicity when he claims that "cultural work was nominated as the new face of neoliberal entrepreneurship, and its practitioners were cited as the hit-making models for the IP jackpot economy."[79] The K-pop industry is prone to the conditions described by Ross, for its dexterous performers parade neoliberal ideals of self-grooming and self-advancement by subtly transfiguring digital technology into creative power. Technologies that literally create K-pop idols' bodies and bodily attributes, such as plastic surgery, auto-tune, and holograms, are celebrated as part and parcel of the creative economy. In this regard, the role of technology in K-pop might not be limited to a mere instrumental way to celebrate creativity; the opposite might be true as well, with the K-pop industry's creativity becoming a subtle form of mediation to ultimately celebrate technology (as seen in the aforementioned creative marketing strategy). This is the implication behind the marriage between imagination and engineering.

But the complexities of digital imagineering are perhaps most illuminating for an understanding of K-pop industry's fascination with liveness. What particular forms of expression and modes of communication does imagineering assume in "live" K-pop? As I investigate how the fluid zone of imagineering conditions the actual performance culture of K-pop that is prone to broad global circulation, I keep my eye on the close partnership between community and commodity, simultaneously being forged under the concept of liveness. Digital technology enables real-time communication around the world and may enable a live community. Nonetheless, live communication is not always equivalent to the creation of a live community, and an often counteracting force is the idea of live connection as a valuable commodity.

K-pop touts rhetoric that blurs the concepts of liveness, community, and commodity and treats them as interchangeable, rather than antithetical. K-pop shows how the music of today has become a key player across various media platforms, traversing TV stations, YouTube, live stages, and holographic performances, which are the converged manifestations of ideology, technology, and imagination. The following chapters will introduce these media platforms—one by one—as fully interchangeable environments where liveness as a valued commodity can be performed along the transmedial spectrum.

2

K-POP FROM LIVE TELEVISION
TO SOCIAL MEDIA

AS IN MANY OTHER PLACES around the globe, television in South Korea served as a central media platform for popular music consumption before high-speed Internet enabled the popularization of digital music and music videos online. Ever since Korea's public station, Korea Broadcasting System (KBS), opened in 1961, popular music has been the crown jewel in the entertainment programming. Starting with the music shows *The Singer of Your Choice* (*Dangsini ppobeun gasu*) and *Pop Song Parade* (*Gayo peureideu*), both of which first aired in 1962, the past fifty years have always featured music, in the format of a variety show or a music chart show. The same goes for the privately owned Tongyang (Dongyang) Broadcasting Company (TBC), which aired pop music through their popular variety show *Show Show Show* (1964–83), Munhwa Broadcasting Corporation (MBC), which began operation in 1969, and Seoul Broadcasting System (SBS), which in 1991 joined the triumvirate of terrestrial networks in Korea. While MBC had six pop song–related programs in the very first year of its operation, SBS started modestly with one pop music show, *Ingigayo*, which continues to this day.[1]

One notable event in the brief history of Korean TV networks is the introduction of color TV in 1980. By the 1990s, a color TV system was established throughout Korea. According to Korean media scholars Gang Tae-yeong and Yun Tae-jin, this development served as a major incentive for various TV stations to pump out more entertainment shows,[2] including music programs. These proliferating entertainment programs were also on a spectacular scale,[3]

laying the foundations for the current music shows to be analyzed in this chapter. Korean media critics Jeong Sun-il and Jang Han-seong even call the 1990s a
time when a vast majority of programs were "entertainment-ized" (*orakhwa*).[4]

The arrival of cable TV channels in 1995 brought about even more foundational changes in popular music programs. On March 1, 1995, thirty cable TV
channels started service in Korea; many, such as MTV Korea and Mnet (Music
Network), included entertainment-focused programming. By the end of 1995,
half a million people subscribed to cable TV, and the number of subscribers
multiplied five times, to 2.5 million, in two years.[5] The emergence of multiple
cable channels meant that the age of intense competition for not only domestic
but also global audiences had begun.[6]

Cable TV also changed TV viewing patterns. Programming followed the
terrestrial stations' simultaneous broadcasting model based on an asymmetri-
cal relationship between producers and consumers (viewers were passive audiences who did not get a chance to participate in program making), where a few
producers transmitted programming to masses of consumers. The transmedia
environment today differs radically from that one-way broadcasting pattern.
The individual-centered consumption pattern of "Me-TV," viewing at a time
and space of one's choosing via IPTV (Internet protocol TV), is rapidly catch-
ing up with the broadcasting model in tech-savvy places like Korea.[7]

How is this "Me-TV" experience different from other concurrent media
practices, such as watching visual content on a smartphone or watching a film in
a movie theater? Film and TV have been compared quite extensively by media
scholars, especially in the early days of TV when it started to disrupt the experience of communal viewing in movie theaters. Philip Auslander makes a key argument that "early writers on television generally agreed that television's essential
properties as a medium are *immediacy* and *intimacy*."[8] These qualities, in large
part, stem from the notion of liveness that early television is known to have fostered. In this context, media studies scholar Lynn Spigel notes the genealogical
kinship between live theater and television: "Television, it was constantly argued,
would be a better approximation of live entertainment than any previous form
of technological reproduction. Its ability to broadcast direct to the home would
allow people to feel as if they really were at the theatre."[9] Using TV's potential
as a vicarious form of live theater, music shows strive to create a semblance of
live performance, despite the inherently mediatized format. Combined with the
intimate viewing pattern of "Me-TV," music performance on TV is much more
capable of staging something akin to "live" than are music videos on YouTube.

Such fundamental differences that separate TV from the rising forms of new media have been noted by Mickey Kim, the head of Google TV Partnerships in the Pacific-Asia region:

> The Internet age evolved rapidly, with a quick transition from PCs to mobiles such as iPhones and Androids as its major platform. But there has not been a smart TV that has changed our lives. TV must be simple and easy, but there have been aggressive attempts to insert features of computers or mobile phones. TV needs simplicity, and we need to be cognizant of the environment unique to TV as a media platform.[10]

Kim teases out the primary factor that makes TV still a prevalent mass medium in the digital age—its simplicity. TV's pervasiveness across generations and command over large screens (often used for communal viewing) still distinguish it from more mobile media platforms, such as laptops and smartphones. Hence, while the modes through which TV's content is transmitted have changed tremendously in the age of new media, from cable TV to satellite to IPTV, TV's function, mostly providing premade visual programming, has not changed much.[11] If smartphones are an ideal platform for multimedia consumption (communication on the phone, checking e-mail, using social media, browsing Web news, consuming audiovisual clips), then TV still is ideal for "monomedia" (consuming audiovisual contents).

Instead of having various features married directly to TV, an increasing number of viewers watch TV while also using other devices, such as their smartphones, tablets, or laptops. As Korean media scholar Yi Dong-hu pointed out: "Television remains the major platform for watching TV programming, but as the proliferation of media platforms that can play the programs as well as the simultaneous action of watching TV while using other media devices is becoming prevalent, a different experience of watching TV became possible."[12] While TV's function remains simple, audiences' viewing habits are becoming increasingly complex, bordering on multitasking and thereby creating intermedial activities between TV and other platforms. This trend is most prominently featured in the following two case studies, where the TV-viewing experience is often accompanied by parallel activities such as texting and tweeting that contribute to the creation of group liveness—an emblematic mode in which media tribalism often plays out.

The two K-pop TV programs analyzed in this chapter—*Music Core* and *After School Club*—will dialogically illustrate a wide range of functions that TV performs in the production and circulation of K-pop. Since *Music Core* is a program produced by one of Korea's largest terrestrial TV stations, MBC, whereas *After School Club* is produced by Arirang TV, Korea's premier English-language cable network subsidized by the Korean government, this chapter illuminates how the government and the private sector reach out to global audiences in ways that are both similar and different.

K-pop Music Chart Shows
and the Meaning of Live Broadcasting

Smartly but casually dressed men of various ages, from their early twenties to late fifties, swarm into their usual hangout coffee shop located near KBS TV, Korea's foremost public television station with the longest history of operation. They are frantically checking their cell phone text messages while comparing notes with one another, whispering rapidly in low voices and frowning at the unfortunate message that doomed their day: "Producer Tak is in a terrible mood today!" "Bad mood warning signal level three!" "Damn, just forget about introducing your rookies to Producer Tak today." Frustration mixed with resignation binds these managers who are hired by entertainment companies to manage pop singers; their sole purpose in congregating near the TV station was to meet with Producer Tak in the hope of lobbying her to feature their new singers on a KBS music chart show, *Music Bank*. As the chief producer, Tak surely wields enormous power as a gatekeeper for K-pop idols who wish to be introduced to a broader audience.

Although a fictional scene lifted from a popular Korean TV drama *Peurodeusa* (KBS, 2015), which centers on the satiric portrayal of TV producers in charge of creating entertainment programming with the sole purpose of garnering high viewership ratings, the scene nonetheless accurately captures the bitter truth about the K-pop industry, where only a certain number of performers can reach the mass audience through the hierarchal structure. This scene cannot simply be diminished into fictitious comedy lampooning the world of K-pop entertainment—the world of glitzy fame with which the general public, and especially young people, are deeply enthralled. There is a documentarian truth to the situation illustrated here: real-world K-pop singers' managers might well find themselves trying to curry favor with the producers of TV music shows and ready to bend over backward to secure airtime for the stars they manage.

The former director of SM Entertainment's A&R Department has testified that the real world of K-pop is not so different from the scene in *Peurodeusa*, especially in terms of how important it is for singers to be on TV: "It is even customary for singers' managers to know the birthdays of TV producers' family members and send presents in currying their favor to get a spot on music programs for their singers."[13] It is no wonder that singers complain about how "producers change when they get to work on music chart programs, since every manager treats them like kings."[14]

When and how did this practice of kowtowing to the producers of music chart shows emerge, and how does television's history of live broadcasting affect the sustainability of music chart shows? When media platforms are becoming increasingly diverse and versatile—a trend that often translates into the rising influence of Internet platforms and a declining share of TV shows in the overall consumption of K-pop—how does TV manage to hold on to its conventional influence over the circulation of pop culture? This chapter surveys the evolution of TV music chart shows, with an eye toward how they strive to maintain their key role in the production and consumption of K-pop in the age of new media. In this process, I will pay particular attention to the practice of "live TV shows" as seen in a case study: MBC's music chart show *Music Core*, a live broadcasting session of which I was personally able to attend and observe.

A Brief History of TV Music Shows

For nearly a decade, from 1981 to 1991, KBS's *Gayo Top Ten* was the one and only TV program in South Korea that provided viewers with a weekly pop song chart. Although SBS's *Ingigayo* (1991–present) and MBC's *Ingigayo Best 50* (1995–98) were close contenders joining the race to produce music chart shows, *Gayo Top Ten* was the undisputed ringleader, unmatched in popularity and authority until its production came to an end in 1998.[15] As *Gayo Top Ten*'s history parallels my emergence from childhood into adolescence and then into young adulthood, the mention of it brings back varied memories interlaced with deep nostalgia. Every week, I eagerly waited for the show to find out which song had landed at the top of the chart. So much class time was spent on daydreaming about skipping school and rushing to the TV station to see the live recording of the program in heart-racing proximity to the singing stars. The Internet was not accessible to provide a constant stream of diverse content, and a show like *Gayo Top Ten* was a rare TV event where one could actually connect faces and moving images to voices heard on radios and cassette tapes, allowing listeners to enjoy music as a total genre layered with visual sensations. It was even a tactile experience, full of heated excitement for those who were present in the studio during the time of recording.

But those days when *Gayo Top Ten* shaped the music chart as the primary authority are forever gone. Now one can hear music through multiple new media platforms—online downloads and streaming services, YouTube and Vevo—all of which play a significant role in determining the ranking on music charts. With the proliferation of high-speed Internet and smartphones, music can be enjoyed as a total performance genre at the time and location of our choosing. As the chief producer of YG Entertainment Group Yang Hyun Suk noted,

> As the Internet is becoming so widely available, fewer and fewer viewers patiently wait for hours in front of a live TV just to see their stars appear. Everyone nowadays just wants to see the portion where their favorite stars appear [on the Internet]; the age of waiting for the stars to appear on TV is now gone forever.[16]

Given this situation, why are music chart shows on TV still wielding enormous power over K-pop distribution and consumption?

Instead of withering away and opening up new spaces for the latest media platforms to provide music, in the Korean music industry, as opposed to its counterpart in the United States, not only did *Gayo Top Ten* survive with a new name, *Music Bank* (1998–), but other, similar shows multiplied so as to provide incessant weeklong entertainment with music chart shows on TV. As of August 2017, there is not a single day of the week when audiences cannot find a TV show like *Gayo Top Ten*. On Monday, the English-language channel Arirang TV airs *Simply K-pop*; on Tuesday, cable channel SBS MTV airs *The Show*;[17] on Wednesday, cable network MBC Music Channel airs *Show Champion*;[18] on Thursday, cable channel Mnet broadcasts *M Countdown*;[19] on Friday, KBS shows *Music Bank*; on Saturday, another network, MBC, broadcasts *Music Core*; on Sunday, yet another network, SBS, airs *Ingigayo*. Of these shows, the last three—as the products of three major terrestrial TV stations—wield enormous influence and broadcast live during weekends to attract high ratings.

The proliferation of TV music shows may seem a bonanza for hardcore music fans, who like to not only "listen" to but also "watch" the spectacular performance by their favorite singers. But similar shows on American TV have pretty much disappeared and are only a chapter in history. The vestiges of TV's golden age as the producer of music charts such as *America's Top 10* (1980–92) can be seen only sporadically on MTV's *This Week's Top 20* in the United Kingdom, or American cable channels, such as Fuse's *Top 20 Countdown* or VH1's *Top 20 Video Countdown*, while most music charts have migrated to cyberspace. The highly influential magazine *Billboard* created the "Korea K-pop Hot 100" chart in 2011, but it exists as an online chart, not as a TV show.

Any explanation of TV music chart shows continuing popularity in Korea must take multiple factors into account, but of primary importance are the specific circumstances the K-pop industry faces, especially the star system used by entertainment companies and the manufactured nature of popularity by various media forces. This issue primarily concerns the shifting power dynamics between TV stations and entertainment companies, both of which vie for control over how K-pop stars are promoted. Before the rise of new media, TV networks had much more influence over which music circulated in the public arena, but nowadays they have no choice but to yield a significant portion of their power to media-savvy entertainment companies that deploy multiple media outlets to promote their stars.

This shift in power dynamics is propelled by the rise of new media that enable consumers to listen to and watch music without the mediation of TV stations. The flip side of increasing music circulation via new media is the demise of music consumption at live performances, which raises questions about the role the TV music chart shows play in this transitional phase, as they still admit live audiences, albeit in limited numbers, to the recording studio to watch and cheer for the performing stars. Understanding this process within the context of the K-pop industry will illuminate how the connections between music production and consumption, fan labor and leisure, can expand the meaning of *live*. If the term primarily designates mere "physical co-presence of performers and audiences" in a live concert format, then in the recording sessions of music chart shows its definition reaches a more abstract level of forging an imagined community.[20] Bound by the idea of synchronicity pertaining to the practice of "live broadcasting," fans certainly play a crucial role in the process as both spectators of the shows and consumers of content on multimedia platforms.

K-pop between Entertainment Companies and TV Stations

Compared to the music chart programs of the 1980s and '90s, the shows that have sprung up in the new millennium on both cable networks and broadcasting stations are radically different. *Gayo Top Ten* could easily amuse all generations, as it covered a wide range of music and singers, but the new shows mostly cover K-pop idol music, catering primarily to audiences in their teens and early twenties.[21] The exact timing of this transition is hard to pinpoint, but it coincides with the turn of the new millennium, when the first generation of idols, such as H.O.T. (1996–2001) and S.E.S. (1997–2002), reached the pinnacle of their popularity and turned into a social phenomenon with an unprecedented fandom consisting mostly of teenagers.

Specialists in the field of K-pop tend to agree that the transition was made in part through a strategic partnership between two forces that shape the industry: TV stations and entertainment companies. According to pop music critic Kim Chang-nam (Gim Chang-nam), this was in large part because entertainment companies and TV networks had something to gain from the joint system of producing and promoting idols through music chart shows that focus on performances: "From TV networks' perspective, idols provided attractive content with spectacular visual performance and hence guaranteed good viewership ratings; on the other hand, entertainment companies used TV networks to promote their idols, which brought about the music shows that predominantly feature young stars."[22] Kim's observation is based on the rapidly shifting contours of the music industry; with the collapse of traditional music sales, the idols needed to take even more aggressive measures to promote themselves as all-around entertainers through dramas or variety entertainment shows to sustain their careers. Terrestrial TV networks, still one of the most pervasive media platforms, became indispensable in the process.

Nonetheless, Kim's point about the high ratings supposedly guaranteed by popular idols does not reflect the latest realities of declining viewership of these music shows. Despite the importance the K-pop industry places on them, these programs suffer an abysmal 2 to 3 percent rating.[23] As pop culture critic Heo Ji-woong (Heo Ji-ung) commented, "Koreans love singing so much, so when music programs get such low ratings, it is a telling sign that something is not working."[24] In addition to the fact that these shows target only a narrow demographic of teenage viewers, the shift in music consumption patterns has diversified the way music charts are produced and circulated via various online music stores, resulting in less dependence on TV music programs for weekly charts.

The increasing influence of online music stores prevents the K-pop industry from having a single credible chart akin to Billboard or Oricon in the J-pop industry. The five major online music stores in South Korea—Mellon, Mnet.com, Ole Music, Bugs Music, and Soribada—each have their own list of recommendations, which greatly influences their music charts.[25] According to research by Gim Min-yong, "90 percent of the songs that end up on top of a given music chart come from its own recommended list" and "The credibility of current music charts is certainly distorted by the recommendation system."[26] This incestuous relationship between chart and recommendations—all managed by the same company—is controlled, in turn, by the music stores' preproduction investment in certain artists and albums; unless artists are managed by well-established entertainment companies, most have to produce their songs and albums by tapping into investments received from online music stores in advance. As online music stores wield increasing power over K-pop production, they inevitably take authority away from the music chart TV shows, which, in turn, suffer poor ratings. But the following question still remains: Why do TV stations, from terrestrial TV stations to cable networks, keep producing the shows with 2 to 3 percent ratings while other variety shows are likely to be discontinued once their rating falls to 4 to 5 percent?

The most convincing explanation to date is provided by the media celebrity Kim Gura (Gim Gu-ra), describing how a strategic partnership is forged between entertainment companies and TV stations:

> Music chart shows are the only mechanism through which broadcasting stations can control large entertainment companies. If TV stations want to increase the viewership rating of their variety show, they have to beg entertainment companies to have their top stars appear on the show. In return, TV stations can feature new stars from the same entertainment company on their music chart program. So the music chart program is like a bargaining chip to invite big stars for other variety programs. This is why many PDs [production directors] want to be in charge of music programs, so that they will be acquainted with top stars' managers and be able to invite them to other programs in the future.[27]

Although not the first one to point out the nature of this partnership, Kim explains well the longevity of K-pop music chart shows despite their extremely low viewership rating.[28] But there is a flip side to this partnership: in rare cases, misalignment between TV stations and large entertainment companies can create noticeable absences of certain stars from a particular TV station. The most conspicuous example is the long absence of YG Entertainment's singers from KBS: for instance, BIGBANG's absence from KBS programs for over four years, from March 2011 to April 2015, which could have been detrimental to their career were it not for their already established stardom and a career structure, unique for K-pop artists, that depends heavily on live concert tours rather than TV appearances.

But BIGBANG's example is really a small exception to the rule; given the working logic of the K-pop industry, most idols place enormous significance on TV appearances when promoting new songs and albums, and this is particularly true for new groups, who need to promote themselves much more aggressively than already established artists. Since most singers cannot afford to have a thorny relationship with music program producers who wield such influence on promoting their songs, K-pop idols usually appear in almost all seven music chart shows on TV, so as not to alienate or single out a certain program and its producer. The frantic schedule of K-pop idols promoting their new songs on TV applies to both established and emerging idols. K-pop megastars like TaeTiSeo, a subunit of Girls' Generation, are no exception. For instance, when they made their 2014 comeback stage on Mnet's M *Countdown,* which broadcasts live at 6:00 p.m. every Thursday, their preparation for the prerecording session began twelve hours beforehand, at 6:00 a.m., when they left their house to have their hair and makeup done.[29]

An even more detailed look at this intense routine is documented in a report titled "24 Hours with Hello Venus," an installment in the serialized coverage of the K-pop industry produced by Tenasia, an Internet media outlet specializing in popular culture and entertainment. Insight into the private lives of K-pop idols can be gleaned from the following account produced by a reporter who followed an up-and-coming K-pop girl group in the middle of promoting their new song. Here I provide a full translation of the report, written in the first-person perspective of the journalist, to capture the intensity of the pursuit of popularity via broad media exposure.

> My date for the day was a girl group named Hello Venus, who are in the middle of promoting their song "Wiggle Wiggle." They arrived at the TV station at 1:30 p.m. for SBS MTV's *The Show.* They got ready and left their house at 10:00 a.m. to get their hair and makeup ready. *To get ready at 10:00 a.m. for a show that airs at 8:00 p.m.!* Upon seeing how surprised I was, the members of Hello Venus responded: "Today is better than other days. We leave our house at 4:00 a.m. for other programs with earlier broadcasting times." Once they arrived at SBS, they put on their costumes, checked their makeup, and did a dry rehearsal at 2:30 p.m. They finished their rehearsal, but it was not an easy start. SBS requested that they change their costumes, since the current costumes displayed

a commercial logo. So they hurriedly changed into different outfits and checked their hair and makeup again. What is shown on camera is very important, so they always check themselves in the mirror. That's why nobody is taking a nap comfortably during a break. Next comes a camera rehearsal. On stage, a large monitor showed how the performance would actually look when aired on TV, and staff members were busy recording it with their tablets [for monitoring purposes]. When the breathless members returned to their dressing room, they got busy analyzing how to improve their choreography while waiting for their prerecording session. They tensely dissected their moves during camera rehearsal and came up with critical comments such as "Let's be bolder with choreography during this part," or "Let's try this here." During the short time leading up to prerecording, they kept analyzing their recorded performance during rehearsals. Once the prerecording started, they put out their best. But because of technical glitches, they were done only after their third trial. When they were finally done, they looked more relaxed and asked for water. Only now did the members look somewhat at ease. Back at the dressing room, they converged and analyzed their prerecording session. They exchanged feedback for about ten minutes and nibbled on snacks that fans had sent them: bananas, oranges, and strawberries. The fans had selected only the best-looking berries and had washed and trimmed them for their stars. The members of Hello Venus said that presents from fans boost their energy after a long tiring day. Since the prerecording was finished, one might have thought that their work was over, but that was not the case. The members were frequently communicating with their fans via their Twitter accounts. They also incessantly took selfies and pondered which photos to upload. *There was no time to rest.* Then they set out to rehearse answers for an interview with the show host. The members discussed who would say what. Two hours passed just like that. *The Show* also conducted a live chat interview with Chinese fans before the program aired on TV. But before that, there was a small window of opportunity to have a meal. I thought they would be on a diet, since this is a group that promotes sexiness as its main image, but I was wrong. The members heartily ate dumplings, *gimbap*, and *tteokbokki*, explaining that they needed to eat well in order to sustain themselves during their tight schedule starting early in the morning. The members told me that they drink lots of water and exercise on a regular basis. Some said they had only some dried fruit and nuts before the prerecording session. Cameras can capture great detail, so it seemed they wanted to be careful in presenting themselves on stage. It seemed surreal that some members could appear on stage five times, covering a dry rehearsal, a camera rehearsal, and three additional performances during the prerecording session. The members said that they might disappoint their fans if they did not present an immaculate image, so they were always ready and alert. It reminded me of college entrance exam takers who pay close attention to their physical condition before the exam. After a short chat, the members got back to preparing for the live chat as well as for an interview scheduled for the next day. They were busy coming up with hypothetical questions, practicing answers, and dividing up their roles for the upcoming interview. After this, an hour prior to live broadcasting of *The Show*, the live chat session with Chinese fans began. Members sent their prepared answers and abundant "*aegyo*"[30] to their fans. As soon as the live chat was over, the live broadcast began. Since their performance was prerecorded, they monitored themselves onscreen in their dressing room. When the top chart winner was announced at the end of *The Show*, all the performers had to appear on stage. Once the broadcast was over, they had to greet everyone who performed, from the most elderly to the youngest. When they finally emerged from the TV station, it was nearly 9:30 p.m. Their following day's schedule started at 6:00 a.m., but all they could say was "Wow, we are done so early today!" (emphasis in original)[31]

This detailed report provides an inside look at how K-pop idols spend virtually an entire day for what turns out to be less than five minutes of TV time. Hugely inefficient as it may appear for a show with a 3 percent viewership rating, K-pop idols nevertheless stick to the practice, not only because TV as a media platform still wields influence over how stars are introduced to fandom, but also because TV content enjoys a second life when transformed into video clips and uploaded onto websites such as YouTube or the TV program's home page. Despite the low ratings, K-pop performers can justify the intensive time investment in TV performance production, since it provides raw materials for new media content to spread over the Internet. Finally, this report also shows how idols actively use social media to promote their songs and keep their fans engaged during rehearsals, indicating that TV and new media are inevitably imbricated in transmedial networks of spinning K-pop machinery as a forum to provide live updates of idols' whereabouts.

While the stars spend virtually all day in the studio, what about the fans? What are they doing on the other side of the busy stage work and long hours of waiting in the dressing room? While the vast majority of viewers of these TV shows may easily spend an hour of live show time in the comfort of their living room, a small number of "live" audience members (usually about six hundred) are admitted to TV studios while the prerecording and live broadcasting sessions take place. What do these fans do while the stars fret over their costumes and constantly announce their minute-to-minute backstage activities on social media in an effort to keep in touch with their fan base?

What Is "Live" in Live Broadcasting?

I often dreamt of going to a live recording of a TV music chart show as a teenager, but I was able to materialize the dream only three decades later, when my burning desire had long since dissipated. Now an exhausted mother of a seven-month-old and a three-year-old, teaching full time at Yonsei International Summer School in Seoul during scorching heat, I would have preferred to watch an hourlong music chart show while folding laundry in the comfort of my air-conditioned living room. But a ticket to attend a live recording of MBC's *Music Core*, which was very difficult to obtain, via favors from acquaintances many degrees removed, was staring up at me from the kitchen counter. How terribly excited I would have felt three decades ago at the mere sight of a ticket like this! But now, having it meant that I would be going out onto the melting streets of Seoul, taking a bus to a metro station, and spending another hour or so on a train to Ilsan, a northwestern suburb of Seoul, where the show would be broadcast live.

So on August 2, 2014, I set out to attend the show in a quite different frame of mind from some thirty years ago; in lieu of thrilling stargazing, I had the desire to learn how these hourlong shows can claim to be "live" broadcasts while featuring nearly twenty songs in just sixty minutes. For instance, on the day I attended the studio, nineteen songs were aired "live." Given that each song takes an average of three minutes to perform, a total of three minutes are left for the MCs to deliver their opening remarks and some other transitional comments. The show's current format hardly allows a second to be wasted. This incredibly tight schedule surely has caused occasional glitches and accidents during live broadcasting time, such as singers colliding with stage cameras, malfunctioning lighting systems, a frightening vision of a collapsing lighting tower that made one singer pass out on stage, and even worse, an announcement of the wrong top chart winner due to a mix-up in voting results.[32] But these accidents are exceptions to the rule, and for the most part, in the eyes of TV viewers, songs are aired seamlessly, without any interval between them. How is this flowing transition possible? Do events on stage unfold the same way for TV viewers as they do for the live audience situated in the same studio with MCs and performers? With a mission to find answers to these questions, I set out for Ilsan.

I was accompanied by three overtly excited students from Yonsei International Summer School—two Americans and one Singaporean—all of whom were taking a class with me entitled "Contemporary Korean Society and the Korean Culture Wave." These three students were chosen out of some sixty applicants who had expressed an interest in attending the live broadcast. The three lucky winners' excitement served as an effective antidote to my sluggishness. When we arrived at the MBC Ilsan Dream Center, where *Music Core*'s recording took place, some two hours before the beginning of the show at 3:50 p.m., the lobby of the building was already jam-packed with fans waiting to enter the concert hall that doubles as a broadcasting studio. This hall space is often featured in MBC's popular variety show *Infinite Challenge*. My students recognized it immediately, feeling the thrill of being present at a place they were usually able to watch only on the Internet, from thousands of miles away.

Hundreds of other fans had already formed neat serpentine lines to accommodate as many as possible in the limited hallway space, since waiting outside on the street would have been unbearable. Most of them were Korean teenage girls belonging to various fan clubs, as distinguished by their paraphernalia in matching colors to mark their tribal affiliation. That affiliation had migrated from online space to offline reality, showcasing that media tribalism is sustained by a strong coordination between the virtual and the material: pastel apple green for boy band B1A4; pearl aqua green for another boy band, SHINee, whose member Minho was one of the show's MCs; black and yellow stripes for another popular boy band, BlockB, whose member Zico (Ji-ko) also acted as an MC for the show and whose song was contending for first place on the chart that week; and so on. But occasionally, I could spot people in their thirties and forties who accompanied their teenage children as chaperons. A small number of Chinese and Japanese speakers were to be found among the waiting as well. There were also pockets of young boys—like small islands in the sea of teenage girls—who were obviously following girl groups scheduled to perform that day. These congregated boys marked themselves as kinsmen by demonstrating colorful cheering card sections with humorous rhymes, such as "Girl's Day *Yeppeuday*" ("You are pretty" in Gyeongsang Province dialect), or "Sistar" banners in the group's signature red and white.

The few hours of waiting in the lobby went by rather quickly as I observed the tribal ties that defined certain cliques among motley fans. The long line slowly but gradually entered the recording hall, which could accommodate a maximum of six hundred. Even in my placid state of mind, my heart started to race at the sight of the half-honeycomb-shaped stage with the familiar logo of *Music Core* in bright azure and pink neon lights. "Wow, we made it!" I muttered, high-fiving my students' sweaty hands. Yes, it felt as if I had finally—albeit much too belatedly—made it to the show.

Soon after we entered the recording studio, we spotted many fans already occupying the standing pit area close to the stage, where they could really see the performers within arm's reach. How had they gotten there while we waited outside for so long? The current practice mandates that these privileged fans, who get to attend even prerecording sessions before the live broadcast time, need to be admitted by either official fan clubs or entertainment companies that manage singers appearing that day. Like the people at the recording of G-Dragon's music video "Who You" (see the next chapter for details), these fans enjoy VIP status determined by their financial contributions to the stars' career in the forms of record and merchandise purchases, account of which is carefully kept by the stars' management companies.

Even as I acknowledged the crass reality of korporate pop's inner workings, I found the buzzy excitement felt throughout the auditorium to be contagious; newly arriving audience members looked around the hall in amazement as petulant guards walked down aisle after aisle, vainly trying to stop stealthy photo takers. The time was fast approaching 3:50 p.m. As the auditorium was finally packed with spectators seated on stairs, the lights dimmed and three MCs—Minho, Zico, and a young teenage actress named Sohyun (So-hyeon)—appeared before the screaming crowd at their MC booth set up close to stage left. At stage right, there was a large flat screen displaying what was being shown on live broadcast TV. As the MCs were preparing for their line on one end of the stage, the screen on the other end was playing commercials, counting down to the beginning of the live show.

When the clock hit 3:50 p.m., the crane camera shifted to the MCs' booth and spotlights converged on three attractive-looking youths. Their announcement in unison, "Welcome, everyone, to the live broadcasting of *Music Core*," was aired live in real time to both live audience and TV spectators, signaling the beginning of what turned out to be an intriguing alternation between live broadcasting of onsite performances and prerecorded shows in the span of sixty minutes.

The first group delivered their performance live, but when they wrapped up their routine, the large TV screen at stage right immediately started to air a prerecorded portion of the next group, hence providing a seamless transition to the next performance for TV viewers only. But for the live audience in the studio, the first group was lingering on stage even after their performance was over, waving to their screaming live fans while exiting—the sight of which was entirely hidden from TV viewers. As the second group's prerecorded performance was still being aired, a transition from the first group to the third performing group took place on the live stage, providing the first glimpse of the intriguing dissonance between the TV screen (featuring the second group) and the stage (featuring the transition from the first group to the third group) for those present in the studio.

This pattern of alternating live performances with prerecorded ones was repeated throughout the ensuing sixty minutes, with an additional pattern of having only established popular groups (Sistar, Infinite, BlockB, Girl's Day, B1A4) perform their songs in front of a live camera. Performances by new faces (such as Red Velvet, who debuted that week, J-min, and B.I.G.) were prerecorded. It appeared as if there was already an established convention of having the new groups start with prerecorded sessions as they got used to the format of the show;[33] if they successfully established themselves in the industry, they would be given a slot on the live performance roster.[34] But even when these rookies' prerecorded portion was playing, they appeared on stage and waved at the live fans, as if signaling *Music Core*'s commitment to liveness. The audience in the studio was treated to split visions as they saw the new singers walking on stage and waving to the crowd while their prerecorded performance was being live broadcast on the TV screen.

One can surmise that this conspicuous division of labor stems from the program producer's recognition that the established groups have more fans attending the live broadcast in the studio and that consequently it makes sense to have the well-supported groups perform live in front of their cheering fans. An additional rationale lies in the program's desire to reduce any potential accidents during the live broadcast, since more experienced singers know better how to perform their routine in front of a live camera, compared to those who are newcomers. As a result, the audience present in the studio can clearly see that they are being treated to a short version of the backstage drama, with the performers going around doing their business outside the time frame of their performance, and that they are consequently viewing the event quite differently than the TV audience, who do not have access to the split vision between stage and screen.

The bifurcation of the audience into a live audience in the studio and an imagined audience watching TV resonates with the performance's split into live and prerecorded parts and makes us consider what it means to claim that *Music Core* and other similar shows such as *Music Bank, Ingigayo,* and *M Countdown,* are "live" at all. In response to "the way in which performance theory continues to characterize the relationship between the live and the mediatized as one in opposition," Philip Auslander has provided a flexible notion of "live" with an eye toward the mutual dependency between live and mediatized rather than placing those modalities in sequential terms.[35] He sees the relationship between the live and the mediatized as "one of competitive opposition at the level of cultural economy" and states that "the traditional assumption that the live precedes the mediatized" must be challenged.[36]

Auslander's perspective offers productive ways to unpack the complex interplay between live and digital. Given that the prerecorded portion is given serious consideration as a live performance—both by the presence of the live audience and by the broadcast of the prerecorded section being dubbed "live"—the notion of liveness attempts to reconcile time lapses and spatial divides. In the narrowest sense of the word *live,* defined as "physical co-presence of performers and audience" or "temporal simultaneity of production and reception," every segment I saw at *Music Core* could be labeled as both "live" and "mediatized," depending on the various levels of the audience and the label we can attach to the show—whether it is a music show or a dance show.[37]

Take the prerecorded sessions, for example; for me, not present during the recording but only seeing the replay on screen, the presentation was not strictly "live," as it would have been for the limited number of fans who were present while the performance was being delivered. By the same token, for the segment where performers appeared on stage and performed in front of the studio audience, the show was "live" to me, whereas it must have been "mediatized" for TV viewers.

But if we were to regard K-pop in the narrowest sense as Korean pop music, the show could not be called live at all, even for the limited number in the studio audience, since the performers were mostly lip-syncing to an MR (music-recorded) track hardly distinguishable from an AR (all-recorded) one. Indeed, the problem of idols' lip-syncing on these TV music chart programs is so pervasive that *Music Core*'s chief producer, Park Hyun-seok (Bak Hyeon-seok), openly deplored in public media that only "10 to 20 percent of performers actually sing live on stage" and said that he would check MRs carefully and "expel those lip-syncing idols whose MRs are hardly distinguishable from ARs."[38] Rebuttals from idols followed immediately, particularly from a member of Super Junior Ryeowook (Ryeo-uk), who pointed out that because of the elaborate choreography that is integral to K-pop music and because of performers' insane schedule, which demands their presence at seven different shows throughout the whole week, it seems almost inevitable that singers will resort to lip-syncing and that very little will change unless circumstances for performers improve. The main point of contention here is that 80 to 90 percent of "live" performances on music chart shows are actually prerecorded as far as the vocal part is concerned, creating the split between prerecorded vocal performance concurrently taking place with live visual performance through various gestures and choreographic movements. In other words, if the show is labeled as a "music" show, then it is not a live show, since it hardly features live vocality; but if it is seen as a "dance" show or a variety show, then it is live, since the technology that allows idols to body-sync or fake-dance has yet to be developed to catch up with the technology that allows performers to lip-sync.

To make matters even more complicated, the meaning of *live* comes under pressure when we scrutinize how the charts are completed by fan voting, which must take place during the hour of the show's live broadcasting time, from 3:50 to 4:50 p.m. This brand of group liveness—where a consortium of online participants determine the outcome of offline reality—posits the meaning of *live* to doubly signify "live broadcasting" and "live voting." These synchronous events tie the in-studio audience to the TV audience, and thereby media tribes to actual tribes. Auslander characterizes this as "temporal simultaneity of production and reception" or "experience as it occurs,"[39] highlighting the fact that liveness in this case is realized around the axis of time, as the live broadcasting time creates an imagined community in the audience, a tribe both online and offline, who are watching and voting at the same time but are not necessarily in the same space.

Is it the practice of voting, then, with its implied participatory spirit of Generation Like and the subsequent possibility for building community, that accounts for the true liveness of the show? The final outcome on the chart is determined by various factors as each program resorts to its own formula.[40] For *Music Core* it is a combination of two broad categories: preregistered scores, the total of which accounts for 75 percent (60 percent from music sales, 10 percent of which is music video score, and 15 percent from the viewers' committee voting score); and the live score (live voting for the top three contenders during the show's broadcast counts for the remaining 15 percent). As can be seen in the distribution of scores, the program prioritizes preregistered scores over live voting scores.

When the moment to announce the winner arrives, all performers, whether they performed live or not during the past hour, converge on stage to congratulate the first-place winner. The announcement is done in real time because the voting result can be computed only at the end of the show's live broadcast. It was a close match between Sistar and Infinite that week, with the final score being determined by the live voting in front of the stars, who intently watched the results displayed on the wide screen.[41] We see in this finale a reversal of the viewing subject and object—if the audience members were watching the stars perform up to this point, in the finale they get to see the resulting performance of the laboring fans. Sistar, in their signature look of hyperfemininity constructed with heavy mascara, tan legs, and bubblegum-colored shorts, gazed intently at the screen to see if their votes measured up to the votes for the boy band Infinite, who also strategically exposed their well-chiseled arm muscles in stylishly cut sleeveless tops in the subtly contrasting shades of brick red and gray. These K-pop stars, who are so used to being gazed at, were now intently gazing at the number of votes they had received—made by busy hands picking up the phone and texting the name of the group they supported. In the end, the spectators were transformed into performers whose collective labor would be seen by the idols.

The fluid alternation of positions between what we conventionally understand as performer and audience makes clear that fans wield enormous power—not only in making and breaking the careers of the K-pop singers in general but also in endowing the show with a unique dimension of "live." Hardcore fans coordinate their efforts to place their idols at the top of the chart, purchasing their singers' albums in bulk, playing official music videos on YouTube incessantly, and coordinating their voting efforts during the hour of live broadcasting time—all done voluntarily.

While fan clubs wield power via social media, the prerecorded portion of the "live" TV show requires the presence of the audience during the rehearsal time, and various kinds of audience members for various levels of rehearsals at that. Just as early TV sitcoms used to be performed in front of a live audience in a TV studio, programs such as *Music Core* still admit spectators to fill the auditorium for the show that is half-prerecorded and half-performed live. Given that early TV dramas started out as live performances in front of actual audiences who eventually were displaced by the laugh track, I wonder whether these music chart shows will do away with live audiences someday. Is there

something special about music chart shows in comparison to other performance genres that demands the presence of a live audience?

Seminal scholars of music performance have pointed out that the sense
of intimacy between performer and audience is an indispensable part of the
ontology of music performance that plays out differently than in other types
of performance. For instance, there are conspicuous differences between TV
dramas and these music chart shows: dramas have always been an audiovisual
genre and have always worked according to the coordinated senses of listening
and watching on the part of the audience, with genres such as radio dramas
being few exceptions to the rule, whereas live music performance before the
age of mechanical reproduction used to be a synesthetic experience in which
the act of spectating was inseparable from listening—audiences heard music
while they saw it being made. This changed with the advent of gramophones,
which eliminated visual experience and turned music into a primarily sonic
genre. Under the predominance of infinitely reproducible music, the sense of
seeing how music is produced by actual musicians was largely taken away from
listeners. Live concerts restore the music as a total performance, requiring coordinated senses of listening and viewing.

Because of this specific history of music as a performance genre, cultural
studies scholar Lawrence Grossberg argues that music's urge to restore and
prove its authenticity endows live performance with a special dimension.
Speaking of rock performance, Grossberg notes:

> The importance of live performance lies precisely in the fact that it is only here
> that one can see the actual production of the sound, and the emotional work
> carried in the voice. It is not the visual appearance of the rock that is offered in
> live performance but the concrete production of the music as sound. The de-
> mand for live performance has always expressed the desire for the visual mark
> (and proof) of authenticity.[42]

Although there is a perceivable gap between K-pop idol music and American
rock, both genres need live performances to restore the authenticity of performance. This is precisely why shows like *Music Core* insist on marrying the
concept of a live concert to mediatized TV broadcasting, even though it generates more work for TV stations, such as distributing admission tickets and
managing various levels of audiences every week. The result is a uniquely hybrid performance that depolarizes what are often understood as the opposites
of liveness and mediatization.

Taking It Live to the Global Stage

While MBC's *Music Core* and SBS's *Ingigayo* comfortably embrace this notion of hybridity in front of domestic audiences, KBS's *Music Bank* has expanded its reach by bringing the show overseas in various formats. Since August 27, 2010, *Music Bank* has been airing live via KBS World to 54 countries.[43] As of January 3, 2014, the show airs live to 114 countries, a staggering number when compared to the relatively small size of the K-pop market vis-à-vis the world music industry: after all, South Korea ranked as the eighth country in overall music market size in 2017.[44] *Music Bank* live shows are accompanied by subtitle services in five languages for worldwide viewers: English, Chinese, Japanese, Spanish, and French, showcasing an imagined audience that spans the globe.

A year after *Music Bank* became available worldwide, the show itself took further steps by sending the performers to global cities that double as hubs of Korean pop culture: in 2011 to Tokyo; in 2012 to Paris, Hong Kong, and Chile; in 2013 to Jakarta and Istanbul; in 2014 to Brazil and Mexico. In the typical format of a worldwide tour, the show transformed the global audience from TV viewers into live audiences, hence transforming the meaning of liveness from live broadcasting to the experience of live music in the moment of its production.

On February 7, 2012, Charles de Gaulle International Airport was packed with screaming fans from all across Europe who waited late into the night to see their K-pop idols arrive in Paris. When the luminaries—Girls' Generation, SHINee, Ukiss, Beast, 2PM, Sistar, T-ara, and 4Minute—performed the next day at a nearly filled Bercy Stadium, which had previously hosted globally popular musicians such as Sting, U2, Madonna, Britney Spears, and Lady Gaga, this seventeen-thousand-seat venue became the temporary world capital of K-pop. *Music Bank* in Paris deftly conceptualized K-pop as part and parcel of the global cultural flow, not only by having K-pop singers travel outside Korea, but also by having them sing a local popular song in order to show the localization of the global cultural phenomenon. When the stage was lit up at Bercy, all the singers appeared singing "Aux Champs Elysées" together. Likewise, when the program traveled to Mexico on November 12, 2014, K-pop diva Ailee sang Tish Hinojosa's "Donde voy," while phenomenally popular boy band EXO-K sang Luis Miguel's "Sabor a mi," a choice that received impassioned appreciation from the local audience. "Live," in this case, was not limited to the synchronization of performance and reception; rather, it pertained to the higher degree of emotional rapport between performers and audience who sang together.

In stepping outside of a Korean TV station and into a live concert arena, *Music Bank* did not attempt to replicate the live broadcasting model used in Korea, letting go of the unique hybridity that emerges from mixing the live and prerecorded formats as experienced at the *Music Core* performance. These overseas performances did not have any live component for TV viewers, as they were entirely prerecorded for later TV broadcasting. The overseas versions also suspended chart ranking determined by audience voting, hence not allowing domestic fans to contribute to the unique notion of liveness as experienced during live broadcasting time. But for thousands and thousands who filled the Tokyo Dome, Bercy Stadium, Asia World Arena in Hong Kong, Quinta Vergara in Chile, and other comparable venues in Jakarta, Istanbul, Rio de Janeiro, and Mexico City, it was a real live concert performed in front of their own eyes. By replacing the unique voting system with a live concert format (and the ensuing recorded broadcast for those who could not be there), the *Music Bank* overseas version effectively converted the invisible voting fans in Korea into visible concertgoers who constituted K-pop's global fandom.

This is a meaningful trade for the industry, given that the overseas market is territory all K-pop artists eventually wish to break into; despite the rise of digital media, the world music market is still very much driven by live music. According to Korea Creative Content Agency data produced on December 27, 2012, of the $49.8 billion global music market, live music accounts for half, physical media (CDs) for one-third, and digital music for one-sixth of the market share. From Korea to the world, from live voting to live concerts, K-pop music shows probe new ways to expand their fandom and ignite worldwide interest in K-pop. After all, those devoted overseas fans will determine whether K-pop will be sustainable beyond the national borders.

Back on the domestic Korean front, the breathless shooting of the prerecorded shows in Korean TV stations, as evidenced by the reporter who followed Hello Venus for a day, points out an analogy between K-pop and K-drama in terms of their intense production mode and their global appeal. Many in the K-drama industry note that airing prerecorded K-dramas is quite akin to live broadcasting, since drama production teams, chronically pressured by various time and budget constraints, shoot scenes until the very last minute leading up to the actual broadcast time. It is quite common to shoot scenes in the morning to be broadcast that evening, just as K-pop idols spend all day in the studio recording their portion that will be broadcast live later. Hence, if we consider liveness as in the present tense, demarcated by the simultaneity of production and reception, these prerecordings are not solely in the past but rather in the recent past and past continuous that stretch into the present moment. The slight time lag between that recent past and now makes us reconsider "live" as an enduring process, a kind of Bergsonian *durée* rather than a disconnected moment-to-moment transition in a linear chronological line.

While my mind was drifting in reverie, the stage of *Music Core* was cleared, with only the winning group, Infinite, half-singing, half-waving to their lingering fans. The blinding spotlights remained on stage for a while, illuminating the subtle crimson/gray costumes of singers that accentuated the sparkly confetti fluttering down from the ceiling. The wide screen next to stage right had long been playing commercials, signaling the end of the live broadcasting time. My students looked disappointed that the show was over, but they quickly grabbed their cell phones to post their latest experience on Facebook, Twitter, and Instagram or to call their friends to talk about the show as someone who had been there. As we descended the stairs to the exit door, I could see the still excited faces of Infinite fans, who must have spent the entire day to witness their stars' five minutes of glory. Seven members of Infinite were still dutifully waving at a handful of fans. I could not but wonder if they would rather be somewhere else, performing live for a varied audience in a jam-packed arena in an exotic foreign city.

Going Live with Global Fandom
in *After School Club*

June 12, 2013. Well over six thousand fans around the world simultaneously have been clicking their mouse to join Google Hangouts with the sole purpose of having a chance to see their beloved K-pop stars and possibly video chat with them in real time. It is fast approaching 5:00 p.m. in Seoul, 4:00 p.m. in Manila, the Philippines, and 5:00 a.m. in Chicago and in Bogota, Colombia. But the time difference means nothing to the zealous fans of EXO, who came to revitalize the somewhat stagnant, post-Psy "Gangnam Style" K-pop scene. When the clock strikes 1:00 p.m. in Seoul, the twelve members of EXO, charming guys in their early twenties sporting a casual style like dashing high school jocks, walk into the TV studio,[45] which looks like a strange cross between a kindergarten playroom and a computer lab, with pastel-colored stools strewn over white studio floors and walls decorated with sparkly rainbow stripes. Over the glimmering chromatic range of red, orange, yellow, green, blue, and purple spreads a large world atlas as well as an enormous flat screen with sharp high resolution.

When the news of EXO's scheduled appearance on Arirang TV's *After School Club* (hereafter *ASC*) spread to K-pop fans, it ignited a flood of trending on the Internet and made the show's content circulate on a truly global scale. Disappointed fans who could not connect directly with their stars flocked to the program's Facebook page or Twitter to dispel their frustration, hoping to get a second chance to connect live with their beloved idols known for their elusiveness.

Switching constantly from Google to Facebook and from Facebook to Twitter on their smartphones is typical for the followers of *ASC*. The program was launched on April 17, 2013, on Arirang, South Korea's English-language radio and cable TV channel that brings coverage on Korean news and culture to foreign audiences both in Korea and beyond. Broadcasting every Tuesday, *ASC* claims to be the first TV program with a unique approach to K-pop as a forum for live interaction between performers and fans around the world. The name *After School Club* unambiguously defines its target audience as teenagers, while its colorful website, adorned with cheerful colors, woos young viewers with the following claim:

> Tired of one-way K-pop? Join the Club! After School Club is the live music request show for K-pop fans all around the world. Connect directly with [the program's MC] Eric Nam, as well as our awesome guests! Prepare to ask questions and request your favorite music videos on air![46]

While promoting the highly interactive spirit of the show, the narrative projects its viewers as a typical TGIF Generation. In keeping with the playful atmosphere provided by its website and studio design, the show seems determined to serve media-savvy users who are well acquainted with the latest platforms and devices: at the beginning of the show is a segment called "roll call" where Twitter users "check in" in real time by identifying their location and time and posting a short greeting for the stars. Some callers fill out online applications in advance to join Google Hangouts for live interaction with the stars. Google Hangouts was released on May 15, 2013, less than a month prior to EXO's appearance on *ASC*—evidencing the fact that K-pop fans are users of the latest technology; moreover, K-pop in conspicuous ways is brokering the spread of technology itself.

Those who cannot get on use Facebook to leave comments and questions for guest stars, who occasionally respond to the callers' requests to sing or dance from their hits or to send them personalized greetings. Many stream the live broadcast on their iPhone or tweet or leave comments about it on Facebook. In fact, the amount of online feedback the program received was so overwhelming that starting in March 2014 it created a spinoff program called *ASC After Show* every Wednesday, featuring behind-the-scenes clips and additional fan tweets and Facebook comments without having guests in the studio, until its last episode aired on February 25, 2015.

Given that there are other K-pop shows that promote "liveness" as their hallmark, such as MBC's *Music Core*, what distinguishes *ASC* from other "live" programs? How does *ASC* expand the level of group liveness to a truly global scale, reaching fans from all five continents as participants in the K-pop discourse? How does their inclusion in live conversation change the dynamics of visibility between stars and fans? What technological circumstances make this global reach possible, and how does it connect to the Korean state's painstaking campaign to globalize itself over the past two decades?

An interview with Sohn Jie-Ae, who served as the CEO of Arirang Station from 2011 to 2014 and presided over the creation of *ASC*, reveals how the idea for the program germinated when Arirang started to play K-pop songs on their radio station. When Sohn stepped to the helm in 2011, Arirang radio was stagnating, broadcasting old-style traditional Korean music from Jeju Island, mostly targeting a domestic audience who wanted to learn English. But as soon as the station started to play more K-pop songs, its message board began to receive comments from listeners in France, Chile, and even Antarctica. This ignited curiosity about how K-pop could suddenly attract so many international listeners, but Sohn remained skeptical about increasing the number of K-pop-related channels at Arirang Station, which was already crowded with other shows on Korean pop culture.

So when a producer suggested a TV show featuring K-pop idols that would emulate radio talk shows with little to no performance, a show in which the stars for the most part would sit and chat with callers, Sohn nearly killed the idea. "Do we really need another K-pop show when there are already a handful of them on Arirang?" was her initial reaction. "What if something goes wrong on a live show? What if nobody calls in?" were subsequent doubts that came to her mind. "We the public broadcasting company play it safe and do not produce programming that is too experimental" was her stance. Nonetheless, she decided to give it a try. *ASC*'s producer, Bak Hui-ju, recounts that "by creating an interactive show that is solely customized for international viewers and having them directly participate in the show, we hoped to strengthen and solidify our status as Korea's global TV station."[47]

But to start out safely, the *ASC* production team decided to target audiences in Southeast Asian countries, such as Hong Kong, Indonesia, Singapore, and Thailand—all of which are known as strongholds of K-pop fandom. The strategy was to guarantee that *ASC* would receive a substantial number of requests from viewers to join Google Hangouts and participate in the program. According to Bak, the show's initial live broadcasting time of 5:00 p.m. was chosen with this specific Southeast Asian demographic in mind, since the likely audiences in Hong Kong, Thailand, the Philippines, Singapore, and Indonesia were precollege students who would have returned home and been able to join the program at 4:00 p.m. But the time eventually changed to 1:00 p.m. in order to accommodate the increasing number of North American and European callers.[48] Sohn humorously mentioned that when the *ASC* production team started to notice that some callers in Chicago were up at 5:00 a.m. to join the program, they realized that "yes, it is certainly after school hours for them, but it's also a few hours before school, so we decided to change the time to accommodate the viewers in the Americas and Europe better."[49]

When the day for the first broadcast of *ASC* arrived and the male idol group ZE:A Five were invited to the studio as the inaugural guests on April 17, 2013, Sohn could not focus on anything out of nervousness. She recalls having cleared her entire afternoon schedule and gone to the studio to observe and monitor how things panned out. Everyone at the station was feeling the tension, hovering over the first-ever live chat show in the world of K-pop. In the few minutes before the start of the show, one news anchor came to Sohn and said: "I don't think we are going to fail. Already more than a hundred people want to join Hangout."[50] Thus began the show that continues to thrive to this day.

ASC claims to be qualitatively different from many other related shows, for its contents are supposedly produced and broadcast in real time so as to allow for the participation of a worldwide audience with access to the Internet. Given that K-pop idol performances—from choreography to what seem like casual comments on variety shows—are carefully rehearsed and calculated, it is rather refreshing to see a TV program taking risks on the air by embracing technical glitches and everything else that can go wrong during a live broadcast as an inherent part of the show. Sudden Internet disconnections and frozen screens during chat sessions have become staples of the show's live streaming. Although it is very difficult at times to follow the conversation because of the mumbled sound of excited fans speaking from thousands of miles away through unstable Internet connections, the program seems to embrace these accidental elements as evidence of the show's true liveness (i.e., "live" as "unrehearsed" and "authentic").

Whereas MBC's *Music Core* establishes its credibility as a live show by having real-time broadcasting coincide with real-time fan voting, *ASC* does so by creating a real-time interaction between guest stars and fans, a constant stream of action and interaction. What is unique about *ASC* is that performers and spectators equally participate in creating the show: while on conventional K-pop programs viewers are expected to be the unseen anonymous multitude, on *ASC* viewers transform into active participants who regularly perform in front of the guest stars. From this unusual role reversal emerge possibilities of obliterating the distinctive boundaries between producers and consumers of K-pop. Moreover, whereas what drives the liveness of *Music Core* is the mobilized voting of Korean fans, *ASC* relies exclusively on the participation of foreign fans, hence opening up ways for them to be key players in the making of K-pop culture.

When I asked the show's chief producer how she chooses Hangout participants from numerous applications, she responded: "We usually look for fans who understand our show and are really able to show off their love for their idols. It's noticeable how big of a fan some of them are because of the questions they ask, or the little details that they know about their artists. We also look for fans who ask really creative or fun questions or requests."[51] Hence, fans' memorable performances, aided by their creativity and knowledge of their idols, are essential to the show's genuine interactiveness, which stands as a hallmark of liveness in this case.

The intimacy created around this unique format is enabled by bilingual communication using both Korean and English, which has come to be the standard mode for the show's participants to interact with one another. With a few exceptions of MCs and guest stars who are fluent in both Korean and English, most participants and viewers are familiar either with only Korean (the Korean idols) or only English (the foreign viewers who participate in video chats with guests). But the show makes a comfortable mix of the two while providing real-time translation services to monolingual viewers, making Korean-English bilingualism the lingua franca of the program.

ASC cannot embrace more than two languages in order to run the program efficiently, but given that a sizable number of guests and viewers of *ASC* are from the Chinese-speaking world and often address each other in Chinese, the program provides an intriguing insight into the linguistic melting pot of the K-pop world beyond Korean-American bilingualism. The MCs often open the show with "Hello," "Konnichi wa," "Bonjour," "Da jia hao," "Hola," and "An-nyeong-ha-se-yo"—using greetings from native tongues of would-be participants and viewers. When I first heard those salutations pronounced in a rapid stream of multiple languages, they immediately reminded me of the streets in fashionable parts of Seoul, such as Sinchon and Sinsadong, that many foreign tourists visit. "Hola, Guten Tag, Bonjour," and many more greetings in many more languages are engraved on the asphalt pavement—a material manifestation of South Korea's "Global Korea" campaign[52]—all visually manifesting that Seoul aspires to claim a place in the global community. *ASC* often features proof of fans' pronounced desire to join the worldwide conversation: many domestic Koreans used to watch Arirang TV to study English once the cable network began operation in 1996, but *ASC* now showcases a reverse trend where Spanish, Arabic, French, English, Chinese, and Japanese speakers demonstrate their Korean-language skills to greet their idols or express their willingness to study Korean during chat sessions.

The technical and logistic challenges emerging from live video chatting among conversationalists who speak different languages were clearly shown in the early episodes of *ASC*, but the flow of the show became smoother and more effective over time. The efforts to make the bilingual live show more seamless become conspicuous when we compare two episodes featuring EXO and GOT7, who were invited to the studio approximately six months apart—on June 12, 2013, and January 22, 2014, respectively. During that time much changed to guarantee the show's signature multilingualism and enhance interaction between guest idols and global participants.

There are multiple reasons for comparing these two groups' appearances on the show. EXO and GOT7 can arguably be called some of the most popular guests to have been on *ASC*. In addition to native Koreans, GOT7 has members hailing from Thailand, Hong Kong, and Canada, while EXO, from its very inception, had the pan-Asian market in mind, as the group was divided into two units that allowed for constant overseas presence: EXO-K, based primarily in Korea and singing in Korean, and EXO-M, based primarily in China and performing in Mandarin Chinese. This strategic alignment with fans beyond

Korea allowed both EXO and GOT7 a huge following in the global market from the outset of their career. Both are managed by giants of the K-pop industry, SM Entertainment and JYP Entertainment, respectively; given their large-scale investment in these groups, both companies inevitably seek financial return from the global marketplace beyond Korea. Because of these circumstances, the stakes of grooming and maintaining foreign fans for EXO and GOT7 are extremely high, and their appearance on a show like *ASC* can be seen as an extension of their service to the fans. But without those global audiences, their career would amount to nothing.

Performing Fans, Spectating Stars

EXO's appearance on the show on June 12, 2013, broke multiple records not only for *ASC* but also for TV shows that feature K-pop content in general. *ASC*'s episode with EXO generated 44,747 simultaneous viewings on Ustream and YouTube's live streaming service, with viewers hailing from 114 countries. The hashtag #EXO ASC made it to the top of Twitter's worldwide trends that day, "creating the highest number of tweets for a non-disaster-related event" in the history of that platform.[53] The program's intense media presence around the world no doubt is music to the ears of the program producers. During roll call, MC Eric Nam exultantly pronounced at the top of his voice, just like an excited cheerleader who was arousing the invisible audience dispersed across the world to participate simultaneously in a live action evolving in real time: "You guys already freaked out our Twitter, the limit has been exceeded!" Indeed, the screen demonstrating the tweets for the program's "roll call" froze a couple of times, but even within the limited display of six to seven entries there were users hailing from all across the world.

Those who wish to have a video chat with the guest stars must fill out an online application on *ASC*'s website prior to the broadcast; for the EXO episode, only ten were chosen from six thousand applications via Google Hangouts. Given the heated competition these fans must have gone through, it is no wonder that those able to participate in the live chat were ecstatic, even screaming and howling in excitement. The first caller to be connected was a fan from the Philippines identified as Ika Santos, who looked barely twelve. But the TV viewers could hardly make sense of her comments as they became muffled in cacophony: in addition to the main caller, six extra girls crammed into the frame of a small pop-up screen, all flustered, waving a portrait of their favorite EXO member and speaking at the same time with the excitement of seeing their favorite stars. With twelve members of EXO in the studio and two MCs constantly chatting and translating Korean into English for those who only spoke one language or the other, the communication inevitably turned into pandemonium. "They are going crazy," one of the MCs interjected, in half amusement and half frustration.

Not every member of EXO spoke English, so Kris of EXO-M, a Chinese Canadian who is fluent in English, Korean, Mandarin, and Cantonese, did most of the talking while other non-English speakers' comments were translated by the show's bilingual MCs. To add to the cacophony, the MCs' question for the fans in the Philippines echoed in their computer, resulting in unnecessary repetition for the viewers of the program. The MCs finally had to ask the fans to put their earphones in to reduce echoing and have one person speak at a time. But despite these challenges, true rapport came when the fans sang an EXO song in unison and both the singers (now turned into listeners) and the fans (now performing in front of the original performers) could share the language they knew best in a hardly containable outburst of *heung*.

When the MCs moved onto the next caller, who identified herself as Erin Qi calling from China, it looked as if this communication would be smoother, since there was only one person on the video chat screen with a much calmer demeanor. But the second chat session brought forth a different set of problems, since her voice could not be heard by those in the studio in Seoul. Several minutes were wasted in vain trying to bring her on board, but the producers had to move on to the next participants while the MCs apologized in Korean that "accidents like these are inevitable in a live broadcast program"—again emphasizing the fact that these imperfect moments were just a reminder of the show's commitment to authentic liveness.

The unfortunate caller from China had to go off screen, and the next caller appeared on the air: Lauren Sheng of Chicago was featured with seven or eight other callers, but since she was wearing earphones the sound was transmitted much more clearly both ways. Once she and others were connected to the chat session, they bowed in Korean style and claimed in unison, which must have required some rehearsal: "We are one, we are Chicago EXO fans!" The caller was able to communicate that EXO served as an inspiration for her dancing and that she had won a dance competition where she danced to EXO's song "Two Moons." When a member of EXO, Suho, asked if she could demonstrate the dance, the callers got up and instantaneously danced to the EXO music, inviting a stream of "Wows" from the guests in the studio. Similar to the first caller's singing of an EXO song, the dance demonstration in front of the group reversed the typical dynamics conventionally assigned to stars and fans in the world of K-pop: highly visible stars usually perform for a multitude of anonymous fans, but in this case a single fan performed for the stars, now turned into spectators. The reversal of dynamics was immediately inverted when the MCs asked Lauren if she had any request for EXO. She asked if Kai could show his ballet moves, which he did in the studio, restoring the conventional role assignments of performing stars and spectating fans.

The fans' love for the stars was made more visible when the program introduced a short interlude by featuring fan art gathered from worldwide viewers. For those who produce such art, the result of their labor is often hidden, since they do not get to see stars opening or enjoying the gifts that they have prepared with the utmost care. The reward of seeing their stars gratified by their work can be given only if the stars are kind enough to thank their fans on social media, but it is rare to witness the stars receiving fans' labor of love in real time on live TV. Hence, the segment on *ASC* where stars enjoy and appreciate fan art adds yet another layer of interactiveness to the program. A segment in the program where EXO gives a signed copy of their album to the first Twitter responder who sends in the right answer to the quiz they provide serves the same function. These prearranged sections are more effortlessly run than video chats where fans are just as visible as the stars sitting in a TV studio in Seoul.

EXO's high-profile appearance came only during episode 9 of *ASC*, when the program was still trying to get on its feet as the first show to introduce a live video chat format involving multiple levels of potential technical glitches. Every episode was a learning experience for the program's producers facing the challenges of simultaneously taming and encouraging the wild beast called live broadcasting. Some noticeable changes were introduced in the ensuing episodes featuring GOT7, the first of which was aired approximately half a year after EXO's episode.

GOT7 appeared on *ASC* three times in 2014 alone (January 22, June 24, November 26) in an aggressive attempt to promote their debut album to international audiences. With each episode, the degree of live interaction was augmented as a way of promoting *ASC*'s commitment to liveness. Their first appearance on *ASC* was on January 22, 2014, only six days after their official debut on January 16, 2014, through Mnet's music chart show *M Countdown*.

The *ASC* episode featuring GOT7 on January 22, 2014, demonstrated noticeable changes from the episode featuring EXO in that it used simultaneous

translation on a pop-up screen, forgoing the often cacophonous live translations provided by the MCs and the show's bilingual guests. Although it was not
the first time this feature had been used (that was during episode 36, broadcast
on December 18, 2013), the pop-up translation created a noticeable difference:
the bilingual communication was much more seamless, without confusion or
wasted time. But there were still many instances when the service was delayed
because of typos and the ensuing corrections, with the cursor moving back and
forth and letters going through the cycle of being typed and retyped. What a
nerve-racking job it must be to listen to the guests, translate, and type their
words in real time while an audience around the world is watching! Nonetheless, rather than concealing these technical glitches as shortcomings, the program openly displays them as inevitable mistakes ensuing from its authentic
liveness, as it does with other challenges, such as frozen screens and poor mi-
crophone connections.

Another conspicuous difference between the episodes featuring EXO and
GOT7 was how the groups entered the studio. When GOT7 appeared for the
first time in January 2014, their entrance was not so different from EXO's six
month earlier, in that the moment of walking into the studio was edited out
and replaced by the premade press review of their performance. This strategy
closely resembled *Music Core*'s use of prerecorded clips as a necessary bridge
between live segments. The viewers did not get to see the guests coming into
the studio in real time, which would have served as evidence of live broadcasting. This pattern of editing out the arrival scene was repeated in GOT7's second
appearance on June 24, but when they returned for the third time on November 26, 2014, a major change was made: the camera captured the members of
the group walking into the studio in real time. Their literal entrance into the
studio embodied the concept of real time in live broadcasting: participants arrived to engage with the live worldwide audience projected on small screens on
the studio walls, performing the idea of spontaneous discovery.

The fans displayed as watching the show in the studio are referred to as
the "live audience" by the production staff in order to distinguish them from
the "Hangout audience" who participate in various other interactions with the
guest stars. The term *live* somewhat belies the mediatized nature of these fans'
appearance on the flat screen; although they are participating in "real time,"
they are not in the same studio as the featured guests (temporal coincidence,
spatial separation). Moreover, the "live audience" is required to rehearse their
appearance with the production team prior to the broadcast. According to

Charlene Jimenez, an American college student who appeared on the show as part of the live audience,

> There is a Google Hangouts rehearsal that the *ASC* production staff does with the live audience and Hangout [audience]. It is usually done about two to three hours before the live broadcasting. It is done to make sure there are no technical difficulties during the live show, and it also determines who will for sure be on the show or not. If not everybody shows up for Hangout, they sometimes pick a person from the live audience and ask them if they want to be on Hangout instead, and it's up to the person whether she wants to go on Hangout or not.[54]

When I asked if the production staff had given her any instructions prior to putting her on the show in the live audience, she replied affirmatively:

> The *ASC* production staff does give instructions to the live audience. In the e-mail, they ask us to make sure we go on the Google Hangouts rehearsal two to three hours before the live show broadcasting. When we appear on the live audience Google Hangouts, they message us to turn off our microphone, so there won't be any background sounds that will play during the show. After that, we just wait until the show starts.

Jimenez's experience points to how *ASC* carefully prepares its "live" content behind the scenes to ensure that what appears to be a spontaneous act is actually a result of careful coordination.

If the "live audience" who do not speak one word during the show must participate in rehearsals, then the Google Hangouts audience who interact with the guests must rehearse as well. Lauren Sheng, who performed a dance sequence for EXO, stated she did not interact with the group before the actual live broadcasting, but each had their own rehearsal, following a loose script that defined their interaction. Sheng confirmed that during the rehearsal process it was made clear that she was expected to dance toward the end of her call and that EXO's member Kai had rehearsed some ballet spins in order to grant Lauren's request to show his dance moves.[55]

The process for those who join Google Hangouts starts early and is carefully moderated by the production staff. For instance, an application to join Hangout with the girl group Lovelyz, scheduled to air on March 24, 2015, was made available online weeks prior to the live broadcasting. The applicants were required to enter basic information, such as their full name, country of residence, and e-mail address, in addition to answering questions and listing requests they might have for Lovelyz if they were to chat with the group. While the questionnaire encouraged the applicant to "be creative!" it also directed them to "avoid the following: 'What is your ideal boy type?' 'If you were a boy, which member would you date?' 'Can you do the *gwiyomi* player (making cute faces and gestures)?'" Editing out potentially risky questions about the group members' romantic interests, as seen in this example, is only a first step to control the content of live broadcasts. To what degree can we call the show "live" if the contents of the broadcast are preselected and rehearsed?

The Anatomy of Live Broadcasting

When I raised this question with Sohn, she responded: "When the show goes live, producers cannot control anything that the participating fans say. Rehearsals try to minimize the risks, but the risk is there. It's the risk that makes it live."[56] The excitement of handling raw and unexpected elements is strongly palpable, not only for global callers and viewers but also for the guest artists and production staff. According to the show's chief producer:

> I think the biggest perk of running *ASC* as a live show is that not only the viewers/fans can feel the excitement, but we, as the staff, also have amazing opportunities to feel the enthusiasm and passion coming from our global viewers firsthand. The fans' love and support are the catalysts that keep us going on *ASC*, and the main elements that keep *ASC* alive. If it were a prerecorded show, I don't think it would've been the same.[57]

Hence, the decoupling of "live" from often related notions of "spontaneous" or "unrehearsed" should not be seen as tainting the purist notion of a "live show"—often understood as "freshly improvised." Instead, this version of "live" should be examined as a unique paradigm of how shows are currently acted and reenacted along the fine line between rehearsed acts and spontaneous improvisation. In the increasingly mediatized world, it is becoming difficult to discern what is purely live (as opposed to mediatized) and to define what is purely original (as opposed to reproduced). The only thing the performers and producers can do is stage a semblance of liveness or authenticity that spectators will believe in. Programs like *ASC* might serve as strong evidence that the criteria for judging liveness rest primarily with how the spectators respond rather than with how producers define it.

In the meanwhile, *ASC* producers do their best to present the freshness of a live show—or more precisely, the impression of it—to general TV viewers.

The practice of including a "live audience" on screen inside the studio was first introduced during episode 17, aired on August 7, 2013. So by the time GOT7 appeared on *ASC* on November 26, 2014, the practice had been in place well over a year. Broadcast in real time as the events unfold in the Seoul studio, with the trappings of a first encounter appearing simultaneously in the eyes of studio guests and TV viewers alike, *ASC* early in its history came to realize the importance of staging the elements of discovery and surprise as evidence of its commitment to live broadcasting. In other episodes, the program took this further by having MCs go out to the street to greet their guests Lee Seung-cheol (Yi Seung-cheol) (episode 15, aired on July 24, 2013), Bizzy (Bi-ji), Yoon Mirae (Yun Mi-rae), and Tiger JK (episode 129, aired on December 23, 2014), who were caught on camera as they were literally getting out of their cars outside the studio.

The risk of going live, despite the show's elaborate rehearsal system, is quite remarkable in the specific context of the K-pop industry: given some K-pop listeners' fanaticism, the program is taking a huge leap of faith, since live broadcasting the fans' chat with the stars always carries the risk of fans acting impetuously outside the sanctions imposed by the rehearsal process. This must be the primary reason the show producers are not able to freely introduce a raw audience into the program; although rehearsals are conducted in order to check technical elements, they are also preliminary processes to filter out potential elements deemed inappropriate for TV. According to the chief producer:

> This is part of the reason why we started doing Monday checks before our show on Tuesdays. We don't have much trouble with impulsive fan behavior, but rather, some of them tend to freeze up and get very nervous when they're chatting live with the idols. We try our best to filter through during these Monday checks to provide the fans with a great amount of enthusiasm and those who are willing to cooperate with our staff, with the chance to chat with their idols live.[58]

The same degree of risk taking goes for the guest stars, whose public image is meticulously prepared and presented with much filtering in advance. As K-pop idols' images are built primarily on fantasy, entertainment companies do their best to staunchly guard it so as not to disappoint fans' expectations, especially during a live broadcasting session, when one misstep can ruin a painstakingly built reputation. Sohn told me during an interview that if the guest stars happen to face sensitive issues or challenges at the time of their appearance on *ASC*, their managers urge particular caution before they go on the air.[59]

Impulsive moves and actions can also damage the reputation of the show, but the benefits of going live seem to outshine the risks by far: in addition to fostering intimacy between Korean stars and foreign fans who are indispensable for the K-pop industry's survival, the program is actively reaping the benefits of live production by taking advantage of real-time social media promotion. Because of the live broadcasting time, *ASC* becomes a player in Internet traffic quite regularly: at least three times in the show's history, when the popular boy bands EXO, GOT7, and VIXX were featured, *ASC* ranked first in the worldwide trend on Twitter. The producers take the utmost advantage of live broadcasting so as to increase real-time Internet traffic by having the program's MCs often encourage viewers to talk about the show on social media as they watch: on every show, Eric Nam prods fans who want to have their pictures shown to the guest stars to send numerous tweets and in particular to "tweet us pictures of you watching *ASC*." In a similar fashion, when the boy band SHINee appeared on the show (episode 29, aired on October 30, 2013), one of the band's members, Jonghyun (Jong-hyeon), took a selfie in the studio during live broadcasting and tweeted it to the program's website, inviting fans who might not have been interested in *ASC* to retweet it and thereby fueling the wildfire of social media to spread more publicity about the program. As observed closely in the documentary "Generation Like," being able to generate and mobilize trends on the Internet is an invaluable asset in the world of digital media.

The simultaneous action of making and consuming the show, jointly performed by the fans and stars in real time, is a strong attraction that recorded shows cannot replicate. This media capital is what the producers of *ASC* seem to target ultimately, and is one of the reasons so much emphasis on liveness, despite potential problems, is woven into the fabric of the program. During episode 16 (aired July 30, 2013), when the program took a retrospective look at its previous episodes, Eric Nam made no secret of his pride about the show's liveness:

> *ASC* is now a hot trend among overseas K-pop lovers. However, it is not easy to make magic happen. Everyone is on high alert for the live show. . . . *ASC* began to write K-pop history as the first global interactive live K-pop request program. *ASC* aired live simultaneously on satellite TV in 188 countries, YouTube live stream, and Ustream, reaching viewers in underserved K-pop markets like Djibouti, Siberia, and Sudan, and has become a new playground for K-pop lovers everywhere.

While the host plays up the amazing geographic range of the show's viewership (I confess I had never heard of a country named Djibouti until I watched this episode), the emphasis on liveness and interactivity was reflected in the studio itself: unlike other episodes, where live guests in the studio met with a virtual audience connected by social media, this one actually featured a live audience in the studio, most of whom seemed to be non-Korean nationals. The audience that day represented a wide variety of races and both genders and interacted with the guest stars face to face by asking them questions in person. The show was prerecorded, but as if to compensate it seems to have brought a live audience into the studio. The show wanted to make the point that it was not really about stars but about these worldwide fans who sustained *ASC* and K-pop as they continued to tweet, retweet, Google, YouTube stream, and constantly press "Like" buttons on Facebook.

What Matters Is Larger Than K-pop

So what is the flip side of tweeting fans in the show's overall production? How does all this look from the perspective of the producers? Sohn revealed some of the program's deeper repercussions.

> The Arirang TV viewership is fundamentally different from viewers of CNN or BBC in that these two channels' main audience consists of men in their forties and fifties. A typical media consumption pattern that you would find among BBC and CNN viewers is they just tend to click the news they want and promptly leave the channel. But women in their teens and twenties compose the main demographics of Arirang TV's viewership. This particular group is likely to expand their media consumption to other activities, such as watching other programs on Arirang TV and having them impact their lifestyle. Hence they can be seen as quite an influential group.[60]

The domino effect that one Arirang TV program can have on other programs from the same station is well documented in the history of expanding K-poprelated shows. Since 1998, *Pops in Seoul* has been covering the popular music scene in Korea, its starting date roughly coinciding with K-pop music's breaking into the Asian market. The show's website claims, "As the No. 1 source of K-pop music that is creating a sensation worldwide, *Pops in Seoul* aims to support domestic musicians' activities abroad and keep its overseas viewers up-to-date with the latest singles and K-pop news." The two-way conversation—from Korea to the world and from the world to Korea—resonates with the interactive spirit of *ASC* as well as later programming, such as *Simply K-pop*.[61] As the show's website proclaims: "K-pop fans around the world get up close and personal with this unique music program! Watch K-pop stars as they perform onstage and interact with the audience throughout the show. No more, no less—only the essentials on *Simply K-pop!*"[62]

> *Simply K-pop* was renamed with the keyword *K-pop* in 2012—no doubt a reflection of the booming popularity of Korean music worldwide at the time when Psy's "Gangnam Style" was sweeping the Internet. The station well knows the most effective way to draw viewers in their teens and twenties to watch its shows, but it cannot increase K-pop-related programs infinitely: according to Sohn, "K-pop related shows occupy 40 percent of the TV station's airtime, whereas cultural programs and news each occupy 30 percent. Since the channel is run in large part by public funds, we cannot increase the ratio of K-pop-related programs simply because they are popular."[63]

The station has managed to ride the momentum of K-pop's popularity while expanding its viewership by introducing shows that are tangential to K-pop music coverage. Those shows closely approximate programs such as *Simply K-pop*, but with a broader perspective on Korea's music scene. *K-populous* is one program that explicitly states its desire to move away from the perception of the genre as idol driven. Introduced in 2014, its mission is "Spreading the K-pop craze! *K-populous* is an interview program that introduces exceptional artists and groups specializing in a wide range of music genres including rock, hip hop, ballad, electronic and jazz. We plan to break the stereotype that K-pop equals idol groups, and broaden the K-pop audience and listeners."[64]

Shows like these are intent on promoting the overall development of the Korean cultural wave, broader than the narrow definition of K-pop as idol music. This is why *Showbiz Korea*, an entertainment show airing since 2002, runs a special segment, "Star and Music," that double-dips into the news coverage about K-drama and K-pop: by focusing on TV drama soundtracks, which are often sung by K-pop idols, the program is able to attract, by natural and gradual association, bona fide K-pop idol fans to watch wide-ranging coverage of the indie music scene, K-dramas, films, fashion trends, and celebrity culture.

Arirang TV ultimately aims to turn this transmedial synergy effect into a valuable asset in branding the nation. When I asked Sohn what was her biggest accomplishment at the helm of the station, she replied:

> We tried to accentuate the attractiveness of Korea to Arirang TV viewers by focusing on Korea's soft power. If audiences started to watch our channel be-

cause of K-pop, we hope they will be able to expand their interest in other programs. During my presidency, the program I created and loved the most was
Arts Avenue, which provides high-quality content covering Korean design, arts,
and performance. We can proudly show Korean culture to the world.[65]

This response prompted me to watch a few episodes of *Arts Avenue*, which was
a qualitatively different experience from K-pop music programs' fast-paced,
stimulating sensationalism. "Each episode is produced and presented aesthetically," claims the program's home page, and the depth of research and the production quality of *Arts Avenue* did not disappoint.

I am well aware that comparing the two programs is like comparing apples
and oranges, but the calm and almost soothing tone of *Arts Avenue* lacks the
lively heartbeat of *After School Club*. The fast, often frantic multilingual mode
of communication in *ASC* is the symptomatic rhythm of the TGIF Generation,
sustained by the idea of real-time connection to the world that we often call
"liveness." Although perpetually risking unscripted improvisation, liveness is
the energy that attracts viewers from Morocco, Oman, the United Arab Emir-
ates, Finland, Poland, Norway, Israel, Bahrain, Slovakia, Hungary, France, Spain,
Peru, Mexico, Germany, and Sudan to skip their day's work or night's sleep and
wait eagerly to see their Korean idols appear on screen. By the way, this country
list indicating where *ASC*'s global callers hail from is far from complete.

3

SIMULATING LIVENESS
IN K-POP MUSIC VIDEOS

THE PRECISE HISTORY of music videos in Korea is hard to pin down, as multiple processes during the late 1980s and early 1990s laid the foundation for the rise of the genre. In the late 1980s, terrestrial television stations started to produce music videos for songs that were featured in their music chart shows and variety entertainment shows. MBC's variety show *Totojeul* (a Korean abbreviation for "Saturday, Amusing Saturday"), which aired from 1985 to 1997 to popular acclaim, was one such forum for introducing pop songs in the form of music videos. These low-quality video productions typically featured rudimentary dramatization of lyrics,[1] especially when compared to today's K-pop music videos on YouTube, but they nevertheless set a trend for a synesthetic consumption that established "listening" and "seeing" music as simultaneous processes.

With the rise of cable TV that included music channels, such as Mnet (1995–present) and KM (1995–2005), the demand for music video production increased exponentially and the quality of production improved accordingly. The cable music channels also signaled the transfer of ownership in music video productions: whereas the videos were produced by terrestrial TV stations in the late 1980s, the 1990s saw a shift in which entertainment companies outsourced the job of producing music videos for their singers to video production companies.

Another important trend that contributed to the rise of music videos in Korea was the increasing popularity of *"noraebang"* (directly translated as "song room") in the early 1990s. *Noraebang* became one of the top national pastimes soon after its emergence. Karaoke machines were used to provide not only lyrics but also moving images accompanying them. Although the images consisted of nature scenes and cityscapes that were not directly related to the lyrics of the song or original singers, they nevertheless taught *noraebang* visitors that music and singing can naturally be accompanied by visuals.

But these videos from the 1990s were rudimentary, even primitive, precursors to the K-pop music videos we know today, which are married to YouTube. Even before Psy rewrote the history of YouTube with "Gangnam Style" in 2012, K-pop was already accruing fame as blue-chip content in cyberspace.[2] Bona fide K-pop groups such as Super Junior ("Sorry Sorry," "Mr. Simple"), Girls' Generation ("Gee," "The Boys"), and BIGBANG ("Fantastic Baby," "Monster") have become household names among YouTubers, each with over a hundred million clicks. In a way, the history of K-pop's global reach cannot be fathomed without YouTube, which became the prime platform for multimedia music to thrive; to put it differently, K-pop's success is highly medium-specific, and the advent of YouTube was a game changer for the industry.

YouTube's rise also coincided with a qualitative shift in K-pop music video contents: if the music videos from the late 1990s to the mid-2000s prioritized a dramatized story line often enacted by professional actors—a narrative form that shared strong affinities with TV dramas—then the videos that emerged after the mid-2000s showcased rising trends that emphasized idols themselves rather than the story line based on lyrics. Much like media art, K-pop music videos in the post–YouTube era featured fragmented visual images designed to optimally showcase idols' charm: their elaborate dance routine, sensational outfits, and physical beauty.

As such, K-pop music videos today prioritize visual images that appeal to multiple sensory systems, and music video production has been soaring, partly because of K-pop's excessive investment in its visual presentation of music and partly because of the global expansion of music consumption on YouTube. Anyone who wishes to talk about K-pop music videos, or any music videos for that matter, cannot avoid YouTube. In 2015 the journalist Fred McConnell claimed, "YouTube, at 10 years old, is the most interesting place on the internet. It's not about the platform or the brand, of course, but rather the sheer amount of content it hosts and its diversity."[3] Ever since the first video, "Me at the Zoo," was uploaded on April 23, 2005, this explosive site with a rapidly evolving media platform and content has grown into an expansive field where visual content is uploaded at such speed that no individual could watch its entirety in a lifetime. Ten years into its operation, in 2015, an astonishing three hundred hours of video are being uploaded per minute, "with more than one billion regular users" flocking to the website.[4]

The fact that the platform is wide open to anyone who has a video camera and a computer to upload video clips created a torrent of moving images in cyberspace,[5] but this meant that initially the vast majority of videos uploaded on YouTube were of low quality. Professionally produced music videos truly shone amid the amateurish crowd. As media studies scholar Carol Vernalis pointed out, "Suddenly music video became a jewel on the top of YouTube's heap. Music video, recently drained of revenue by the music industry, and with no place to call home, suddenly busted out."[6] Music videos regained the surging popularity they had once had on MTV, but far beyond MTV's viewership.[7]

Music video is now enjoying "a major renaissance,"[8] as it is distributed, viewed, and downloaded across different forms of media and national boundaries. The fact that music videos can more easily transcend cultural specificities, compared to feature films, for example, also has to do with the genre's inherent nature that is constantly mutating into something else. "Music videos are media hybrids," as Kay Dickinson aptly declared in her study of the genre:[9] they dominate the aesthetic, commercial, and experimental fields of vision. They have come to present a wondrous realm of senses, evocations, empathies, and kinesthesia, a mixture of melody, light, rhythm, costumes, beat, and movement that can be infinitely repeated at a touch of the fingertips. As a way of grappling with this overwhelming quality of music videos, Dickinson uses the concept of synesthesia, defined as "the transposition of sensory images or attributes from one modality into another."[10] The term points to the hybrid processes of transposing senses that result in atypical associations, such as "seeing music" or "tasting shapes."[11]

The spirit of blending is at the core of how music videos work as synesthetic experience, producing their own set of phenomenological rules and a complex set of sensibilities that also mutate distinctively depending on which media platform is under discussion. Hence, media studies have confronted this issue very specifically by investigating how this media environment developed. Contemplating the discursive effects of the unusual transmedial and transtemporal blending of YouTube, cell phones, and other new media, Vernalis observes that "contemporary digital media present forms of space, time, and rhythm we haven't seen before."[12] Newly emerging paradigms of time and space are related to the fact that often "viewers are unsure where they are in the media streams; where a phenomenon was initiated or where to find content. . . . A viewer can become confused about what platform and genre they're participating in."[13] This out-of-time-and-place experience, which, as Stephen Epstein and James Turnbull have pointed out, is inherent in music videos, is the defining texture of the genre and consequently makes it difficult to endow a given music video with conclusive meaning: "The rapid crosscutting between shots and decontextualizations of music videos do far less to foreclose particular interpretations than the generally more coherent narratives of film or fiction."[14]

While music video might seem to be veering away from its filmic counterpart in its compression of time and space, there is also a noticeable tendency in the K-pop industry to emulate filmmaking conventions in music video productions, such as adopting music video teasers that are akin to film trailers,[15] and adopting concepts of seriality and intertextuality that are akin to those of franchise films with characters that appear in a set of related films.[16] But the most prominent affinity between film production and K-pop music video production is generated by K-pop industry's conscious appropriation of iconic genres of cinema.

What film genres have not yet made their way into K-pop music videos? Spaghetti westerns with stock characters (Super Junior's "Mamasita"), detective-mystery flicks set in the Victorian era (SHINee's "Sherlock"), Hong Kong noirs shot in gritty slums (BlockB's "Nillili Mambo"), sci-fi horror featuring cyborgs gone wrong (VIXX's "Error"), pop art inspired by comic strips and animation (Lee Hyori's "Bad Girls"). Tear-inducing Korean TV soaps (Speed's "That's My Fault"), high school drama (BTS's "Boy in Luv"), and kitschy local comedy that places mundane life on a psychedelic roller coaster (Psy's "Gangnam Style," "Gentlemen," and "Hangover") have made their way into K-pop music videos as well. In an attempt to fit the exponentially growing medium of cell phones, there is even a music video that uses a tall (vertical) screen rather than a wide screen, signaling the rise of smartphones as the predominant platform to consume music videos (for example, Epik High's "Born Hater").

Anything and everything goes to promote the featured stars and their music as the pulse of the moment. As a result, K-pop music videos embrace a broad spectrum of global cultural icons, which effectively suggests that the "K" in K-pop stands for "kaleidoscopic" rather than for "Korea." K-pop music videos have distinguished themselves with a flamboyant mixing of classical and kitschy, old and new, foreign and local elements, precisely to be able to travel across cultural borders in the age of global media, when particularities of nationally defined music industries are becoming less and less indigenous.

The phenomenon that combines these opposites also gives the "recorded" music of music videos a semblance of "live" performance that exudes the freshness of here and now. The two music videos that will be analyzed in this chapter—"Twinkle" by TaeTiSeo, a subunit of the representative K-pop girl group Girls' Generation, and "Who You?" by G-Dragon, a leader of the boy band BIGBANG—attempt to achieve the aesthetics of live performances, unlike most other contemporary K-pop music videos, which are happy to accept the predominance of digital forums. I choose to analyze the exception (the two music videos with an emphasis on liveness) rather than the rule (the vast majority of K-pop music videos) primarily in order to investigate how effectively the digitized ecosystem of music video production and consumption can simulate liveness. But why would music videos, whose genealogy does not show any conscious efforts to embrace live performers or a live audience, want to simulate liveness in the first place? Taking a closer look at the pastiche of live performance styles, such as Broadway-style musicals, Motown-style performance, revues, and even avant-garde performance art, that have influenced the two videos I propose to analyze, I contemplate the efficacy of liveness beyond spatio-temporal coincidence between performers and audiences, interactiveness, and risk-taking improvisations.

Shades of Revues, Motown, and Broadway in "Twinkle"

Facing the blinding white light of flashbulbs and the whirring of clicking cameras wielded by a mob of raincoat-clad journalists, a female trio decked in glimmering sequin minidresses step out of their limo. Their high heels are suited only for risky catwalks on a red carpet, designed to create a subtle sway in their torso as they take measured, model-like steps down their imaginary runway. Quick flutters of thickly mascara-enhanced eyelashes and lips painted with candy-colored gloss define the expressions of their oval faces as the trio strike a series of poses, each one stirring up green- and pink-shaded constellations embroidered over shimmering gold sequins on their dresses. To the dismay of their worshippers, who incessantly take photographs to the beat of popping flashes, they disappear into the brightly lit theater where they are scheduled to perform that night. Thus begins the music video of the song titled

"Twinkle," infused with an eclectic blending of funky soul and a sense of languid self-indulgence.

The mannequinlike trio, composed of Taeyeon, Tiffany, and Seohyun (Seohyeon), is collectively known as TaeTiSeo in the world of K-pop. A subunit that branched out from the K-pop industry's most celebrated girl group, Girls' Generation, TaeTiSeo operated under the auspices of SM Entertainment Group from May 2012 to December 2015. The music video further follows the stars into the theater's vestibule and eventually to their dressing room, where they sport an array of equally glitzy outfits, all brought to them by a small army of staff members. Bubbly anticipation behind the curtain sets the stage for the culminating performance of the music video, when they descend a sweeping staircase reminiscent of a typical center-stage ornament in a beauty pageant or a Broadway musical; one can almost recall seeing a line of beauty queens or chorus girls descending such a magical staircase in countless performances and videos (figure 4).

As the TaeTiSeo members take measured steps down the ethereal staircase, they closely simulate a seductive, yet readily recognizable femininity and a feline agility that was the hallmark of revue-style performances of the 1920s and 1930s. At that time revues not only were enjoying their heyday in Europe and the United States but also were introduced to Korea through Japanese performers, complicating the global circulation of pop culture that takes place

FIGURE 4. A scene from the music video "Twinkle," performed by TaeTiSeo, a subunit of Girls' Generation. Source: YouTube.

across disparate times and spaces.[17] At the same time, TaeTiSeo's physical presence strikes the same chord as that of numerous pop divas hailing from all corners of the globe—Taylor Swift, Katy Perry, and J-pop girl groups too numerous to count. In this dizzying matrix of rapidly shared performance styles, it is nearly impossible to certify cause and effect of cultural influences, or before and after of cultural flows. Cultural citations from various times and spaces have become not accidental mutations of the past and present but an inevitable way the present acts as a cross-shaped conduit, through which bygone moments from global and local cultural productions freely travel. So what do the cultural references and flows in today's K-pop videos, or their omnivorous appropriation of recognizable tropes of Broadway, Hollywood, Camden Town, and Harajuku, mean? If such elements are ever-identifiable, what is their epistemic valence in "Twinkle," and how does it aid the analysis of K-pop's liveness? I hope to create an epistemic disruption in the understanding of K-pop music videos, showing that they are not something that naturally and gradually evolved from the local Korean cultural scene but a genre that flexibly associates itself with old and new, local and global, while interweaving both retrospective and anticipatory vectors of cultural modalities for the sake of gaining a competitive edge in the ever-globalizing entertainment world.

In an effort to place themselves on the global pop chart, many K-pop artists collaborate with popular American musicians and producers: celebrated hip-hop artists, such as will.i.am, Nicki Minaj, and Snoop Dogg, to name just a few. However, not all who work with K-pop artists are American. According to Cha U-jin, SM Entertainment works extensively with European songwriters and producers to create a soundscape that closely approximates the Eurodance genre of the 1980s—a style not often found on today's Billboard chart.[18] For instance, Anne Judith Wik, a former member of a Scandinavian group, SODA, and now a chief songwriter for DSign Music based in Norway and Los Angeles, is one of the most prolific songwriters for SM Entertainment, with credits that include songs for Girls' Generation, EXO, BoA, SHINee, and f(x).[19] The blending of K-pop aesthetics with Eurodance trends has gone so far beyond such temporary collaborative models that in 2017 SM Entertainment co-founded EKKO Music Rights Europe with DSign Music and with Pelle Lidell, the former head of A&R for Universal Music Publishing in Europe.

While the K-pop industry is at the cutting edge of the neo-pan-Asian pop culture movement, parading as the very vanguard of "the new" and branding itself as exemplifying the latest fashion, many K-pop music videos are presented as prized memorabilia from the past. In light of the overwhelming digitization of media culture, is it a mere accident that a small number of K-pop music videos, such as "Twinkle," Lee Hi's (Yi Ha-i) "1,2,3,4," and Girls' Generation's "I Got a Boy," with their colorful neon-lighted streets and buildings, actively invoke a distant past when entertainment thrived on live stages, in cabarets, and on street corners by featuring Broadway-style musical sets as metonymic evidence of live stage performance?

The contours of twenty-first-century digital music video production are partly created by the shadows of American musicals, a complex combination of pre-digital-era revues, vaudeville, and burlesque, all of which helped lay the cornerstone for America's first global cultural production, the Broadway-style musical. To be sure, musicals in the K-pop industry carry multiple significations: actual show productions, distinctive visual and sonic spheres, a business model, a quintessentially American cultural product with a spectacularly global reach.[20] But before morphing into a metaphor or index, Broadway is an actual street and a physical location where shows go on night after night. As a metonym, it stands for physical spaces with stunning entrances, hallways, vestibules, dressing rooms, and dark auditoriums and bright prosceniums temporarily separated by heavy crimson curtains—all of which accentuate the contrasts and continuums between backstage and stage front (figure 5).

FIGURE 5. TaeTiSeo's music video "Twinkle" begins with the opening of crimson curtains reminiscent of a live Broadway stage. Source: YouTube.

This section closely examines the figure of Broadway-style musicals, including their precursors and derivatives, embedded in K-pop music videos as part of digital media's nostalgic nod to the live stage performance. For a music video to exist, a live performance of some sort must precede it, whether a recording of live music or a lip-syncing performance that accompanies the acted portion of the music video. Live performance formats today, as powerfully manifested in Broadway-style musicals, stand as a glamorous inspiration of current digitized performances, yet paradoxically are unable to regain the enormously popular status they once enjoyed. With this in mind, I propose that Broadway in K-pop music videos doubles as an actual theater space and a figurative ideal of the iconic American culture while embodying both the splendid legacy of the past and a pale specter that lingers in the heavily mediatized world of the present. I offer a deep reading of the image of the live stage captured in K-pop's music videos as a way of tracing the ontological crisis of mediatized shows in the digital era, where the notion of live performance becomes an etiological marker of the music video's imagined origin. In the process, close attention will be paid to how the simulation of live stage performers gives K-pop an invented historical authority by associating the genre with other global pop scenes that have survived the tests of time. Liveness as such becomes a recognizable trope not only in the music industry but also in other multimedia performance genres, especially in theater and film.

K-pop and Broadway as Happy Bedfellows

The eclectic nature of K-pop is well evidenced by the songwriting camp that SM Entertainment hosted in October 2013, bringing in some twenty composers from Sweden, Denmark, Norway, England, and Germany. Yi Seong-su, the director of the A&R department at SM Entertainment, notes that SM collects four hundred to five hundred demo songs from foreign composers per year and that "mixing jazz composers with dance music composers will result in unusual chemistry" in the color of SM music.[21] Anything and everything goes into this mishmash of styles, in terms of both soundscape and visual presentation.

In this world of excess, an overarching visual concept is of tantamount importance. It is no wonder that the biggest and the most successful Korean entertainment companies, such as SM and YG, have in-house visual design departments instead of outsourcing the work, since the role of a visual director is crucial for bringing together logos, album design, posters, music videos, costumes, and stage design. SM Entertainment's Min Hui-jin, who plays a triple role as a graphic designer, a visual director, and an art director, noted:

> My work consists of producing an overarching concept, graphic arts, and the overall visual presentation of an album. It is not simply to decorate an album jacket and interpret a producer's intention. My work includes capturing the concept of the stage costume and overall visual direction. . . . When I listen to the artist's music, I first visualize a central item and ask the stylist to execute it. The main thing about costumes is to capture well the central concept of an album and to communicate it effectively on stage.[22]

Likewise, YG Entertainment's former creative director, Jang Seong-eun, claimed:

> Visualizing music is the most important aspect of my work.. . . . From designing the album logo, posters, and merchandise to creating any visuals that will express a group or artist, I work on the entire process. Collaboration with the producer, artist, photographer, and stylist is necessary, since I am involved in every aspect of album production, styling, and promotion.[23]

The rule of prioritizing the central concept no doubt applies to making music videos: Jang Jae-hyeok, a renowned director who has made videos for K-pop stars such as Rain and Wonder Girls, said: "When shooting Wonder Girls' song 'Nobody,' JYP told me that retro is their major concept in this album and that it would be nice to go with the *Dreamgirls* feel."[24] Indeed, "Nobody" is like the music video version of the 2006 film *Dreamgirls*, with similar retro hairdos, sequinned dresses, and black funk soundscape, thereby announcing loudly to viewers that it is adding to the genealogy of Motown aesthetics.

K-pop as a total performance genre that emphasizes a key pictorial concept resorts to many iconic visual aesthetics in the history of pop culture to create an eclectic style: Broadway musicals, Hollywood films of all genres, Motown, manga, anime, Harlequin novels, and so on. Among all these influences, Broadway casts a long shadow, in part because it left an indelible mark on the subsequent pop cultural fields, including Hollywood. So many successful Broadway musicals have been adapted into Hollywood musicals, incorporating virtually every other cultural wave of each generation along the way. These cultural encounters do not travel a straightforward route from Broadway to Hollywood or from the United States to Korea; rather, they are entangled networks that can hardly be assembled in a unidirectional and chronological order in the age of rapid information exchange.

A case in point, a crisscrossing of multiple temporal destinations and spatial zones that illuminates the interface among K-pop, Broadway, and Hollywood, is a segment in the music video "Twinkle" that closely approximates a Motown stage performance. It not only features black musicians onstage but also creates a scene similar to the iconic image in *Dreamgirls*, where the three singing divas are silhouetted by a blinding stage light. But which *Dreamgirls*? The Hollywood film starring Beyoncé and Jennifer Hudson, or a theatrical show? If a theatrical show, then which version? Beyond that, *Dreamgirls* is not "real Motown" but a nostalgic, glossy, fictionalized, and fantasy rendering of the real-life story of the Supremes and other Motown groups. Hence, copying that scene turns the music video into a simulacrum of a simulacrum.

When the citation of other cultural productions is facilitated by the assemblage of widely available digital sources, fluid exchange and appropriation of cultural flows prevail while the chronological order of production history, as in the case of *Dreamgirls*, loses its epistemological authority: the global success of the 2006 Hollywood film, an adaptation of the 1981 Broadway musical (music by Henry Krieger and lyrics and book by Tom Eyen), ignited the revival of the musical in 2009, letting the story play out in its original theatrical form once again. But the 2009 revival was not on Broadway in New York City but in Seoul, where a pilot project was tested. David Savran commented on the transnational trajectories of Broadway-style musicals as a way to illustrate the deterritorialized nature of productions nowadays: "In the twenty-first century, what theatregoers call a Broadway musical need no longer originate or even play in the United States to glow with an unmistakably U.S. aura."[25]

It was no coincidence that the 2009 theatrical revival of *Dreamgirls* was tested in Seoul, of all places. No doubt the financial benefit of having a Seoul tryout before the show landed at New York City's Apollo Theater was a significant factor in the production model. According to Savran, "The Seoul Production enabled Breglio to save $6.5 to 7 million, about 60 percent of the estimated budget, while the Korean backers covered 'the lion's share of the entire tryout costs,' including scene and costume designs and wages and expenses for the twenty-member, U.S.-based creative team."[26] But more notable than this economic rationale was that, by the end of the first decade in the new millennium, the Korean public had been thoroughly exposed to Broadway-style musicals, which had become popular as middle- to upper-middle-class entertainment. "There emerged a new backbreaker for the men in their twenties and thirties— it's the musicals. Nowadays, if you want to enjoy a memorable evening with your date, you need at least 400,000 won. VIP seats in musical performances cost at least 300,000 won and 100,000 for dinner," was the sardonic comment made by a director of a research center at a large Korean stock brokerage firm.[27] But even those who do not frequent musical theaters, which generally charge higher admission fees than other forms of popular entertainment, such as films or other theater productions, are still well initiated into what "Broadway style" might look like, precisely because of freely available K-pop music videos such as "Twinkle." In short, live Broadway-style musicals became a familiar cultural reference point because of digital networks that propagated the genre's quintessential, albeit fragmented visual, choreographic, and sonic landscapes.

But a key question remains: Why would K-pop, whose primary market is in Asia—most notably Japan and China—choose Broadway as a dominating visual icon? The suggestion by performance scholar Lee Hyun Jung (Yi Hyeon-jeong) that Broadway is "the great symbol of affluence and . . . the epitome of the global" sheds light on the nature of this complex engagement between the United States and postcolonial, postwar Korea.[28] Lee goes on to note that Broadway "has become first and foremost a marketing tool, a megabrand with a unique power to sell the experience, music, spectacle, and thrills of the live theater people round the world love most."[29]

To be sure, the glimmering image of America, as manifested in extravagant Broadway shows, presented an attractive destination of desire in South Korea in the 1960s and '70s. For instance, Gim Seong-hui points to 1962 as a seminal year for the history of musicals in South Korea: it saw a Broadway adaptation of *Porgy and Bess* at the Seoul Drama Center and a new Korean-style musical, *A Feast for Thirty Million People*, by the Yegreen Musical Troupe, which later became the Seoul Municipal Musical Troupe.[30] However, only in the mid-1980s did Broadway-style musicals become more widely available to Korean spectators. According to the costume scholar Gim Hui-jeong, in 1983 three separate troupes—Minjung, Daejung, and Gwangjang—all staged *Guys and Dolls*, which turned out to be a commercial success. This further ignited an adaptation boom in the Korean musical market, resulting in the staging of well-known titles such as *West Side Story*, *Les Misérables*, *Cats*, and *A Chorus Line*.[31]

But the view that Broadway has become an attractive paragon of prosperous America is too generic, and might as well apply to any other culture's desire for Broadway-style musicals. More crucially, it does not necessarily address the particular circumstances of Korea as one of the most exciting cultural hubs today, at least in Asia. While the fundamental premise of seeing Broadway as a cultural modality rather than a specific American location is clearly delineated in Lee's observation, it implies the problematic assumption that Korea—or any other local culture, for that matter—can only react to the dominant cultural flow that makes inroads into national and local cultural scenes. This stance is reminiscent of Allan Pred and Michael Watts's conception of "multiple modernities," reworkings of dominant invasion and submissive reception produced in confrontations between local cultural forms and the global forces associated with capitalism. But as Ong and Nonini argue, such an approach "seems to suggest that modernities in non-Western countries are only reactive formations or resistances to Euro-American capitalism," and they suggest that "we see these instead as cultural forms that are organically produced in relation to other regional forces in the polycentric world of late capitalism; forces with new cultural ecumenes independent of older centers of power have arisen."[32]

Ong and Nonini's definition of newly emerging cultural centers may well apply to the recent rise of Seoul as an important location in the global cultural network and the change in Broadway's status from a traditional locus of uniquely American culture and a center of world cultural hegemony to merely one of the decentered loci of multidirectional cultural flows. Just like Hollywood, Broadway in the twenty-first century is a thoroughly deterritorialized notion freely and creatively associated with a broad spectrum of values, genres, media platforms, and regional hubs like Seoul, which can now claim to be in the vanguard of rapid cultural exchange. Propelled by digital technology, the speedy rate at which various cultural modalities become available prompted Seoul to appropriate productions proven successful elsewhere without necessarily paying homage to them as the "origin."

This stance is very much in line with the argument of Korean cultural studies scholar Joo Jeongsuk (Ju Jeong-suk):

Since globalization was largely feared as the influx of foreign cultures in Korea, this dramatic reversal of fortune for Korean popular culture [*hallyu*] presents a unique and fertile ground to critically reexamine globalization. For example, with Korean popular culture increasingly flowing out, the Korean Wave is one of the latest examples refuting the view that equates globalization with an undisrupted advance of American popular culture. What is interesting in this regard is that it is often indigenized and hybrid versions of American popular culture—hip-hop, the blockbuster, and soap operas—which came to not only replace foreign cultural contents in Korea, but also build up export profiles of

Korean popular culture in Asia. Thus, instead of Americanization, intensified global flows of American popular culture have come to unsettle its own hegemony by inadvertently invigorating local popular culture industries.[33]

It is against this backdrop of a motley assemblage of music and play, live and digital, and the blurring lines between cultural origins and derivatives that "Twinkle" introduces visual motifs associated with Motown.

A popular trope for Broadway, as seen in the well-known production *Motown, the Musical*, Motown has been a natural intermediary along the fluid continuum between live Broadway productions and their Hollywood adaptations. K-pop's alignment with Motown is not limited to conspicuous stage presentations, where flashy black backup bands are incorporated into performance scenes,[34] but includes both industries' training style—the manufacturing machinery of talents. Much like the record labels of the Detroit area, K-pop management companies today carefully deliberate on how to package superstars in a way that will enthrall the global marketplace. *New Yorker* writer John Seabrook goes so far as to claim that K-pop has completely outdone what Motown set out to do with a regulated training style; K-pop's typical training model "would make the star factory that Berry Gordy created at Motown look like a mom-and-pop operation."[35]

It is no wonder that *Dreamgirls*, which centers on the process of "making" a star, was a popular hit in South Korea; the audience saw a conspicuous parallel between the musical's Broadway origin and its own national pop industry. Even less surprising is that, much like *Dreamgirls*, music videos like "Twinkle" feature both the onstage and offstage lives of their stars, as a way of creating a self-referential commentary on the practices of the industry that these stars actually inhabit. Both "Twinkle" and *Dreamgirls*, with varying depth, capture female stardom in the music industry, the stars' determination to live a life onstage, and their illusory world made by the media's presence. It is precisely this affinity that makes certain K-pop music videos a form of "compressed musicals." The parallels between the training style heralded by Motown and Seoul management companies, the self-referential commentary by Broadway musicals and *hallyu*, and the fact that Broadway musicals in South Korea concurrently rose with K-pop while featuring many K-pop stars indicate that a complex genealogy and cross-pollination are at work in cultural flows along the Pacific Rim.

When SM Entertainment decided to cast Taeyeon, Tiffany, and Seohyun as embodying the quintessential stardom of Broadway musicals and Motown productions, the company must have wanted to seal its image as the leader of the ever-prospering Broadway entertainment style in Korea. In the new millennium, the comfortable transmedial symbiosis of K-pop and Broadway has piqued the interest of artists and businessmen alike. Bolstered by the enormous potential of Broadway musicals and the financial success many musical production companies have come to enjoy in South Korea, SM Entertainment started to flirt with the possibilities of producing its own musicals rather than occasionally outsourcing its singers to star in other companies' productions. In 2008, to celebrate the launching of its branch SM Art Company, SM Entertainment staged a Broadway-licensed musical, *Xanadu*, with Kangin (Gang-in) and Heechul (Hui-cheol) of Super Junior as leads. Although the production garnered much attention from the press because of the K-pop stars' presence in the cast, it "did not win critical acclaim of the public and the critics alike."[36] Nevertheless, it initiated a series of experiments by SM Entertainment in training itself as the potential producer and its celebrated K-pop stars in Broadway musical performances: the company invested in the musical *Catch Me if You Can* while having its leading K-pop stars, such as Kyuhyun (Gyu-hyeon) and Ryeo-uk of Super Junior, Onew (On-yu) and Key (Ki) of SHINee, and Seohyun of Girls' Generation, star in various productions to prepare them for an alternative career beyond the life of K-pop idols.

In 2014, six years after its first dance with Broadway musical productions, SM Entertainment announced that it would produce *Singin' in the Rain* under its company label, this time starring Kyuhyun, Sunny of Girls' Generation, and Baek-hyeon of EXO. The critics had a lukewarm response: the overall musical was of passable quality and lacked the kind of distinctiveness for which other musical production companies had come to be known. One review noted: "Seol and Company is known for its luxurious style, Seensee Company for its appeal to the public, Audio Musical Company for creating mania in fans, EMK Musical Company for its grandiosity, Musical Haven for its experimental spirit, CJ E&M for its spectacular style. . . . SM Entertainment proved that it can make an ordinary musical with *Singin' in the Rain*, but it needs to show what SM musicals are like vis-à-vis other musical companies which already consolidated their brand image."[37] This will not deter SM from moving forward with a more distinctively styled musical of its own, featuring its lineup of stars and their enormous publicity-generating power, since K-pop and Broadway, similar in so many aspects of production making, are bound to enjoy their companionship for a long time to come.

Flappers and "Twinkle" as a "Compressed Musical"

As a compressed musical with eclectic elements, "Twinkle" does not just re-imagine Motown-esque musical scenes but actively converses with Broadway re-vues. The visual presentation of perfectly coiffed, sylphlike Taeyeon, Tiffany, and Seohyun in glittery outfits draws a transhistoric parallel with the famous *Ziegfeld Follies*, or the kind of ensemble of exquisite women who composed the revue tradition from 1907 to 1932 on live stages. Beginning in music hall revues, the *Ziegfeld Follies'* live theatrical heritage of the early twentieth century finds an un-likely partner in K-pop music videos of the twenty-first century, but not without intermediary steps, having been rendered in multiple digital recordings—most notably in the form of Hollywood musicals and by interfacing with music vid-eos from the early MTV era as well as with the contemporaneous music videos widely available on YouTube. The 1946 film version of the Follies' "Here's to the Girls," Marilyn Monroe's performance of "Diamonds Are a Girl's Best Friend" in *Gentlemen Prefer Blondes, Dreamgirls*, Madonna's "Material Girl," Taylor Swift's "Mean," and Katy Perry's "Unconditionally" all establish their kinship with "backstage musicals" using the immediately recognizable tropes of theater space and proscenium stage, which become a crucial backdrop to illustrate the lives of the performers.

The history of the digitization of live performance—the film adaptation of live shows presenting iconic femininity, particularly performances of the Zieg-feld Follies—is not surprising given that their French predecessor, the Folies Bergère, founded in 1869 in a Parisian music hall, also went through multiple cycles of digitization.[38] The Ziegfeld Follies, in turn, have seen many trans-medial reincarnations: the 1929 Technicolor sound film *Sally* (First National, 1920–22 run at New Amsterdam Theater), *Rio Rita* (RKO, 1927), *Glorifying the American Girl* (Columbia Pictures, 1929), and *Whoopee!* (Goldwyn, 1930). In 1932, Florenz Ziegfeld took his troupe to CBS Radio in "The Ziegfeld Follies of the Air," which lasted until 1936. In 1941 a feature film titled *Ziegfeld Girls* was made, and in 1946 the revue was created exclusively to be filmed in MGM's studios and given the same title as the long-running theatrical success— *Ziegfeld Follies*.

The 1946 MGM production embodies the happiest marriage between live and digital—the opulent and flamboyant legacies of the live revue immortal-ized by the golden age of Hollywood cinema—and thus is the most recogniz-able parallel with K-pop. Particularly important, in this film the performers consciously acknowledge the presence of the proscenium stage while the directors take advantage of filmic interventions, such as close-ups and phantasma-gorical editing sequences that create an effect of optical magic.

The 1946 film can be seen as a devolved form of the 1929 *Glorifying the American Girl*, produced by Florenz Ziegfeld himself with Columbia Pictures, which devotes a substantial part of its ending, roughly a third of the entire film, to pure stagings of revues as they existed live onstage, with occasional reverse shots of the audience. The grammar demonstrated in one film sequence the crowd or stars arriving at the theater, the backstage dressing-room scene, the onstage performance, and the reverse shot of the audience leading back to the stage, seen in "Twinkle"—is already found in this film. *Glorifying the American Girl*'s devotion to the revue for a full third of the screen time has shrunk in the new music video format, where the performance lasts less than five minutes, on the average. The length of a music video is perfect for one major skit lifted out of a long sequence of acts in a traditional musical or revue.

Starring Fred Astaire, Lucille Ball, Fanny Brice, Judy Garland, and many other luminary entertainers of the time, the 1946 production of *Ziegfeld Follies* was advertised as the superlative of all forms of diversion in America:

> *Ziegfeld Follies* marks the beginning of a startling new era in the world of en-tertainment. The *Ziegfeld Follies* is music and magic, laughter, romance, and America's most beautiful girls. The *Ziegfeld Follies* is big beyond all comparison, spectacular beyond your most fantastic dreams. It is entertainment unequaled in the history of motion pictures. Bringing to this theater the greatest assem-blage of celebrated talents ever to appear in one show on stage or screen.[39]

The grand scale of *Ziegfeld Follies*, on both stage and screen, deserves the su-perlative adjectives. Echoes of this self-congratulatory narrative from nearly seven decades ago reverberate in Korean entertainment today. Just replace "*Ziegfeld Follies*" with "K-pop," "America" with "Korea," "motion pictures" with "music videos," and all these declarations have the ring of truth. Not only is K-pop made of something more fantastic than fantasy itself, but also it is one of the most conspicuous claimants to be the most magnificent entertainment form of the moment, on both stage and screen.

The persistent engagement between live and digitized, stage and screen plays out in intimate perspectives created within the boundaries of produc-tions—all intended to generate the feeling of watching live stage shows. Spec-tators of *Ziegfeld Follies* and "Twinkle" find an entire array of alternative spectators embedded in the scene, disguised as bystanders who enjoy close proximity to the stage and stars. When TaeTiSeo step out of their limousine in "Twinkle," an army of photographers greets them, heightening a sense of viewership and a closer proximity to the object of viewing. When the group enters the theater building and flirtatiously marches through the vestibule, two male performers ogle them and join them for a short dance. Like the male photographers swarming outside the theater building, these two men highlight the desire to view the female stars through their brief contact.

But the close onlookers embedded in "Twinkle" do not confine themselves to spectatorship—they also act out their desires to interact with the stars. Collapsing the boundary between performer and spectator, an emerging "spect-actor" can blur and cross boundaries, such as those between viewing and acting, passive and proactive, consumer and producer, labor and leisure.

Similar impulses appear in the most extravagant part of the 1946 film, where Fred Astaire and Lucille Ball assume the roles of the handsome gentleman and the beautiful damsel in a sequence titled "Here's to the Girls." The sequence features a bevy of decorated female performers: pink-tutued ballerinas, an ensemble of ladies in pink boas and silvery garments, and a horde of cat women scantily clothed in shimmering black dresses. In their collective performance (which would be a prime target of feminist censure today for objectifying female beauty for the pleasure of the male gaze), Fred Astaire transitions from a singer/emcee who introduces the arrival of the main act into an onlooker. The act begins with Astaire's introduction of the female ensemble with the following lyrics:

> Here's to the beautiful ladies
> Here's to those wonderful girls
> Adeles and Mollies, Lucilles and Pollies
> You find them all in the *Ziegfeld Follies*
> Here's to the silks and the satins
> Here's to the diamonds and pearls
> This is the mixture to start the picture,
> So bring on the beautiful girls.

The allure of heightened femininity as spelled out by Astaire, simultaneous actor and spectator embedded in the onscreen action, provides a loose sketch of the visuals unfolding in front of the film spectators. Similarly, "Twinkle" is structured around loosely connected vignettes—the stars' arrival at the theater, their preparation for the stage, and their final performance—to best showcase the sylphlike beauty of its three stars, much like a promotional video or commercial film, rather than providing a tightly knit dramatic narrative. To be fair, the music video's brevity simply does not allow for an extended narrative structure; rather, it necessitates the compressed or impressionistic fragmentation of the entire narrative arc. "Twinkle" features fragmented lyrics that glorify the singers' stardom, which cannot evade the close scrutiny of onlookers. The refrain ("Even if I hide it, I twinkle / What can I do, I just stand out / Even under the veil I twinkle") draws attention to layers of perspectives provided by the spectators within and the viewers of the music video that transform voyeurism into an explicitly acknowledged performance of seeing.

The kinship between the revue and the music video is strengthened by the structure of both genres: the revue's lack of plot is similar to the absence of narrative in the music video. Revues have roughly sketched themes and identifiable acts, but not narratives, mostly because they are visual rather than verbal genres. The distinction between revues and musicals depends on whether a recognizable, verbally communicated plotline exists or not. As Thomas Hischak noted, "A theater revue is a collection of songs, dances, and sketches that are written, scored, and staged to hang together in a plotless entertainment. It is not the same as a vaudeville show in which a bunch of individual acts are created separately and then strung together to fill out a program."[40] Like revues, many K-pop music videos comprise loosely connected themes or vignettes, which partly illuminates why these videos place so much emphasis on presenting a pastiche of lavish visuals in lieu of hammering a memorable story into listeners' minds via lyrics. As Kay Dickinson stated, the music video's central paradox lies in that the "composite parts are compatible yet incompatible and the 'dominance' of any given element is constantly under negotiation."[41]

Such fluidity—or lack—of sustainable "plot" prompted Hischak to pinpoint the reason behind the demise of large-scale filmic adaptations of live Follies.

> [1946 MGM] *Ziegfeld Follies* was not a smash hit, and never again would a studio try and re-create a Broadway revue on the screen. Just as Broadway itself turned back on the revue format in the late 1940s, so, too, would Hollywood give up trying to capture this unique kind of entertainment on film. Plot would continue to drive most musicals and even the idea of a film climaxing with the Big Show would go out of fashion by the end of the 1950s. The revue became a thing of the past, both on Broadway and in the cinema. But what glorious moments passed away with it![42]

What might Hischak have said, had he seen how "Twinkle" conspicuously references the tropes of revues, especially *Ziegfeld Follies*, while capitalizing on the sensual and lithe female stars as its primary attraction? Hollywood feature films, with their length and format, might not have found a comfortable way to dance with revues again. Take, for instance, Marilyn Monroe's performance of "Diamonds Are a Girl's Best Friend" from the feature film *Gentlemen Prefer Blondes* (20th Century Fox, 1953). This iconic sketch, pulled out of a two-hour-long film, became the sole basis for Madonna's equally iconic music video "Material Girl," which openly claimed to pay homage to Monroe's performance. But what gives the two acts continuity, more than anything else, is the spatial setup: a proscenium stage as a neatly demarcated unit to distinguish the featured number from the film's narrative flow.

Music videos, with their brevity and freedom to do away with grand, cohesive plots, became the perfect media format to recapture the characteristics of the revue once again. Loosely connected performance vignettes, one after another without any necessary narrative continuity, offer a series of easily adaptable motifs that can individually provide structure for music videos, which generally do not exceed five minutes—perfect for shortened attention spans in the TGIF era. Hence the connection that at first glance seems quite unlikely—the American revues of the early twentieth century and the Korean music videos of today—composing a new hybrid genre akin to what a 1946 film termed "a dance story."[43] The genres share the characteristics of brevity, a mediatized history of live entertainment, the presence of internal spectators, and a suggested or entirely absent narrative.

Nonetheless, to most contemporary Korean audiences, the *Ziegfeld Follies*, or even a more generic category of revue, would be unfamiliar. To be sure, revue-style entertainment was not entirely absent from Korea in the formative years of the genre's popularity. As early as 1913, revue dance was first introduced to Korea by the Japanese Denkatsu Circus Troupe, which performed spectacular dances around the themes of Salome, orchids, and birdlike movements. The Denkatsu Circus Troupe would remain influential in Korea until the 1920s, to the point that by the end of that decade revue was recognized as an inherent part of mass entertainment, according to dance historian Gim Yeong-hui.[44] Bae Gu-ja, one of the pioneers of modern Korean dance, learned revue dance from the Denkatsu Circus Troupe starting in 1915 and eventually established her own troupe in 1926, a group of young girls who presented "neither traditional ballet, nor modern dance, but cute and esoteric dance sequences" in the style of revue entertainment,[45] where dance performance was interlaced with solo and chorus singing, violin performance, and screening of films. Despite this local history, Koreans of the new millennium would more readily recognize more recent examples of Hollywood and MTV featuring Broadway-style performances because of their proven success in the global marketplace; that success prompted Korean producers to engage with such performances closely, after the original revue had been filtered through various degrees of local and global sensibilities. Song-and-dance sequences from revues provided the basis for Broadway musicals after they had been mostly sanitized; their lingering images of bawdy female nudity are the remnants of far-back origins in the smoky music halls of the late nineteenth century.

Broadway is a hallmark of respectable entertainment, even a property of cultural elitism in South Korea today, just as K-pop stars are revered by most young members of its society. The undeniable contempt for the demimonde often associated with the entertainment world of singers and performers in premodern Korea is long gone, and the rise of K-pop serves as an emblem of South Korea's soft power. So it is under the rubric of respectable entertainment that Korean audiences have noted the obvious references to Broadway in "Twinkle," as one blogger mentioned in response to the music video: "I can tell the style Tiffany [one of the trio] prefers. *Broadway musical kind of feel*?"[46] Another, in a more professional analysis, praised the song as having "a strong beat, familiar melody, and a sound overall composition. A nice song that has a power to *compress an entire musical in itself.*"[47] "Musical," in the latter remark, obviously is a foreign notion to the indigenous Korean music scene, referencing the modern allure of the West in postwar Korea. With the patronage of a younger, middle-class generation that sustains the Korean economy, Broadway-style musicals, when melded with globally famous K-pop acts, provide the image of family-friendly entertainment for all to enjoy.

The deterioration of such wholesome aesthetics associated with Broadway revues, or the more risqué elements of *Ziegfeld Follies*, borders on the burlesque of the late nineteenth and most of the twentieth century in the United States; in some cases, K-pop girl groups hew closely to this line by accentuating piquant feminine charms with sexualized elements, such as pole dancing and striptease, that echo Las Vegas showgirls. Starting around 2012, many K-pop girl groups began to give salacious performances that would not come across as family-friendly. For example, the girl group After School featured a pole dance onstage for their song "First Love," and a song called "Marionette" (restricted version) by another girl group, Stellar, included dances akin to striptease. The tantalizing tension between the dual legacies of Broadway revues—wholesome and darkly sexual, like the older music hall performances—delineates the overall contours of K-pop girl groups' performances today.

It is no wonder that when TaeTiSeo came back as a unit in 2014, two years after the release of "Twinkle," to launch their second album, *Holler*, they tapped into the previously successful reworkings of the Broadway musical theater theme. In a cable TV reality show centering on their everyday lives and fashion choices, Taeyeon commented on the visual concept for their new album: "We chose passionate red costumes for the song 'Adrenaline' and emulated the 1920s flapper style. But we also used collars to hint at the showgirl style. Just by looking at the costumes, you feel a tension right away."[48] Given that the term *flapper* entered the English vernacular with the popularity of the silent film *The Flapper* (1920), starring Olive Thomas—once a highly successful Ziegfeld girl—it is no wonder that the association between Ziegfeld revue and flapper culture is reaffirmed. The eclectic appropriation of styles that were once inseparable in the performance roots of Broadway continues in today's K-pop.

The Show Continues . . .

Every glamorous moment in the limelight eventually fades into memories, and before long the glitz of live revues, transposed to film, gave way to the rising popularity of television shows. Sheldon Patinkin, in a tone similar to that of Hischak, mourns the downfall of the *Ziegfeld Follies*, but this time names a different culprit, the new medium of TV:

> Ironically, although television killed the revue, present-day economics prevents it from resurrection. The television variety show that interred the Broadway revue in the 1960s has all but departed from the living room or bedroom screen. What remains of it, in tattered reflections, is relegated to late nights and is so overwhelmed by commercial breaks that any sense of form is forever fragmented. Nay, annihilated.[49]

True, the revue tradition would never be revived on its original grand scale onstage. The last production to join the *Follies* genealogy was the 1971 live Broadway show *Follies* (lyric and music by Stephen Sondheim)—another version of a filmed show, which took its cue from the live show, returning to the format of a live stage performance. What Patinkin did not anticipate, however, was that the beautiful glory days of the revue would be reincarnated in an unexpected time and space, some one hundred years later and seven thousand miles away across the Pacific, in the form of music videos that eventually came to enthrall many audiences across the globe.

"Who You?" on the Margins of Performance Art

With its rich references to a wide range of proscenium performances from a bygone era, "Twinkle" is an exception to the general rule of K-pop, as the vast majority of K-pop music videos do not have a direct relationship with live performance or even make conscious efforts to carry any vestiges of it. Like "Twinkle," G-Dragon's "Who You?" is an anomaly in that it playfully courts the ontological traits of live performance, even as the clear boundary between the mediatized world of music video, which the performers inhabit, and the actual world of spectators is rapidly vanishing.

What is to be gained by creating a music video that borders on performance art, forgoing sets of visual grammar already proven to be successful in the world of K-pop? What are the specific perks of appropriating the often-esoteric language of performance art for a mass medium like K-pop music videos? While "Twinkle" deploys conspicuous signs of a proscenium stage to invoke the notion of live performance, "Who You?" realizes a different manifestation of liveness by including fans as the audience to be incorporated into the fabric of the music video. "Who You?" uses a highly interactive process by having live fans at the music video set, yet paradoxically, the final cut of the music video is bound to circulate in prerecorded, nonlive form, like other examples in its genre—creating an ambivalence that is neither entirely an observation of a live event (like music videos that are solely based on the recording of a live performance) nor all recorded (like music videos that do not make any attempt to reference live stages). A rare example that stands on the margins of K-pop music videos, "Who You?" calls for a closer look as it charts the far-reaching terrain of K-pop's visual experimentation with performance art.

"Who You?" or How to Make a Music Video without a Plot

No other male singer in the current K-pop world can claim the title of Mr. Flamboyant more deservingly than G-Dragon. The leader of the enormously popular boy band BIGBANG, he is a delightful crossover between Michael Jackson and Lady Gaga, with a heavy dose of androgynous charm that befits David Bowie more than Annie Lennox. With the charisma of Prince, G-Dragon has been capturing the imaginations of fans in multiple music videos where he takes on fantastical personas as a fallen Lucifer, a decadent king ("Fantastic Baby"), a dysfunctional cyborg ("Monster"), a beast master, a fashion queen, a convict ("One of a Kind"), a troubled punk ("Crooked"), a nihilistic revolutionary ("Coup d'Etat") and an Afro-haired freak with excessively large feet ("Crazy Go").

An eccentric fashion icon with a thousand faces, this star is difficult to associate with the concept of mundanity. But in "Who You?" G-Dragon lets go of his deep commitment to dramatic transformation and appears as "himself" in an allegedly nondramatized, nonsituational narrative. Compared to the previous music videos featuring G-Dragon and his group BIGBANG with futuristic sets that create a world in outer space, this video exudes a highly intimate, DIY approach. As if having G-Dragon appear as himself was not enough, the music video staff invited fans to participate in shooting—in a unique attempt to counter excessive theatricalization or conspicuous separation between the star and the fans.

The making of the music video was a highly advertised event. YG Entertainment announced on their website that they were planning to invite one thousand fans to be present at G-Dragon's music video shooting session; furthermore, the company claimed that excerpts from fan-shot footage would be selected to become part of the music video itself, effectively turning fans from bystanders into proper makers of the video. On October 1, 2013, YG Entertainment posted an announcement that it was accepting applications from fans to participate in the shooting. On the 6th, it posted another notice that the fans would be able to upload their clips from October 6 to midnight on October 7.[50] This provoked an intended flurry of responses, creating a wildfire on social media about the music video even before it was shot and released. G-Dragon himself was at the center of the social media campaign to promote the event. On October 1, 2013, he tweeted: "10.5. 'Who You?' I am the director. Please shoot me and make the music video yourself."[51] When the shooting was over, he also posted a shot of himself in the studio set on Instagram: "The End! Thank you everyone!"

True to the company's promise, on October 5, one thousand selected fans, or a typical assemblage of media tribes, were invited to enter the Ilsan Kintex convention center, where an intriguing set had been constructed. The indoor studio was large enough to accommodate all the fans, with high industrial ceilings and austerely white walls well illuminated by footlights that conjured up images of an urban loft doubling as a contemporary art gallery. But the centerpiece of this shooting location was a slightly elevated T-shaped runway structure, approximately fifty meters long, part of which included a gradually descending slope, with all sides covered with transparent glass. Huge spotlights from the ceiling illuminated this center space, in which G-Dragon was about to perform.

Inside this glass cage with no ceiling, many props signifying G-Dragon's private life were on display. A series of material objects, G-Dragon's personal belongings as well as obvious props for the occasion, were casually placed inside the glass case. A white Lamborghini actually owned by G-Dragon occupied the very end of the runway, and smaller props were strewn all over: a skateboard custom made for G-Dragon by a heavy metal fashion brand, Chrome Hearts; a large leather teddy bear and a smaller rabbit figure bearing the logo of MCM, a luxury brand that became prominent in Korea and China with its sponsorship of G-Dragon; and various shoes, clothes, sunglasses, toiletries, and travel trunks that were made to appear as G-Dragon's own personal items. Props such as a Mae West sofa, flower-shaped floor cushions in baby blue and pink, a white armchair, and a couple of black-shaded lamps indicated that this was a space invoking everyday life. The presence of a white grand piano and scribbled papers gave the idea that this set might be G-Dragon's music studio.

In this intimate space of self-display, what was supposed to be private was openly displayed, inviting thousands of fans to gaze, video-record, and share their version of the scene on social media. This supposedly "private" space calling for conspicuous staring is far from paradoxical; once privacy is staged, it becomes too theatrical, immediately betraying the intention to seclude the star from the multitude of spectators. This effect primarily stemmed from the fact that the walls separating G-Dragon from his fans were transparent, allowing viewing from the outside. But spectators were bound to stare inside through occasional obstacles, such as white graffiti and tape sporadically obstructing the view. Graffiti would ordinarily mark the exterior of a wall that separated inner and outer spaces, but here the wall, instead of shielding private lives that inhabited the interior space, was transparent glass, permitting the gaze to penetrate the space and reach the desired object.

In place of its typical functionality as a demarcator of inside/outside, the wall in this music video, with its all-seeing, all-permitting transparency, becomes a symbolic part of the décor, playfully denying separation and integration at the same time. Since visual transparency nominally disallows a complete separation between inside and outside whereas inaccessibility disallows true tactile intimacy, the wall in "Who You?" is radically different from the fourth wall in the theater of realism; its transparency is a tongue-in-cheek signal that nothing is private in this world of media surveillance while also signaling that there is no definite boundary between stage and everyday life space.

The transparent wall itself is already an ontological paradox, since in proper concerts performers are fully aware of being seen by the anonymous multitude, whereas in private space the presence of the fourth wall is the requisite for privacy. What we see in this video is a titillating alternation between these registers and their varying politics of vision—dually inviting the pleasures of seeing and being seen while also signaling the inescapable horrors of surveillance (figure 6).

The liminal nature of this set is well reflected in G-Dragon himself, who comes out to inhibit the interior space during the music video shooting (he never steps out of the glass cage). Stripped of fancy stage costume, he wears what could be regarded as mundane casual clothing: a denim shirt, pants, and lug boots. The ordinary nature of his clothing is accentuated in contrast to his outlandish stage costumes on display, which are not worn in the music video but simply hang on the rack inside the glass cage: a silvery sequined jacket long enough to be a frock coat, a snow-white jacket that would have been simply elegant were it not for large rainbow-colored puff stripes stitched onto the sleeves; a silky pink

FIGURE 6. The music video "Who You?" maximally emphasizes media surveillance of a K-pop star by having openly invited fans to help shoot the music video. The live interaction between G-Dragon and fans is mediated by the presence of cameras. Source: YouTube.

jacket with a tiger's head on the back; a black leather jacket with metal studs and images of white skulls strewn over it; and a pop art jacket with blue and green figures, most eye-catching of which is a pair of female legs spread wide open in center front.

Against the backdrop of bemusing sartorial theatricality, G-Dragon is rather plain in what looks like his everyday wear. And yet, rather than showing his bare face, he still sports thick stage makeup with smoky raccoon eyes, for which he would have easily used up half a bottle of gel eyeliner. G-Dragon's heavily made-up face reminds us that his ordinary-looking denim shirt and jeans, plain as they appear, are a theatrical costume meant to be seen by a thousand pairs of scrutinizing eyes and recorded by a thousand cameras.[52] In the ensuing scenes of the music video, G-Dragon's actions flow casually from playing piano, singing, and dancing to reclining on a sofa, throwing his composition notes into the air in a mixture of delight and frustration, riding a skateboard down the runwaylike slope, and talking to the fans while making eye contact with them. As G-Dragon stages an ostensible performance of himself, blinding flashlights constantly pop from fans' cell phones like luminous stardust, augmenting the dazzling professional lighting provided by the music video staff.

Bordering on Performance Art

In an interview for Japanese-speaking fans on the subject of making the music video, G-Dragon stated: "In other music videos, I appeared very strong. In this one, I want to let go and be natural, just like I am doing a live concert. So I asked my fans to come and shoot me and we promised to use their clips for my music video."[53] In a calm, prosaic manner, G-Dragon nevertheless emphasizes the word *natural*. For a star known for his unusually vivid stage persona, what was at the heart of his desire to let go of the usual theatrics? If he was trying to feel as intimate as possible with the fans, then why was he coyly locked up behind the glass walls, shielding himself from immediate contact? Was he truly striving to eliminate the gap between his stage persona and his authentic self?

The question of whether there can truly be a performance of an authentic self is something that performance artists have been struggling with. Artists such as Marina Abramović and Sam Hsieh have explored the frontiers of selfhood by using their bodies as the most perceivable marker of being in time. Over a long duration, these artists push their bodies to the breaking point as a way of mapping their limits, to pursue "the interrogation and destabilization of subjectivity."[54] Consider Marina Abramović's renowned performance piece at the Museum of Modern Art, *The Artist Is Present*. Abramović sat still on a chair and faced audiences who volunteered to sit in the opposite chair every day, from March to May 2010, totaling 736 hours and 30 minutes of stillness. Or consider Sam Hsieh's one-year performances,[55] all of which took place over the course of one full year, during which the body became the only reliable marker of intangible time. Most illustrative of this point is a piece titled *Time Clock*, in which Hsieh punched the clock every hour for the duration of an entire year; as a way to provide material evidence for his endlessly repeated action, he took a single photo of himself every time. In a compilation of these photos, we see his hair grow: he started out with a shaved head but ended up having disheveled shoulder-length hair at the end of the year-long performance.

Performances like these are contingent upon the durability of self-exposure and the continuity of the gaze placed upon the artists' bodies as they bear the traces of time's flow. Despite the conspicuous display of self met by the intensified gaze in the music video—often marked by the presence of cell phones as not only a medium but also an extension of sight—G-Dragon's performance certainly is not meant to be, and cannot measure up to, these classical performance artworks. G-Dragon's performance in "Who You?" lacks the uneventful duration of everyday life, which is what art critic Adrian Heathfield saw as essential to Hsieh's works:

> Long durations such as those of Hsieh's lifeworks can be contrasted with the temporality of eventhood as ascribed to much performance work. . . . Extended duration lacks the distinction that separates the event from the mundane, the everyday: the bracketing off and casting out of experience into the domain of the "uneventful" through which the event, as heightened experience, must necessarily be constituted. Resisting time's spatialization in cultural measure, duration deals in the confusion of temporal distinctions—between past, present, and future—drawing the spectator into the thick braids of paradoxical times.[56]

Extended durations that erase the boundaries of the everyday and the specific time of the performance are not part of G-Dragon's music video shooting process. The making of "Who You?" took less than a day, whereas according to K-pop music video director O Se-hun, shooting a typical K-pop music video would take a full day or two.[57] What is left in "Who You?" is only mediatized traces of live interaction based on an intense gaze and brief self-exposure. After all, the final cut of the music video circulates via mediatization—a kind of heavy editing meant to interweave professional shots by the music video crew with amateur shots captured by fans' cameras and cell phones—which ultimately dictates what should be seen in the final cut.

G-Dragon's performance bears a closer resemblance to a kind of performance art that places much emphasis on display, as demonstrated by the Australian performance group Urban Dream Capsule (UDC hereafter). Both UDC and G-Dragon are interested in staging how visibility works by walking a tightrope between stage and home, effectively creating a show "of" and "out of" everyday life. UDC is known for making "interactive window theater" by taking up residence in well-exposed public spaces. This unique blend exploring simultaneously the ideas of site-specific theater and performance art started in 1996 at the Melbourne International Festival of the Arts in the Myer Melbourne windows. Since then, UDC's work has been showcased around the globe in Europe, Asia, and the Americas.

UDC made their US debut in 2001 in the window of a newly opened Sears department store in downtown Chicago. For two weeks, from June 12 to June 25, four Australian artists lived in four display windows. Much like G-Dragon in a glass cage in "Who You?" the men displayed their daily activities around the clock in a show window without shades or shutters. According to the Sears publicity statement that advertised the performance:

> The windows will be equipped with a full kitchen, bathroom, living room and bedroom, where UDC will make the ordinary extraordinary. UDC shows how everyday interactions can be transformed into artistic expressions, reflecting the goodhearted nature of humankind and the creativity of communication.[58]

The unwarranted optimism in the Sears statement shows the corporation's aspirations to turn its everyday products into part of a special happening; the members of UDC were human agents who carried out the magical transformation of department store merchandise into essential props of art making. The newly decorated Sears flagship store's show windows inhabited by the resident artists were filled with crisp bedsheets, cubic furniture pieces, puffy cushions, shiny stainless-steel kitchen appliances, and a brand-new shower booth with frosted glass doors—all brilliantly lit to create an immaculate impression. There were no traces of the boredom, repetitiveness, and purposelessness that can often suffocate daily lives. UDC's interactive window theater was a benign, five-star-hotel version of Sam Hsieh's *Cage*, where the artist was confined in an 11.5 by 8 by 9-foot cage for an entire year without speaking, reading any books or newspapers, or communicating directly with the outside world.

Having personally witnessed UDC's Chicago performance, I could not stop wondering whether G-Dragon's music video was partly inspired by this interactive window theater. Both performances deployed simple material objects from daily life—furniture, clothes, writing tools—but turned them into heightened theatrical props, inciting wondrous fantasies that belied the quotidian. Both G-Dragon and UDC were embodying the image of a desirable life by placing themselves inside the showcase as the focal center. But most significantly, both performances took place in a glass cage separating the performer from the audience while heavily relying on the presence of an intimate onlooker who would bring a new dimension to the action taking place inside the cage.

However, although the nature of the live exchange between performer and audience that constitutes this interactiveness is similar for both performances, a noticeable difference exists between G-Dragon's music video and UDC's Sears window performance. G-Dragon's spectators were handpicked fans invited by his management company to corroborate in the music video production, but the pedestrians in downtown Chicago were a mixture of incidental onlookers and intentional gazers who were aware of UDC's artistic direction. Moreover, whereas G-Dragon communicated directly with his fans during the shooting, the spectators had to communicate with UDC by means of written language, such as e-mails, faxes, and erase boards that were provided both inside and outside the show window. The dynamics of direct verbal communication are different from written communication, which is one step removed from the more intimate exchange of gestures and facial expressions in face-to-face communication.

The fans' investment in G-Dragon's performance (they had to apply to be a part of the shoot, be selected, travel to the location, shoot the video, and upload the clips to the designated website in the hope that their work would make it to the final cut) was radically different from that of casual bystanders of the UDC performance in Chicago. And it is this zeal that drives fans to create the impressions of authentic participation around liveness; their desire to partake in the music video production establishes a qualitative difference between intentional gazing and accidental onlooking in performance making. But was their authentic participation a marker of genuine liveness?

Music Video with a Thousand Versions

The official music video "Who You?" clearly does not have the duration of a performance artwork that lives and thrives over long stretches of time, nor does it have visceral live interaction with an open audience. But because of the participation of fans who were invited to shoot the video, "Who You?" paraded as a unique participatory piece into which spectators were projected to become proper cinematographers.

The final cut of the music video was released on Mnet on November 11, 2013, approximately a month after the studio shooting on October 5. The opening sequence starts with a caption, "This music video was made by G-Dragon and the personal recordings of one thousand of his fans," appearing over the bird's-eye view snapshot of the dark studio, temporarily illuminated only by scattered flickerings of fans' cell phone screens and flashlights. This shot captured by a professional camera from an elevated crane introduces the scale of the entire set from above ground level. The scene immediately cuts to low-resolution fan video clips shot with cell phones (figure 7). This pattern of rapid transition—from high-definition professional shots to shaky fan shots recorded by handheld cameras, then swiftly back to professional shots—defines the overall rhythmic flow of the video sequence. The result is an interesting alternation of pixel textuality, from low to high, high to low, close up and stable to shaky.

To make the music video more multidimensional, the final cut introduces complex layers: screens within a screen and screens gazing at other screens. While the professional cameras of the music video crew capture the way the fans capture G-Dragon through their handheld screens, one of the professional crane cameras also features a large display screen inside the transparent glass wall. This large screen displays a close-up head shot of G-Dragon, immediately fol-

FIGURE 7. The music video "Who You?" interwove professional shots with amateur shots to emphasize fan participation in its making. Source: YouTube.

lowed by the same shot from the ground level captured by a fan's low-resolution camera. In terms of soundscape, a stream of G-Dragon's professionally recorded song "Who You?" is temporarily interrupted by the fans' lively buzz at the music video shooting location, as G-Dragon cheers them to follow his command. The conventional language of K-pop music videos—the smooth flow of stimulating images made by piecing together highly professional shots against the backdrop of professional sound recording—is interrupted by the cacophonous sounds and images made by fans. Creating a stark contrast to the professionalism of the conventional music videos, "Who You?" introduces an unrehearsed authentic view of fans as a way of creating an impression of liveness.

"Fans have been featured in music videos before, but this is the first time that fans actually participated in the shooting of the music video itself," wrote one journalist.[59] By having a substantial part of the music video made by the fan cameras, passive consumers became active creators in this case. The music video production team well anticipated the multiple potential versions that would exist beyond their final cut and gave proper credit to all who participated.

Taking this inverted relationship between conventional producers and consumers even further, not only were a handful of fan shots included in the official music video but also thousands of individual fan recordings that did not make it to the final cut truly shed new light on the overall participatory practice. Numerous fans who went to the event posted their footage on YouTube, revealing many hidden processes of video making, not simply as "behind the story" scenes but as the "front story" of their YouTube account, thereby fully exposing the event from their own vantage point.

Many fan-posted clips reveal how this shooting event achieved various purposes by reassembling multiple functions: a live concert, a fan meeting, and, not too surprisingly, a sales event (k-pop as "korporate" pop). In terms of how the video shooting doubled as a live concert, take into consideration that G-Dragon's second regular album, *Coup d'Etat*, in which "Who You?" was listed, was released in September 2013, a month prior to the music video production. So the sound track was already available to fans by the time the music video was shot. In this regard, the shooting of the video was like a proxy concert in front of one thousand fans, many of whom were holding BIGBANG light sticks, staple items in live concerts.

Fans were not left to their own devices in attending this "concert"; rather, they were thoroughly directed by the star and his crew. In one piece of fan-posted footage, G-Dragon monitors the clips recorded by fans: "Can you show me your footage?" He peeps through the transparent glass and watches a clip of himself on a smartphone held by a fan on the other side of the glass. During another interval, G-Dragon directs his audience to lower their cameras and asks if they can participate in the performance more proactively: "Some people are busy shooting, some are just having fun, so the picture might come out as neither this nor that. Let's show how much fun we can have! Even if you raise your hands a bit, I think we are going to have a much better picture."[60] De facto director on site, G-Dragon further encourages his fans: "Is it possible to have more fun? Can you dance along?"[61]

In this directorial effort to arouse *heung*, a uniquely Korean conceptual link between joy and liveness, the boundary between performer and director disappears not only for fans but also for G-Dragon himself, just as the boundary between spectating fans and performing stars disappears when everyone is featured in the final cut. Rather than placing the makers and the recipients of the performance in contrapuntal terms, the music video deploys the dynamics between the two as totally alterable and fusible with each other. In this field of openness, live concert comes to approximate performance art charged with unexpected possibilities.

Perhaps it was this rapport between what are normally understood as opposite poles that made this event a forum for communication, serving the function of a fan meeting for the star. Fan videos attest to the fact that many breaks scattered around the official shooting time gave ample opportunities for G-Dragon to directly address his fans. A fan with YouTube ID "seino772" shared a clip where G-Dragon addresses the crowd: "I was not able to host a fan meeting this time [catches his breath] so this . . . just simply is . . . [like a fan meeting]." If this was part of the purpose, the event provided an ideal ground, since this setting in which performer and spectators were separated only by a glass wall was much more intimate than usual fan meetings, where there is a greater distance between the stars on a stage and the fans in the auditorium.

But not everyone was invited to this intimate forum, and the selection process reflected the cold-hearted marketing and promotion strategy of a profit-driven corporation. Invitations to join the video shooting went first to loyal VIP members of the official fan club, whose status is defined by quantifiable contributions to their stars' career, usually in financial terms, such as purchasing the stars' albums or merchandise. The few remaining spots went to non-VIP members, who had to provide proof of purchase of G-Dragon's latest album by bringing either the receipt for the album download or the actual package (disk and enclosed poster). In short, every single guest who participated in the video shooting had to purchase G-Dragon's album in order to be there. Not only that, numerous other applicants who wanted to be in the shoot most likely would have purchased G-Dragon's album in happy anticipation of their potential participation. The irony here is that fans bought a commodity in order to participate in a live interaction with the star, but in the end they themselves became commodified as props in the final cut of the music video.

In this generous offering of voluntary time, one paying fan can easily be substituted by another, making the fans and their affective labor fungible. According to Shannon Winnubst, "Fungibility [in neoliberal economics] refers to those goods and products on the market that are substitutable for one another. For example, a bushel of wheat from Kazakhstan is fungible with a bushel of wheat from Kansas, assuming the quality and grade of wheat is the same. . . . While this may all make sense at the level of economics, the problematic neoliberal twist is translating it from a dynamic of capital to a dynamic of 'human capital': this is arguably the site at which the neoliberal episteme appears to become ethically bankrupt."[62]

Hence, beneath an event that approximates an open forum of fusion and rapport lies a marketing campaign to promote album sales, turning what seems like a spontaneous gathering of a tightly knit community into a monetary transaction in a neoliberal marketplace. While G-Dragon and YG Entertainment reaped the benefits in this transaction in tangible terms, participating fans walked away with a more amorphous sentiment of having created something with their favorite idol. The parallel between UDC's Sears performance and G-Dragon's music video shoot is once again confirmed in their promotion of corporate interest, while the naked face of capitalism is subtly veiled by the attractiveness of live events.

Indeed, the crassness of korporate pop is masked by the highly masterful editing done by mixing professional shots with amateur ones. Given that the process of making the video becomes the video itself, turning the rehearsal into the final product, and that a thousand different versions exist, "Who You?" is a unique case in the panoply of K-pop music videos. As such, it highlights the biggest paradox of how K-pop maintains its dynamic liveliness, made available around the globe via YouTube videos while its stars carry out minimal live tours. G-Dragon's "Who You?" cleverly resolves the paradox by making a live event out of the process of producing digital music and the accompanying music videos. Although this video cannot emulate the audacious destruction of boundaries between the extended time of everyday life and the limited framework of a performance, it ultimately appropriates from the performance art a commitment to interactiveness,[63] which we often term "liveness."

HOLOGRAM STARS
GREET LIVE AUDIENCES

WHEN WE THINK OF DIGITAL REVOLUTION prompted by the pervasive use of telecommunication, high-speed Internet, and virtual reality, we generally tend to regard it as a huge leap forward in bringing humanity to a new level. People separated by temporal gaps and spatial distance can now converse with the help of a mediated audio and visual interface. A father on a business trip to Berlin can talk to his son in Santa Barbara via FaceTime despite the distance between the two. Video-conference software will continue to reduce the need for businesspeople to travel and meet in person.

But can we really call this a step forward? Taking a closer look at all the marvelous technological interventions so pervasive as to reconfigure our perception of actual time and space, we notice that they reduce the dimensions of the represented object: the three-dimensionality of actual space, in which synchronous presence of live bodies of performers and spectators is at best captured by a two-dimensional screen, no matter how high the resolution of the 2-D display might be. In truth, we are gladly enthralled when we replace an actual space of 3-D inhabited by living bodies with a flattened 2-D surface.

In an attempt to counter the restrictions that come with the 2-D flat screen, various technological devices such as augmented reality (AR), virtual reality (VR), and hologram technology have been introduced to restore the vivacious contours of the actual body in real time and space. Hologram technology leads this restorative trend. A compound word made of *holo* (complete) and *gram* (picture), it is one of the most sought-after technologies in information and communications technology (ICT) in that users do not need any devices such as 3-D glasses to fully enjoy the realistic rendition of objects. Based on the optical illusion of expanding a 2-D surface to a 3-D space through multiple layers of 2-D projections, it nevertheless presents a protracted sensory experience otherwise trapped on the 2-D flat surface.

One of the popular introductions of the hologram as future technology may have been the first installment of the *Star Wars* film series, *A New Hope* (1977), in which R2-D2 projected a small holographic image of Princess Leia to Luke Skywalker in her plea to save the Rebel Alliance. The scene provided the first well-known instance of what it would be like to communicate with a 3-D projection; but in terms of the actual technology involved the filmmakers used a flat 2-D image projected on a sheet of Mylar to give an impression of a 3-D projection in the film. It was a pale imitation compared to more recent examples. A widely viewed 1992 intergenerational collaboration between Natalie Cole and the late Nat King Cole, who appeared on stage as a hologram singing "Unforgettable" alongside his living daughter, comes closer to our contemporary definition of hologram as fully conveying the image of three-dimensionality on stage.

In the new millennium, an animated cyber celebrity by the name of Hatsune Miku is an undisputed leader of this trend, performing in sold-out 3-D concerts worldwide with performances in Los Angeles, Taipei, Hong Kong, Singapore, and Tokyo while commanding nearly one million fans on Facebook. A creation of the Hokkaido-based firm Crypton Future Media, she debuted in 2007 as a vocaloid, eventually assuming a corporeal form of a sixteen-year-old girl with two voluptuous turquoise pigtails in the 3-D projection on stage. Then there is the much-talked-about resurrection of Elvis Presley in hologram projection via rotoscoping technology to sing next to Celine Dion for the 2007 *American Idol* stage. And there is the late rapper Tupac Shakur, who was shown on stage as a hologram with Snoop Dogg and Dr. Dre during the 2012 Coachella Music Festival. In the United Kingdom, there is even a TV show called *Impossible Duet*, in which stars can sing along with their favorite idols from previous generations, making an appearance on stage as holograms.

But it is not only popular culture that voraciously experiments with hologram technology. Holograms also find successful applications in "higher" echelons of culture and society. Queen Elizabeth II sat for a full-size holographic portrait in 2003, and in 2011 an Italian composer, Franco Battiato, relied on virtual presentation of singers via hologram to stage his new opera dedicated to the sixteenth-century philosopher Bernardino Telesio. In a form known as "Telesio" lyric opera, the production featured live orchestra music while the acting and dancing on stage was performed by holographic projection.[1] Transmedial applications of hologram technology like these indicate that incorporation of holograms, whether met by popular approval or resistance, seems to be an escalating trend that will command a larger presence on future stages.

In the future, the use of hologram technology will inevitably expand from its current applications in concerts and displays to more mundane uses involving household electronics and portable electronic devices. In The growing demand for it was shown by its inclusion in IBM's 2010 "Next Five in Five" list, which highlighted five rising technologies that would create differences in our lives in the following five years. In 2015—the last year in the span of IBM's projection—the world had yet to see the widespread everyday usage of holograms, but there is an ever-growing trend in development by the large industry giants: Microsoft introduced Windows Holographic, a technology that presents a "world with holograms," during its Windows 10 release event on January 21, 2015.[2] Not to be left out, in January 2016 the *Financial Times* announced that Apple had hired Doug Bowman, one of the top VR researchers in the United States, "to catch up to Facebook, Alphabet, Microsoft and Samsung in what many see as the next big shift in computing platforms."[3] Not only tech companies but also those that produce daily consumable goods like Ikea, AMC, and the Food Network are working to launch "new augmented reality applications, which let you overlay slices of the digital world on top of the real one," according to a 2017 CNBC report.[4]

South Korea is not a bystander in this race, as the *Financial Times* reference to Samsung indicates. What makes the South Korean case quite noticeable is the intimate—and often destructive—ways the government-affiliated corporations and the private entertainment sector collaborate under the banner of the "creative economy." The administration of Park Geun-hye (Bak Geun-hye) (February 25, 2013–March 10, 2017) set out an initiative for economic development based on technology, culture, and media, under which the creative economy (*changjo gyeongje*) was projected as an extension of the government campaign to brand the nation in a positive way.[5] The creative economy was Park's intended political legacy, a response to a trend in postindustrial South Korea for export-driven manufacturing to gradually give way to the export-driven service sector. Park's choice was also in line with a broader global trend of using creativity as a strategy to survive postindustrialism. "The creativity complex" is one of the main soft-power analogues to the hard-power "iron triangle"—"the policy-making relationship among legislative committees, state bureaucracy, and interest groups that consolidate elite power"—complementing and often even overwhelming hard power.[6] Hologram technology received special grooming from the South Korean Ministry of Science, ICT, and Future Planning,[7] the newly created ministry that stood as the symbol of Park's presidency itself.

A colossal scandal shook South Korea in the fall and winter of 2016–17, exposing the government's corruption and abuses of power under the auspices of the creative economy initiative that eventually led to Park's dishonorable impeachment.[8] Nonetheless, the campaign facilitated some groundbreaking innovations, such as South Korean researchers' creation of the world's first 3-D hologram in 2015,[9] bringing the Korean ICT sector closer to the K-pop industry than ever before. Therefore, rather than emphasizing the sensational political scandal, I reflect upon the drive behind the alliance forged between the K-pop industry and the government-led initiative.

For instance, in 2013, SM Entertainment signed a joint business agreement whereas YG Entertainment established a consortium with KT Corporation, formerly state-owned Korea Telecom, with overwhelming ownership in Korea's broadband Internet market. Together, K-pop entertainment companies and KT have been actively pursuing a partnership between hologram projection technology and performance through which both K-pop celebrities and made-in-Korea technology will attract a wider range of global audiences.

In addition to collaboration with KT, SM Entertainment has been partnering with KAIST (Korea Advanced Institute of Science and Technology)—formerly Korea Advanced Institute of Science, founded under the auspices of former president Park Chung-hee (Bak Jeong-hui) in 1971—in carrying out a joint project creating synergy among science, technology, and entertainment sectors. "Robots, software, applications, big data, screen, display—all these aspects require collaborative work between celebrities and technology," pointed out the head of SM Entertainment, Lee Su-Man (Yi Su-man), who obviously saw SM's hologram musical as the brainchild of such a vision.[10] Likewise, YG Entertainment company has been making similar strides to expand its hologram performance in Korea and beyond, with the backing of government-invested agencies.

Hologram collaboration illustrates that private industry leaders, such as YG and SM Entertainment companies, are very much partners in the South Korean government's vision to promote its image as the leader in future technology. Their stars' holographic bodies, by analogy, fabricate the ideal national body: a technologically savvy futuristic body created by the convergence of culture and ICT. Times have changed in that the display of an ideal national body in robust bronze statues (as most nation-states have their national heroes commemorated) or of a mightily coordinated populace to symbolize the ideal collective (as socialist countries do in national parades) has given a way to the display of flimsy holograms.

But the new millennium is an age when digital technology has come to be a major yardstick for measuring a nation's strength, and in this respect, ideal national bodies have to be pixel-perfect. Holographic renditions of K-pop idols' bodies are disciplined and controlled, but they also have a cool factor: they are disciplined in the sense that they are carefully recorded and edited before public release, but cool in the sense that they are the closest simulations of living bodies capable of interacting with the audience.

The two case studies introduced in this chapter—YG Entertainment's hologram performance at Klive and SM Entertainment's hologram musical at COEX Artium—are prime examples of the private entertainment companies' and the South Korean government's collaborative attempt to create a win-win situation: if the nation is set on enhancing its soft power under the banner of promoting "creative economy," then companies are eager to explore how to transform ephemeral live shows into permanently reproducible performances that can enhance profitability. Although YG Entertainment's hologram show closely observes the format of a music concert while SM Entertainment's production identifies itself as the world's first "hologram musical," both reaffirms the convergence of public and private, entertainment and technology sectors that propel our desire to lay claims to the future.

Klive, the Hologram Theater, and the Restoration of the Body

The body is the most revered, fetishized, contested, detested, and confused concept in contemporary cultural theory. Moreover, that is just the natural, corporeal body—things become even more complicated with its virtual counterpart.

Steve Dixon, *Digital Performance*

As the leading cultural icon of novelty and trendiness, the K-pop industry cannot be left out of the recent boom in hologram technology. While the boom is riding on the broader trend of technologically enhanced performance on stage, K-pop's courtship of hologram performance has a special implication: as much as hologram technology makes its best attempts to capture human bodies in 3-D that closely simulate the actual living body, the fact that such efforts can generate only digital simulations points to the location of the hologram's natural habitat, namely the intermediary zone created by the intermixing of live performance and prerecorded digital performance.

Holograms can be a titillating remedy for the lack of lively interaction between the audience and the K-pop stars who find it difficult to appear on live stage; when K-pop artists go on a live tour, they usually focus on overseas markets, which tend to be more lucrative and more effective in promoting their music in the global arena. When they happen to be in Korea, their time is mostly dedicated to preparing for the new album, shooting MVs, and making appearances in music chart and entertainment shows on TV, all of which remove them from live spectators and fans. When they do make appearances in person, by either attending promotional events for commercial products or appearing on TV programs ranging from music chart shows to entertainment variety shows, they face only a handful of live fans committed to being there in person. So when do the idols get to perform live in front of congregated fans in a proper concert setting? How is it possible to quench the thirst of fans who desire to have intimate interaction with their stars?

Klive, which opened its doors to the public on January 16, 2014, might not be a perfect solution to this conundrum. But at least it attempts to fill the gap in the K-pop scene left by the conspicuous lack of live performances. Located on the top floor of Lotte Fitin, a newly decorated commercial space for youth with trendy clothing shops and posh cafeterias, it features 3-D performances by the most prominent YG Entertainment artists, such as Psy, BIGBANG, and 2NE1. Boasting a 270-degree view, the venue was created as a result of a joint investment of approximately $9 million by the KT Corporation and private sectors (d'strict and YG Entertainment), hoping to attract global tourists to the Seoul metropolitan area as the mecca of the K-pop industry and cutting-edge fashion.

With an eye on becoming the world leader in the field in terms of setting industry standards and charting new product development and business opportunities, Park's administration had intended to invest approximately $250 million by 2020 and to create fifty-one thousand new jobs by 2025. Keen on propelling various projects that would link the IT industry, entertainment, media, and tourism, the Ministry of Science, ICT, and Future Planning established the Strategic Planning Committee on ICT in May 2014, the same year Klive opened its doors to the public. Seeing Klive as the focus of its future vision, the committee even hosted its second meeting there on August 27, 2014, over which the prime minister presided.[11] Among many forms of marriage between the K-pop industry and South Korean government sectors, this one stands out in its shared vision to project the live performing space as a venue for future digital technology.

Understanding the partnership between the South Korean government and the K-pop industry always requires getting stories from both sides. While the question of why and how K-pop stars will reap the benefits of hologram performance has been raised already, the flip side of that question—why did the Korean government decide to dedicate its energy to, of all things, the K-pop industry as the prime area to showcase its developing hologram technology—needs further elaboration. The South Korean government surely could have chosen film or video games instead of K-pop as its designated banner to flaunt the country's advanced ICT. Why elevate K-pop stars, such as BIGBANG, 2NE1, or Psy, to a project of national significance? What does the government gain by aligning itself with these pop stars, who often face public criticism due to various scandals involving illegal marijuana smoking (G-Dragon and TOP of BIGBANG), sex scandals (Seungri [Seungni] of BIGBANG), evasion of proper military service (Psy), and smuggling of illegal drugs (Park Bom [Bak Bom] of 2NE1), other than the obvious fact that these YG stars already have a huge global fandom and recognition?

A Day at Klive

I visited the venue on August 9, 2014, when the summer heat was already melting everything down in Seoul. Leaving behind the ferocious intensity of bustling streets, I stepped into Lotte Fitin, a nine-story department store, to find myself instantly surrounded by the respite of chill, faintly aromatic air. With rows of glimmering showcases displaying everything from colorful phone cases to irresistible cute stationery, Lotte Fitin can be called a hip place; it is adjacent to the newly opened Dongdaemun Design Plaza (DDP), situated in one of the longest-surviving mercantile centers of Seoul—the Eastern Gate Market. Even prior to the establishment of modern markets in the twentieth century, the Eastern Gate Market was a famous commercial hub that fed the bustling life of Seoul, the capital city of the nation since 1392.[12] In the late twentieth century, its reputation was built mostly as a wholesale clothing market that eventually earned a global reputation around the turn of the century, attracting retail and wholesale buyers alike from Korea, China, Japan, Russia, and beyond.

DDP was erected on the grounds of now-demolished Dongdaemun Stadium (1984–2008), which witnessed the district's bustling commercial boom throughout the twentieth century.[13] DDP's silvery and amorphous contours, designed by the renowned architect Zaha Hadid, reflect Seoul's ambition to revamp its image as the global center of urban design and architecture. As its slogan "Dream, Design, Play" illustrates, this new tourist landmark is aspiring to be the command post for the Korean cultural wave, serving as a prime destination in global tourism, which has been on the rise with Korean culture's growing popularity, especially among Asians.

For instance, a special exhibition of a popular TV drama, *My Love from Another Star*, was staged at DDP, hoping to attract tourists from China, where the drama had enjoyed enormous success in early 2014. A promotional ticket combining an admission to both Klive and the drama exhibition, which are separated by just a ten-minute walk via underground passage, was on sale during the high summer tourist season—from June 10 to August 15, 2014—testifying to how both venues target the same clientele made up of young local fans of Korean pop culture and foreign tourists.

Rather than being isolated experiences, the act of visiting Klive and becoming a spectator of K-pop stars' hologram performance should be considered as networked events along the continuum of consumption, somewhere in between intentional visits by K-pop fans who see this trip as some kind of pilgrimage and non-K-pop tourists' visits to general attractions, often defined by tour guides' recommendations. In many websites promoting Korea tourism, Klive makes an appearance as a must-visit place, exposing foreign tourists who are not necessarily K-pop consumers or followers of YG Entertainment's K-pop artists. The reverse is also true: YG artists' fans who did not plan on shopping will have to go through multiple floors and be exposed to K-products.

Such a win-win scenario—drafted by K-pop industry and its partners, of course—applies to other tourist sites. But Klive distinguishes itself from other experiences of viewing K-pop, such as watching music videos online or going to live concerts, since it hopes to produce a distinctively symbiotic experience of liveness and digitization while parading South Korea's technological savvy.

Visitors to Klive are introduced to the world of optical phantasmagoria—created by the playful integration of the live body and the prerecorded digital body—even before they land on the ninth floor. Enter an elevator and you will find yourself standing right behind G-Dragon. But the star coexists with the visitors merely as a digital phantom—a photoshopped projection only in the screen hanging over the elevator door. Nonetheless, he looks back and waves at the visitors, creating an augmented reality where corporeally absent (but digitally present) star and corporeally (as well as digitally) present visitors inside the screen can seamlessly coexist.

With this intimate greeting from the pixel star, visitors enter a K-pop heaven glimmering with well-lit K-pop souvenir shops and multiple exhibition items that encourage the conflation of visitors' reality with the stars' reality: a paparazzi panel will encourage visitors to peep into what look like private moments from stars' daily lives while a large-screen panel will project visitors to be riding in a van with their beloved stars. Or visitors can step into a star photo box where they will end up getting a photo of themselves posing with Psy or BIGBANG (figure 8). At the other end of the foyer is a larger-than-life photo of G-Dragon

FIGURE 8. A photo booth at Klive will produce a seamless image of visitors with YG stars. Source: Kim Suk-Young.

in front of a sports car made of transparent material, brightly lit up with ice-blue neon lights. This was an actual prop used for his "One of a Kind" world tour, and to augment the idea of a live tour, the background photo flanking G-Dragon features a constellation of yellow lights, which immediately remind the viewers of yellow concert light sticks found at BIGBANG live concerts. The installation gestures toward bridging the live concert and the fake live concert, that is, the hologram show, by way of displaying the actual prop once used on live stage as if it could carry the aura of the live event.

The highlight of this shrine dedicated to idol worship is the tall screen tower soaring up to the ceiling with large vertical digital panels, which project high-definition images of singing stars that visitors can choose. This tower of K-pop has a screen at the bottom commanding visitors to "touch your favorite stars," fostering the illusion of tactile intimacy even though they are only touching a cold screen (figure 9).

FIGURE 9. Visitors to Klive project the image of G-Dragon on a digital tower. Photo by Kim Suk-Young.

In this dazzling space filled with a sleek chromatic patchwork of pink and azure design panels planked by silvery metal columns, sharp fonts in grayish and black shades spell out the names of popular K-pop acts everywhere you look. From basic Photoshop to a more complex hologram projection using rotoscoping technology, virtual reality reigns over visitors, who are ready to suspend their belief in actual time and space and submit themselves to an altered reality made of optical illusions.

Yet Klive does not completely let go of the tensions between actual material reality and the manufactured pixel reality. Before visitors are allowed to enter the hologram theater, they are greeted with an expertly executed mime-dance in the theater's smartly decorated foyer. A trio of break dancers wearing white masks and red suits emerge in front of the congregated audience who have been waiting to enter the auditorium. Their corporeal presence in front of high-definition pixel images of YG stars calls into question the long-standing duality of the physical body and the digital body: What do these live dancing bodies hope to achieve with the audience who arrive at Klive prepared to see a hologram show, or a simulation of live performance packed with the digital doubles of live bodies?

The trio dance within an arm's reach of the audience, and the space between performers and spectators is marked only by a flimsy barricade. Across this easily crossable boundary, a strong kinesthetic connection between the dancers and the audience emerges, since the dancing bodies are not separated by the division between auditorium and proscenium and the fast-beat music invigorates the audience to join the groovy moves being performed. The introduction to the hologram theater incorporates live dancing bodies, signaling to the audience that they will be treated to a hybrid show that makes use of both live and digital bodies; the holographic bodies are obviously hollow projections without material substance, yet they gain their spectacularity when juxtaposed against the live bodies.

While contemplating the symbiotic nature of this presentation, I want to pay close attention to Steve Dixon's argument that "the virtual body operates as an index, as another trace and representation of the always already physical body."[14] The precedence of actual bodies over digital bodies underlines the fact that "audiences cognitively and empathetically perceive the performing virtual *human* body (as opposed to a computer simulated body) as always already embodied material flesh."[15] For Dixon, the virtuosity of the pixel bodies, no matter how convincingly they may have been executed in their fullest 3-D reality, is only an extension of the actual body, without which the optical illusion of the holographic body cannot exist.

If we entertain Dixon's view, the presence of the actual human body introduced by the dancing trio in the foyer of Klive signals how live bodies become the indexical foundation for holographic bodies to emerge later inside the auditorium: once the visitors enter the house, they find themselves mingling with the mime actors who will later appear as hologram images on the proscenium. Having set the tone for hybridity between live and digital performances in the foyer minutes ago, three dancers are now dressed in new costumes as a joker, a motorcyclist, and a man in a lemon-colored suit in emulation of characters who make appearances in Psy's "Gangnam Style" music video. They busily go around and interact with the audience, who, once again, find their anticipation to see "fake" hologram bodies betrayed. Once they make their live presence known to the audience, the mime actors step onto the proscenium stage.

As the audience starts to feel familiar with the trio's live dance on stage, suddenly Psy appears next to them as a 3-D projection, signaling the beginning of a hologram show. The world-famous Psy as a hologram, standing next to live bodies of three dancers, appears hollow and pale. The show does not make a secret out of the fact that Psy is "fake" (read "not live"); rather, it emphasizes the blatantly phantom-like nature of hologram projection by splitting his single body into five figures, making a point that digital bodies, unlike actual bodies, are more susceptible to optical manipulation. To augment the sense of illusion, the audience members are invited to see multiple Psy figures flying over famous geographic landmarks, such as the Statue of Liberty, the Egyptian pyramids, the Mausoleum of the first Qin emperor, the Leaning Tower of Pisa, and the Eiffel Tower.

In the space's chilly air-conditioned environment, the fast-moving global attractions introduced by holographic Psy throw me into dizzying confusion: What to make of it all? Don Ihde's seminal book *Bodies in Technology* (2002) introduces a three-tiered register of bodies, which provides a useful framework to understand the Klive show: body one is our physical and phenomenological being-in-the-world; body two is the culturally and socially constructed body; and body three exists in "a third dimension," "the dimension of the technological."[16] To borrow this framework, holographic Psy, or what Ihde calls body three, remains a valid reference point for the actual singer's body, or the combination of Ihde's "body two and body three." The relationship between actual Psy and the digital Psy is indexical: without the former, the latter does not exist;

without the latter, the former is confined to the singular register of corporeal reality. After all, the holographic image of Psy (body three) cannot exist without the actual body of Psy (body one), but how many Klive visitors have encountered Psy (body one) in real time and space? Most of us encounter Psy in the virtual space of YouTube music videos (body three) as an inevitable substitute for the presence of his actual body (body one) in our mediatized world. The reference to the "real" singer, in this case, has no other choice but to be predicated on the virtual space of YouTube.

The Klive performance seems to embody the idea that the digital and the real are no longer phenomenologically separable entities: in other words, hologram technology collapses the difference among the three levels of the body presented by Ihde. By having the holographic Psy (body three) shoot a laser gun aiming straight at the live audience, it claims that we have entered an age in which digital performers and live audiences are no longer disturbed by their ontological breaches—no matter how differently their bodies are materialized. Taking this fusion further, when holographic Psy pulls his trigger, the three live dancers simultaneously shoot a water gun into the audience in an effort to ignite a kinesthetic response in the audience. But what really illustrates the entanglement of the three registers of body types is the moment when the projection on stage incorporates three photos of the actual audience, who are present in the auditorium (body one) as well as in 2-D renditions (body three), interacting with holographic Psy on stage.

This instant transformation of the actual audience into digital projections on stage is made possible by the fact that audiences have gone into the photobox inside the auditorium while waiting for the show to begin, providing the show producers with the opportunity to select a few audience photos and incorporate them into digital projection. When holographic Psy talks to the "freshly digitized" audience who are actually standing in the auditorium, it reaffirms Dixon's point that the actual 3-D body has to exist prior to the creation of holographic images. As Dixon aptly noted, "Irrespective of the medium, performance's ontology has for centuries been virtual and simulacral, and the flesh of even the virtual performer remains too solid and will not melt."[17] But given the mutual dependency of actual and virtual bodies on the stage at Klive, the flip side of this statement is equally applicable—the virtual reality inhabited by digital bodies liberates the actual bodies from their time-and-space confinement.

The mutually dependent relation between the virtual and the actual in Psy's performance continues in the following sections featuring 2NE1 and

BIGBANG. Tricks such as instantly digitizing the faces of the live audience and transposing them onto the holographic bodies on stage to interact with holographic stars, or holographic images of stars addressing the audience directly in their effort to break the fourth wall, are embodied examples of how live and digital bodies are inextricably entangled. Digital Psy's flight over various landmarks, 3-D projection of 2NE1 members' flight on a magic carpet, and BIG-BANG members' levitation in defiance of the laws of gravity remind viewers that these figures' status as "just holograms" is not being concealed; yet the digitally fabricated reality does not cease to interact with material reality. The show takes this attempt even further when a digitally projected giant hand appears on stage to shatter life-size holographic figures into pieces, preemptively dispelling any potential belief that holograms are realistic renditions of human bodies. All in all, there is really no confusion between virtual and the digital in this show, although they might be mutually dependent on each other. As my three-year-old son confirmed after the show, "Those people on stage were NOT REAL."

In light of this symbiosis of the digital and the actual that acknowledges the artificiality of the digital, it is ironic that the promotional videos on YouTube cite visitors who provide their testimonials in Chinese, Japanese, and English about how "realistic" the holographic images appeared. Comments such as "It was as if G-Dragon was standing next to me" or "It was like a real concert" attempt to sustain the fragile illusion that holograms are a dependable framework for capturing the realness of the material body. But my observation tells me that the Klive performance is nothing but evidence that digital body and actual body can never truly transform into each other. All they can achieve is the creation of a field of vision whose spectators get to realize that they live in times when the intermingling of those bodies is something to be celebrated as a high-technological virtue. The notion that "the quotidian is jealous of the telepresence, jealous of the virtual," is only partially true in this case,[18] since there is neither any particular desire for various registers of bodies to emulate one another nor any confusion to pass off one as the other. This might have been the compelling reason why the South Korean government regarded idols' physiological bodies as ideal material for holographic projection: idols' bodies are already well disciplined and malleable to outside pressure and needs, and after years and years of modification through training, cosmetic surgery, and strict diets, idols make their bodies a vacuous playing field where technology of all sorts can be tested out. In the case of Klive, they happen to be performing the nation's highest technological aspirations.

Virtuous Technology for the Nation

The technological complexity and the labor intensity involved in the production of this show are hidden from the sight of the audience. Most spectators just enjoy the outcome in its seamless form, but the show at Klive involves three technological components: holograms, virtual reality (VR), and augmented reality (AR). The beauty of hologram technology lies in that it does not require special devices to fully access its three-dimensionality. VR, on the other hand, requires special gadgets for a full 3-D effect, such as goggles and gloves to enhance visual and tactile sensory systems. It is a kind of technology that depends on a user interface with the software. AR, on the other hand, is differentiated from VR by its reliance on "overlap" of real and virtual images to create a seamless field of vision.

Shooting the hologram video for one song usually lasting four minutes takes around three days minimum, and for performers in high demand such as Psy, 2NE1, or BIGBANG it must have been a huge time commitment to make themselves available for the recording of the Klive performance. Since each artist presents three songs on the average, approximately a week must have been spent—a much longer time than that required for shooting a music video, which is normally from twenty-four to forty-eight intensive hours. But the payoff moment for the stars arrives when the film can be interminably reproduced and circulated. The infinite reproducibility of holograms has led some artists to claim without qualification that the future of music will change. London-based singer-songwriter Emmy the Great, for instance, wrote in 2015 that holograms will do the hard work for singers in the future:

> We'll be able to spend our tour dates in bed watching Netflix 2.0, while our avatars shake their little blue booties out on sweaty venue stages. Holograms can't smell, and don't sleep or eat, so grueling schedules of hops-soaked bars, miles away from the last motorway Waitrose, will work out fine. Basically, you hear "hologram," I hear "music slave."[19]

As if conforming to this prediction, the music slaves of real K-pop stars have been working incessantly for the live audience since their creation. According to Korea Economy TV (*Hanguk Gyeongje TV*), a paying audience of thirty thousand attended the Klive show in the course of seven months. The same hologram show is played in a theater in the Samsung-owned amusement park Everland, and a free admission to hologram shows is guaranteed with the price of an admission ticket to the park. There, some 750,000 people attended the show in the course of one year.[20] Considering that each of these venues can accommodate only 350 people per show, the numbers are staggering when compared to attendance at live K-pop shows. While real K-pop stars have been shooting commercial films or vacationing abroad, their hologram slaves have indeed been working hard in front of a live audience.

Just like films, holograms can easily circulate overseas. Many instances of K-pop acts have made their appearance as holograms outside Korea, especially in the second decade of the new millennium: 2NE1 was one of the first artists to lead the trend, as their holographic debut took place at London Old Billingsgate during Korea Brand and Entertainment Expo (KBEE) 2013. The hologram performance of YG's biggest star BIGBANG was displayed as a part of YG Exhibition in Japan in Kisarazu Mall located in Chiba Prefecture from February 22 to April 20, 2014.[21] By popular demand, the show was extended for another month.

To ride the momentum and take the holographic show to even a bigger overseas market, in partnership with d'strict Holdings, KT, and Paradise Group, YG Entertainment established a joint venture, Next Interactive Korea (NIK), to open a digital theme park PLAY K-POP in Chizhou in Anhui Province, where their hologram performance will be shown to Chinese visitors. This performance in effect also serves as a demonstration of Korea's advanced ICT technology—3-D, 4-D, VR, and holograms.

The creative economy campaign hoped that holograms would embody the symbiosis of state planning and private business, precision and spontaneity, industry and culture, thereby obliterating the traditional division between cultural content and IT and uniting them into one and the same force in today's South Korea. Foreign media, such as the following BBC report in 2014, noted the efforts to promote a synthesis of technology and arts.

> The wave of music is part of how the country is trying to change. Under its new female president, Park Geun-hye, South Korea has embarked on what she says is a new way for the country to run. . . . Korea wants to create the so-called new creative economy and K-pop is part of it. Korean TV soap operas, Korean films, and of course, this music. At the base of this creative push is technology South Korea has embraced over the past two or three decades. The country has one of the highest uses of smartphones in the world, and almost every household has broadband internet connections.[22]

Written in a largely positive light before the eruption of the massive political scandal, which exposed the corruption involved in creative economy–related projects that led to Park's impeachment, the article highlights successful co-ordination between the private and public sectors as South Korea's national virtue. Nonetheless, the article fails to capture critically the South Korean gov-ernment's opportunism in taking a free ride on a spontaneous cultural boom that was not created by a top-down approach alone. The critical gap between the discursively developing private sector and the more regimented as well as opportunistic government policy has been pointed out elsewhere:

> South Korea's economy has yet to catch up to its people. They are the world's most-wired citizenry and the most advanced at using smartphones. Korean stars are Asia's most popular; Korean gadgets and fashions the coolest. Yet at home, huge manufacturing conglomerates, or *chaebol* [*jaebeol*], such as Hyundai Motor Group, Samsung Group and LG Group remain the mainstays of an export-focused system established after the Korean War by strongman Park Chung-hee.[23]

As this *Korea Herald* article shows, the top-down approach of grooming a cul-tural movement and the bottom-up discursive flow of pop culture cannot be so easily reconciled. Only the South Korean government's aggressive push gen-erated a special brand of creative economy with mixed results—from the ex-perimental merging of music and technology to absurd schemes that dragged artists and producers into one of the most bizarre political scandals that cor-ruption-familiar South Korea has ever seen in its contemporary history.[24]

The conspicuous push for a creative economy became nowhere more evi-dent than at the 2014 conference of the International Telecommunication Union (ITU), which was hosted by South Korea. The United Nations' special-ized agency for information and communication technologies, the ITU opened its plenipotentiary conference in Busan, South Korea on October 20, 2014, where two of the best-known South Koreans—Park Geun-hye and Psy—made an appearance.[25] The only difference was that the South Korean president was there in person to give an opening speech to the world delegations from 193 countries, whereas the goofy singer was there in a holographic incarnation to perform his signature horse dance that made "Gangnam Style" famous. Here was a clear collaboration between politics and entertainment to raise the pro-file of IT Korea, but which presence was more effective in supporting the ide-ology of a creative economy—the real body or the holographic phantom?

The live presence of the nation's head at the opening ceremony would impart much significance to the occasion by highlighting the important place ICT has come to hold in South Korea's destiny.[26] In her speech, Park emphasized:

> We thus have reached an inflection point in the hyper-connected digital revolution—a revolution defined by increased connection, smarter connection, and faster connection. This hyper-connected digital revolution will lead to new converged industries and services such as smart vehicles, smart health care, and smart cities. It will transform the way we live and contribute to the development of our economies and societies.[27]

Park's comments primarily pointed to the rapid convergence of networks that used to mark distinctive sectors, such as technology, culture, economy, urban planning, and travel. Flexible crossover of these categories—marked by a holo-ecosystem where industry, entertainment, and media will create a fluid continuum—would give rise to new challenges.

There is little doubt that the application of holograms will only increase in the future and that the idea of a holo-ecosystem is not just hype. In light of this trend, the idea of having hologram technology become a part of our mundane life is an important lesson to be learned in civic education. The lesson has been well rehearsed in Klive shows, as well as at the 2014 ITU conference, where live bodies and digital bodies mingle seamlessly without interfering with one another to present a vision of wholeness. The actual presence of the South Korean president next to holographic Psy extends further the kind of coexistence of live audiences and holographic K-stars that takes place at Klive. They mirror each other in that the fabric of liveness today is inherently made of the fabrication of mixed reality, where the aura of a pixel image and the material presence of flesh and blood weigh equally.

The holo-ecosystem will have a few enduring consequences in the K-pop industry. Just as music videos have reinforced the notion of K-pop as total performance capitalizing on all sensory modalities rather than just being a music genre, holograms will do the same—but much more aggressively than music videos, since there is an embedded notion of "liveness" in the hologram theater, especially with the congregation of a live audience, that is lacking for the most part in music videos.

Liveness, as we saw in the Klive performance, with its displays of technological marvels to a live audience, provides awesome opportunities to forge a new kind of public space where technological advancement will be displayed as a national virtue to both domestic and foreign audiences. This is precisely why the South Korean government is so keen on investing in the technology during its nascent stage and providing a fluid ecosystem to capture the dynamic networks connecting culture, economy, digital technology, and tourism. To have K-pop stars—albeit in holographic projections—be the iconic representation of Korea's future is a strong indication that the kind of public space and social discourse the government wants to foster is not deeply polemical. Just like British royalty, K-pop stars do their best to avoid any political statements and controversies by remaining vacuous icons to appease the public. The consumers of K-pop industry, on the other hand, see K-pop stars as the focus of their consumerist desire, and their commercial transactions regarding those stars assume the form of affective labor (more on this point in the following chapter on KCON).

The public space fostered by K-pop and the South Korean government is a perfect embodiment of neoliberal transactions, which seek "to bring all human action into the domain of the market," as David Harvey once described.[28] When the Klive show was over, the audience was brought out to exit the venue once again through enticingly displayed K-pop merchandise. Although not holograms, this merchandise bears images of the virtual stars and therefore performs the idea of absence to the utmost commercial effect, all under the auspices of the South Korean government. All in all, the spirit of live performance can be commodified in the service of the neoliberal state, which is only too happy to dance with hollow holographic stars.

School Oz and the Musical Holo-Ecosystem

While YG Entertainment has pioneered a new K-pop performance paradigm with a full-fledged hologram theater, Klive, and other overseas hologram projects, SM Entertainment has also been making steady attempts at hologram business. Not to be left out in the race for hologram applications in the cultural industry, SM Entertainment opened Hologram V-Theater in 2013 in Japan to have holographic renditions of their popular stars, such as TVXQ, Super Junior, SNSD, SHINee, and EXO, perform along globally recognizable icons such as Elmo and the Cookie Monster in collaboration with Universal Studios Japan. Such an attempt to test out hologram performance in the Japanese market—home to world-famous hologram performer Hatsune Miku—turned out to be so successful that SM Entertainment opened another hologram concert show in Huis Ten Bosch Theme Park in Nagasaki from April 3 to July 5,

2015; there, the company's biggest stars presented themselves to visitors in their holographic best. According to a media report, SM's latest hologram project featured superlative facilities where the hologram theater is "bigger than an IMAX theater" with "a 33-meter large-scale screen with 12K resolution quality, to bring a more real-life effect to the performances."[29]

The pattern shows a contrasting development strategy between YG and SM: while YG tested out the Korean market and brought the hologram show overseas, SM Entertainment took the opposite route by testing out the foreign market first and then building a physical space in Korea. It is still too early in the process to estimate which strategy will prove to be more viable, but one thing has been made very clear: though SM Entertainment has joined the still highly experimental project of combining K-pop and holograms somewhat belatedly, it has nevertheless devised a new transmedial experiment and developed its own hologram projects quite divergent from those created by YG Entertainment. If YG Entertainment has created a show in which hologram technology captures YG artists' concerts with occasional forays into optical illusions, then SM Entertainment's hologram musical *School Oz* does exactly the opposite by centering the show on the conventional format of a musical complete with a story line, acting, singing, and dancing. While YG resorts to holograms as a technological instrument to augment its artists' live music performance on stage, SM sees them as a magical tool kit for creating a brand-new musical genre that can extend performers' K-pop careers.

As already mentioned in chapter 2, SM Entertainment's investment in, and penchant for, Broadway-style musicals significantly influences its idols' creative activities. If TaeTiSeo's music video "Twinkle" was deploying the tropes of Broadway musicals to simulate the aura of the live proscenium stage of a bygone era, then we are left to wonder what the genre of musical can achieve in the case of *School Oz* when it interfaces with the unmistakably digital texture of hologram technology. As the first known instance of "hologram musical," a hybrid genre that purports to be the one and only example of holographic ingenuity, what can we surmise with regard to its ability to produce unique modalities of liveness? And how do those modalities articulate major concerns of national branding and the creative economy? We need to situate these questions within the spatial venue where the hologram musical is played; hence, my analysis starts with a closer look into one of the most impressive K-pop shrines that exists to date—SMTOWN—where the world's first hologram musical is being regularly staged.

A Day at SMTOWN

Enter SMTOWN, the imposing center of K-pop veneration. Its grandeur and central location turn Klive into a mom-and-pop store by comparison. Like an austere temple receiving pilgrims who travel across distant lands and seas to reach the holy site, it has become a hot destination since it opened its doors to K-pop fans and tourists on January 14, 2015. Located in one of the most prosperous sections of the Gangnam District on the south side of Seoul, the seven-story structure is illuminated by a brilliant combination of natural light shining through bluish glass panels and dazzling spotlights that strategically accentuate its futuristic architectural details.

I visited SMTOWN on April 26, 2015, roughly three months after the venue opened its doors to the public. The overall impression was one of freshness and brilliance. Stepping into SMTOWN is like walking into an "SM box," K-pop lingo for a brightly lit, ultra-sleek studio set often found in SM artists' music videos (think of the sets in Super Junior's "Mr. Simple," SHINee's "Your Number" dance version, and Girls' Generation's "The Boys," to name just a few). SMTOWN is a motley assemblage of high-fashion flagship stores, luxurious beauty salons, comfort-inducing spas, futuristic spaceships, multiplex film theaters, and clinically immaculate cafés, in which hologram theater is just one extension of an overall feast of consumerist desire.

The monochromatic entrance to SMTOWN amid the busy shopping mall resembles that of a high-end Las Vegas hotel for its unabashed stylistic mixing of austerity and kitsch (figure 10). Glossy black granite slate columns flank both sides of the spacious entrance; like brilliant constellations in the dusky sky, thousands of mirror inlays showcasing SM band names and geometric signs that resemble the symbols designating each band are found on the onyx-like surface in a neat pattern, surrounding a large "SMTOWN" logo. Once visitors enter the first floor of the "Welcome Zone," featuring a "light-emanating fantastic media wall," on which members of SM boy band SHINee greet them with irresistible smiles, they are led upstairs by an escalator to SUM, the celebrity shop on the second floor.

In SMTOWN, visitors enter through the gift shop as well as exit through it. If the entrance set the ambience for SMTOWN to signify ultimate trendiness, then SUM on the second floor turns that ambience into fuel for the machine of consumption. Walking through SUM provides an actual litmus test for how long visitors can go without shopping. It is a space designed to showcase "unique lifestyles presented by celebrities," with merchandise ranging from

FIGURE 10. Entrance to SM TOWN in Gangnam District in Seoul. Photo by Kim Suk-Young.

jerseys, snap bags, and shoes to sunglasses, perfumes, and notepads—all featuring SM idols' faces and logos.

On the third floor is SMTOWN studio, or what the SMTOWN website calls an "EDUtainment studio where visitors can experience the life of the artist with the assistance of a professional staff." Here visitors can get a total K-pop makeover, record their own music, or shoot music videos like the idols themselves. While SUM is a place where visitors are able to consume idol-related merchandise, the studio is where they can simulate the idols themselves. SMTOWN provides a fantasy of imitating them at various prices.

The idea of total consumption continues on with the LIVEary Café on the fourth floor, which, again, is a space of combined functions: "café," "music," "media," "books," and "special goods" appear as subtitles to this café. Indeed LIVEary functions as an SM artists' music archive where visitors can make their own CD by arranging SM artists' songs in a specific order or can treat themselves to overpriced, idol-themed baked goods. Cupcakes with baseball-hat toppings displaying idol logos in pastel hues, so irresistibly adorable as to justify their exorbitant prices, go well with equally overpriced soda water in transparent bottles named after SM Entertainment idols: lemon "BoA" water, hot pink "Girls' Generation" water, aqua blue "SHINee" water, deep violet "f(x)" water, bloody garnet "TVXQ" water—impeccably displayed on snow-white melamine shelves—lure fans who are thirsty to consume the idols of their pursuit.

As the visitors travel between floors on escalators, they are treated to photo panels of SM artists, museum-like displays of trophies, and expert installations of costumes worn by various idols in their music videos (figure 11). *Larchiveum*, a compound word standing for a library, an archive, and a museum describes the multiple purposes that SMTOWN fulfills, and if the word could be hyphenated with *storine*, a compound word I devised to stand for "store" and "shrine," it could be coming close to capturing the entire range of functions the place has come to perform.

Just like Klive in the previous section, SMTOWN can be another destination for lay tourists, but for die-hard fans of SM idols it can signify much more; it is a place designed for religious pilgrimage where commodity-idol worship is openly professed. What sustains SMTOWN's authority as a place of adulation is its ability to convey the aura of stars' live presence, much as religious temples

FIGURE 11. SM TOWN display case dedicated to SM's stars, Girls' Generation. Photo by Kim Suk-Young.

can be regarded as sacred spaces where the object of worship is believed to be authentically present. As emphasized in the café's name, LIVEary, the notion of "live" very much signals multiple possibilities: live music, authentic presence of the idols, and most significantly, live interaction between absent stars and present audiences. The last meaning of "live" is especially crucial for understanding hologram musicals performed at a theater on the top floor of SMTOWN.

When visitors reach the fifth floor, they enter a bright open space illuminated by skylights and a fifty-foot-high media wall that stretches out across the entire side of the hallway. During my visit, the latest SM music videos—EXO's "Call Me Baby" and Red Velvet's "Automatic"—were constantly being looped to an overpowering effect. In front of the screen were white cubic stools displaying autographs of popular SM artists, strewn over the glossy floor like material remains of evanescent idols. Yes, they had been here in person, and we could see the material evidence of their live presence that had preceded our visit. The foyer to the hologram theater already sends strong signals that visitors have entered a negotiated space where remains of live presence attempt to override the conspicuous absence of idols. Similarly, the hologram theater lends itself to both live idols' performance and their holographic projections, marking itself as a place where the play between illusions of presence and disguises of absence will be the main feature on stage.

As if to complement the impending tension between the absent stars and the present audience, the vestibule of the hologram theater is marked by other titillating signs of intimacy that potentially signal interactions between stars and fans. Life-size cardboard figure of idols, which visitors can touch and take pictures with, are everywhere. The airy atrium houses interactive screens where visitors can find the best match between their hands and the hands of the idols generated by the similarities in shape and size; on the basis of the match, the screen goes on to provide personality traits shared by the visitor and the star. As with the "touch your favorite star" command on the media tower at Klive, the imagined tactile intimacy works to give concrete form and character to absent stars.

The final entry to the hologram theater reinforces the idea that the distance between the physically present visitors and the absent stars can be easily abolished by a simple visual trick, much like the one already done in Klive. When I was about to enter the theater, a staff member with a camera, having decided that I was a Japanese tourist, started asking in Japanese which idols I wanted to take photos with. I chose TVXQ, the popular SM male duo, one of whom was cast in the leading role of the hologram musical I was about to see. In a couple of seconds, the staff handed me my "photo ticket" to SMTOWN theater, where I was seen smiling with the handsome duo. The making of a K-pop apparition is based on a quick simple logic: what bare eyes cannot see, technology can.

School Oz

Unlike Klive theater, which was imagined as a standing area in a concert arena with no designated seating, the hologram theater at SMTOWN was built as a typical auditorium with 746 generously upholstered seats.[30] Honey-colored oak wall panels flanked the barely occupied seating area, accentuating how there were only slightly more audience members than staff, even to the point that I could count everyone on my ten fingers. All the media hype about this new venture that SM was undertaking, and about hologram performance as the next big thing for K-pop, was immediately subject to doubtful scrutiny.[31]

Though school was still in session and April might not have been the peak tourist season to visit Korea, it was hollowing to see that this highly publicized hot spot, which on opening day only three months earlier had been so crowded that visitors had to wait more than three hours to enter the gift shop, was now virtually empty.[32] Approximately US$25 million was said to have been invested in the making of this hologram theater. According to an analyst at KDB Daewoo Stock Market Research Institute, "Forty percent occupancy in SMTOWN theater marks the break-even point. In the case of 50 percent occupancy, there will be an annual increase of sales in the amount of US$10 million."[33] Some analysts stated that a full-fledged promotion of the venue to attract more audiences would launch in April 2015, the month of my visit, but with a 1 percent occupancy rate, the promotion obviously was not having the desired impact yet.[34] Not only were stars absent, but the audience was nowhere to be seen.[35]

As the lights went dim, three members of EXO-M—Tao, Xiumin, and Chen—appeared on a 2-D screen to promote their newly released album *EXODUS*. This promotional pitch was promptly followed by a general announcement in four languages—Korean, English, Chinese, and Japanese—asking the audience to turn off their cell phones. These languages also appeared in subtitles during the hologram show, addressing the imagined multinational audience members that SM would have liked to have in the auditorium.

Thus began the first hologram musical in the world, featuring six luminary stars of SM boy bands and girl groups: Key of SHINee, Luna of f(x), Seulgi of Red Velvet, Suho of EXO-K, Xiumin of EXO-M, and Max of TVXQ. While fans of these groups can dispute eternally whether these artists are the most popular of their respective groups or not, by virtue of being a part of popular K-pop groups, all of them command substantial global fandoms. And yet, with the exception of Luna of f(x), an expert singer who had starred in a few Broadway-style musicals, it was the first time for all other members to have appeared in a musical of any sort, whether a live production or a prerecorded hologram musical.[36] To add even more star power, the production also featured other well-known SM idols (Yoon-ah [Yun-a] of Girl's Generation and Lee Teuk [Yi Teuk] of Super Junior) as cameos, while supplementing the quality of performance with professional musical actors such as Jo Eun. Although Jo played a crucial singing part as a character, "Betty," in the production, she was not credited in posters that broadly circulated in the media promotion, most likely because of her lack of celebrity status.

School Oz concocted a narrative out of broadly known productions from various periods and places, such as The Wizard of Oz, Harry Potter, and even some elements of The Hunger Games. Also incorporated into the story were rudiments from various K-dramas, such as the lingering legacies of the premodern value system, especially the emphasis on family background and the class system. Supernatural elements culled from fantasy graphic novels also featured prominently. The story roughly centers on the fantastical events unfolding at a magic academy where students hailing from powerful wizards' families hone their magical gifts. Max plays a character named Oscar, who is introduced as the successor of Oz Corporation in accordance with the typical K-drama cliché of the rich heir who is expected to continue the family business. (In one scene, his father appears to him and pressures him to understand that the future of Oz Corporation depends on Oscar's success.) Key plays David, a mischievous friend of Oscar; Luna plays Diana, a strong-willed witch in the making; Suho plays Hans, who hails from a clan capable of shape-shifting into a wolf; Xiumin plays Aquila, a human vulture who is in the process of learning how to fly. The fantasy elements of the plot are possible on stage, since holograms, as hollow projections, are not bound by rules of gravity, natural scale, or shape. Holograms can perform many actions that the physical body cannot, thus becoming the front line for the full expression of technological possibilities.

As the main characters prepare themselves for the school's magic competition that constitutes their culminating graduation project, Dorothy, an orphaned girl played by Seulgi of Red Velvet, becomes a captive of black witches when jealous Diana intentionally misplaces Dorothy's magical red shoes—an obvious homage to *The Wizard of Oz*—in the forest, forcing Dorothy to venture out into unsafe territory. The narrative centers on how the other students eventually get over feelings of competitiveness and jealousy toward one another and become united in order to rescue Dorothy from eternal nightmarish sleep—the curse imposed upon her by the black witches—and bring her back to safety.

Elements of competition among young teenage students to win at the price of others' loss provide the major dramatic conflict, which comes across as a watered-down version of the desperate struggle to survive in *The Hunger Games*, as if to meet the low age requirement set for the show (children of age eight and above are admitted). Rather than emphasizing the rules of the harsh survival game, *School Oz* stages safe morality lessons: the opening sequence of the production, which features 2-D animation, expresses a clear Manichaean division of the world into good and evil that often sets the tone for fantasy animation or graphic novels. In short, what seems like a simple children's musical reveals a complex entanglement of various cultural elements.

The anthropologist Néstor García Canclini would use the notion of "multi-temporal heterogeneity" to reference the multifaceted nature of the musical,[37] referencing how modernity is a process of compressing not-always-synchronous processes of geographic and cultural hybridizations. Much as TaeTiSeo's music video "Twinkle" straddled manifold performance elements from various eras and cultures, *School Oz* compresses various story lines and styles to create multiple points of identification for audiences to enter the story. From the preteen idol fans to their chaperon parents, the show anticipates that everyone will find something to enjoy in the familiar components of *School Oz's* clunky plotline.

What ironically enables the facile identification between the holographic actors and the actual audience is the vacuous nature of the performing bodies on stage. As holographic projections, they are able not only to absorb fantastic elements, which defy the rules of physics, but also to serve as empty icons for various desires and perspectives to play out upon them in a flexible manner. Hologram characters in *School Oz* can circumvent the rules of gravity and material dimensions, as they are often seen levitating during their magic shows or teleporting themselves through time and space. But such scenes also perform the idea of replication and inauthenticity by lacking the actual performing body.

The physical freedom of disembodied holograms, no doubt, is granted by the fantastic effects of technology, yet at the same time, the optical illusion stemming from free-flying holograms preempts any potential for materially grounded interaction between the performer and the audience. At first glance, what the actual audience sees on stage—the holographic projection of already illusive idols performing unreal magic tricks and time-space travels—has nothing to do with the real world. But could vacuous holograms embody multiple potentials that the body generating them can realize in the future?

In his study of Japanese idols, Daniel Black noted that "idols exist primarily as a carefully constructed mode of performance. While, of necessity, this mode of performance is most commonly generated by a living body, dependence upon a physically present performer is not inevitable."[38] Black's position presents a counterpoint to what Dixon suggested in the previous section—that digital bodies have an indexical relationship to live bodies, and that digital bodies cannot exist without physiological living bodies. What Black proposes is not to negate the necessity of the physical body that eventually generates digital bodies but to emphasize the illusive nature of the live bodies, especially if those bodies concern idols.

As artificially constructed agents created to maximize the profitability of their performance across media, K-pop idols' physical bodies are heavily altered to emulate the ideals of body types that frequent graphic novels and animations—the impossibly beautiful bodies that exist on the 2-D surface, without any organs, without any flesh or bones that give volume to the body. In this respect, holographic bodies are not a radical departure from real bodies of idols, which are constantly struggling to emulate 2-D aesthetical standards. As explored in the previous section on Klive, for most of the audience idols already exist in the pixel world of digital media apart from tangible reality, and therefore any attempts to distinguish real bodies from digital bodies, and 2-D bodies from 3-D bodies, inevitably lead to futility.

Hence, it is not only limiting but potentially misleading to claim that the only referent for the holographic figures on stage is the actual physiological bodies of idols. Two-dimensional mangas and animes are equally significant referents that the holograms are supposed to embody. This circular movement, in which human bodies in manga and anime are indexical to human bodies while live human bodies of idols constantly approximate the impossible standards of 2-D bodies, posits *School Oz* as a self-referential production. Not only are the bodies looped in the circular move as a way of referencing each other, but thematic and performance registers of the musical are also working along with the logics of self-referentiality; this may be a way of creating a holistic system in which holographic reality and actuality outside the theater will converge into a fluid continuum—if not ideologically, then at least technically and affectively.

Given the self-proclaimed musical genre, songs in *School Oz* inevitably play a seminal role in this production. But what constitutes the core of the musical score, rather than original scores composed for the musical, are well-known SM idol songs: BoA's "Atlantis Girl," TVXQ's "Mirotic," Super Junior's "Mr. Simple," Girls' Generation's "Genie," TaeTiSeo's "Twinkle," SHINee's "Shirlock," f(x)'s "Pretty Girl," and EXO's "Howl"[39] and "Mama," all of which have distinctively themed merchandise attractively displayed in the lower-level store of SMTOWN. The original versions of these songs were revamped into musical scores by the in-house SM songwriters and producers Yu Yeong-jin, Yu Han-jin, and Kenzie (Ken-ji). Although a song like "One Day One Chance" (coproduced by Yu Yeong-jin and DSign Music) was also composed just for this musical, the fact that a vast majority of the songs are derived from immediately recognizable SM hit songs effectively creates a transmedial bridge between the events in the musical and the mediatized networks in which these songs circulate along TV channels, YouTube videos, and smartphone screens. To revamp the songs from actual albums for musicals, once again, reaffirms the importance of transferrable media formats while also pointing to the continuing overlap between the performance of music to the live audience in the hologram auditorium and its digitized replay on other media formats.

The transmedial interplay between the realities within the musical and the broader products of SM Entertainment shows up, once again, in a scene when students from School Oz travel through various places in search of missing Dorothy. One scene features a nocturnal skyline of Seoul with variegated neon light billboards, one of which clearly displays a "School Oz" sign, laying bare the self-referential trick the scene engages in with the audience. SMTOWN now becomes a part of the holographic landscape on top of being a real building in which audience members find themselves; *School Oz*, on the other hand, is both the hologram musical the audience watches and a musical within a musical by becoming a part and parcel of the reality within the holographic landscape.

The double vision is realized by a looping system in which a hologram and real human figures are not necessarily confused with each other but flexibly share a vision of the musical as a phantom object that simulates but cannot become the reality itself. For instance, when hologram projections of Dorothy's friends arrive at SMTOWN theater on stage and wander around in search of their missing friend, real human actors appear in the auditorium to extend the link between hologram figures and the real audiences as a way of establishing the parallel between fictionality and reality. On stage, David, a jokester figure played by Key of SHINee, claims, while looking around the nearby area of the SMTOWN theater, which is part of the holographic projection: "Oh, there are so many people here!" This self-referential remark, humorously intending to mark the success of the *School Oz* production in general, would have been another instance establishing the connection between the stage and the auditorium had the auditorium been filled with viewers. But in this case, it paradoxically accentuated the disconnect between the illusory world on stage and the reality of the near-vacant auditorium. The auditorium was far from matching Key's observation, and the commercial failure of *School Oz* created a moment of rupture in the show's continued attempt to sustain self-referentiality.

After this moment of Brechtian alienation effect, the characters in the musical promptly teleport themselves from Seoul to New York City, to the Metropolitan Museum's Asian art collection. In this scene, SHINee's song "Sherlock" foregrounds the action as a major score, attempting to create a continuum between the hologram musical and the song's music video. The "Sherlock" music video is set in a museum, naturally tying the music to the museum scene in the hologram projection. The following sequences are much like the Klive hologram show in that the images of global landmarks, such as the Forbidden City, Osaka Castle, and some generic cosmopolitan cityscape with Chinatown gates fly by in rapid succession. As bright spotlights descend on the hologram characters on stage, real spotlights also shine upon the auditorium, an attempt to erase the gap between the stage and the audience.

The fast-moving panoply of hybridized story lines and global tourist attractions prominently features technological achievement, which can flexibly compress temporal and spatial gaps that are distanced by linear history and spatial geography. If *School Oz* teaches anything to the multigenerational audience, it is that the dizzying vision stemming from multitemporal heterogeneity is characteristic of our times. We live in a post-tourist world, where virtual travel is no less valued than actual travel, and the real-time encounter between stars and fans over Internet forums is no less immediate than the copresence of the two parties in a large concert arena.

In this regard, the musical becomes a shorthand education for extolling the virtues of technology that fosters intimacy, and it could not have been more appropriate to have "school" in the title of the musical. When the musical was first revealed, some fans and critics questioned why SM Entertainment had to cast a twenty-eight-year-old Max to play the role of a pupil in a school fashioned after Hogwarts School of Witchcraft and Wizardry. The obvious age gap between the actor and the student character brings critical attention to the analogy between SM Entertainment and a school. SM Entertainment's strict training system, fostering not only expert performing skills but also the idea of respectability, positions the company as a prime example of a pedagogical institution training young people in their formative years.[40] According to Cha U-jin, SM is just like an alternative school to which parents can entrust their children without the fear of tainting them.[41] SM Entertainment has accrued a reputation for fostering attractive yet polite performers, who present themselves as paragons of virtue, at least to the eyes of the public.[42] Training malleable and young K-pop star hopefuls to become both technically accomplished and docile-mannered members of the community resonates deeply with the strict authoritarian education system that South Korea has come to be known for.

As a testimony to how the technocracy of K-pop's training system integrates with broader fields in the technology sector, SM Entertainment's investment in education is not limited to training would-be stars in singing, dancing, acting for camera, foreign-language training, and polite manners but extends to a broader spectrum of education. As a case in point, in 2006 SM Entertainment forged a relationship with the Graduate School of Cultural Technology at KAIST to pursue how cultural technology, a term Lee Su-Man famously coined to designate the systematic ways in which SM content production should be regulated, could bring together media, technology, culture, and consumption.[43] In a speech given to commemorate the ten-year anniversary of the Graduate School of Cultural Technology, Lee declared: "I always tell SM employees to think about everything in a creative fashion with the focus on robots and celebrities, who are going to be at the center of the future."[44] Sure enough, we do not have to wait until some distant future; in the world of K-pop, that future is already here.

Hologram performances are the first steps taken to envision that perfect marriage between the celebrities and technologically constructed bodies. As early as the 2000s, SM was invested in applying hologram technology to concerts. In 2004, during BoA's tour in Japan, SM used hologram technology to create double images of its immensely popular teenage idol for a stage performance, in which the live performer was also present. Since then, holograms have come a long way: *School Oz*, with all its trappings of institutional rigor and competition, is developing real magic that can teach us how to sustain the mirage vision of seeing holograms and real human idols as a continuum.

At the heart of that union is the intersection marked by converging media platforms and hybrid performing agencies like holograms, whose ontological underpinnings are grounded simultaneously by the biologically live and the digital projection. As Lee noted, "SM is always searching for ways to create a nexus among music, videos, and SNS [social networking services] in the age of robots."[45] True to this vision, a music video of *School Oz* was created and posted on YouTube, whereas an original soundtrack of the musical was released as an MP3 file on January 20, 2016. Although the commercial drive that motivated such transmedial duplication of the musical has not been satisfied, the attempt illuminates how hologram technology, as a pilot project of fully realized future robots bearing the image of celebrities, can boast its versatility.[46]

When the musical credits rolled and the lights came up, even fewer people were present than at the beginning of the show. The auditorium, now fully illuminated, revealed not only the absence of an audience but also the absence of technology that had not been fully mobilized. In 2017, holograms have yet to be fully integrated into everyday life, and it may take some time for them to become the next thing. But in the meantime, perhaps SM Entertainment should create not only hologram stars but also hologram audiences to fill its state-of-the-art auditorium.

5

LIVE K-POP CONCERTS
AND THEIR DIGITAL DOUBLES

SOME MEDIA CRITICS hailed K-pop's emphasis on digital music as something of a future model, but as K-pop is gaining more and more traction in the global market, it is facing the growing need to adjust to the increasing overseas demand for live concerts. The rise of digital music is an irreversible trend, but the global music industry outside Korea is still very much dependent on multicity live tours to sustain artists' careers. As a result, the K-pop industry is trying to meet the demands of global music consumers by setting out on multicity tours to get closer to the overseas fans. For example, the K-pop girl group Wonder Girls, in their most wholehearted attempt to land the US market, suspended their highly successful K-pop career in Korea, which mostly consisted of TV appearances and commercial endorsements, and went on a multicity live tour in the United States in 2009–10. Although this strategy turned out to be unsuccessful—garnering very limited response from the US audience while their extended absence from Korea negatively affected their K-pop career—the group's effort to reach live audiences overseas was a pioneering one and became a trend that kept growing in subsequent years.

Around 2011–12, the number of live tours both domestically and overseas started to grow. For example, according to the statistics provided by the Korea Creative Contents Agency (KOCCA), the revenue garnered from live music performance in the Korean domestic market was roughly US$323 million in 2011, a 25.5 percent increase from the previous year.[1] Similarly, the number of overseas tours by K-pop bands, especially outside Asia, started to rise dramatically in 2011: whereas in 2010 there were only three notice-able overseas concerts, 2011 saw a massive increase in the number of K-pop tours, which included US cities as well as cities in Germany, Canada, France, the United Kingdom, Australia, and Brazil.[2] Not only did the number of tours and continents on the tour list increase, but also the format of the tour started to shift from variety acts by multiple artists who came up on stage to sing only a couple of their hit songs to a show by a single artist or a single band where fans were able to experience the distinctive musical style of a given artist.

In 2012 and 2013, efforts to reach out more aggressively to a global audi-ence continued, with groups such as BIGBANG and Super Junior embarking on truly global-scale world tours. Unlike most K-pop "world tours," which were worldwide only in name but not in scale, BIGBANG's Alive Galaxy Tour in 2012 included forty-eight concerts in total: forty-one in Asia, four in North America, one in South America, and two in Europe. Although most shows were concentrated in Asia, especially in Japan, it was the first K-pop tour to reach four continents. In 2013, Super Junior embarked on Super Show 5, with twenty-two tours in Asia, four in South America, one in North America, and one in Europe. Although the scale of Super Show 5 is far less ambitious than that of the BIGBANG Alive Galaxy Tour, it is noteworthy that Super Show 5 included stops in Brazil, Argentina, Chile, and Peru, marking it as the first extensive tour in South America by a K-pop band.[3] In 2013, another boy band, Teen Top, tried a similar strategy of touring extensively in Europe during their Teen Top Show, with stops including Munich, Dortmund, London, Paris, and Barcelona. These tours have set a precedent for other bands to try out similar, and at times more ambitious, world tours. The trend continued well into 2017, when K-pop rook-ies like K.A.R.D., who had debuted just a year before, toured five North Ameri-can cities and five European cities.

The Korean government paid close attention to the rapidly changing mode of exporting music and contemplated how it could further assist as well as ben-efit from the spread of live touring as a new model for generating Korean Wave momentum. In a 2015 white paper, KOCCA suggested that live concerts could be one of the main "short-term strategies" for the K-pop industry to land new overseas markets.[4] This intriguing perspective on live tours implies that long-term strategy would involve sales of digital music, which do not require K-pop artists to go through long hours of travel and extended absence from their home base, where their frequent media presence is required. Such a way of looking at live tours as a "hook" to bring fans to purchase digital music places a highly commercial value on "liveness," turning it into an advertisement to sell digital music as something more permanent and profitable.

The 2015 report also points out the untapped potential for a live concert to be part of a broader spectrum of festivals designed to promote nation's soft power:

> In the case of Korean culture festivals sponsored by overseas Korean cultural centers or the Korea Trade-Investment Promotion Agency (KOTRA), Korean drama, film, food have been the main feature, but rarely did K-pop artists make an appearance at these events. In the future, it will be ideal to have K-pop artists participate in these events and turn them into a large concert.[5]

Much as KOCCA viewed live concerts as a way to sell digital music, here it views live K-pop music as a device to spice up other promotional events to propagate Korean culture rather than as an event in its own right. As a matter of fact, many K-pop acts are serving such instrumental functions already, as will be examined in the case of KCON, where live concerts have become glorified sideshows for the convention, where the affective interaction between performers and spectators has become highly commercialized.

This chapter looks at BIGBANG's Made tour in Seoul (2015) and KCON LA 2015 to compare and contrast the technological and ideological workings of live concerts. Beyond the obvious fact that the former took place in Seoul, Korea, to entertain domestic fans, whereas the latter took place in Los Angeles for a multiethnic audience, BIGBANG's Seoul performance and KCON LA feature two different models of organizing a live concert in the preproduction stage. While the former presents a model in which artists and their management companies find an outside production company to organize concerts, the latter showcases how production companies seek out artists via their management companies to assemble a line of performers. The differences result in varying dynamics of the live event: the former focuses on presenting the consistent visions of a single band, whereas the latter focuses more on creating lively dynamics out of a motley assemblage of different music and performing styles.

But both events are similar in that the durational practices outside the live event provide the true vector that shapes the meaning of "live" on stage. In other words, liveness is shaped as much by what happens outside the concert arena as by what happens on the live stage. BIGBANG, for instance, used its

Seoul concert to make an announcement that it would be releasing two songs per month—from May to August 2015—as a way to keep offering "presents" to its fans on a continuous basis. While such a piecemeal release was in effect a savvy marketing strategy to sell both digital songs and the complete album, which included eight songs when they were all released, it also created an extended unfolding of the album over the course of four months, with live concerts in the Made tour series being the first forum to introduce the new songs. Such a strategy fashioned the revelation of digital songs into an ongoing live event, and the fact that their initial release unfolded on live tour stages countered how songs are released on an online music market.

KCON's tremendous social media campaign, on the other hand, is a nearly year-round campaign with little recess and is in many ways more important than the three-day convention itself. The convention may feature a forum for stars and fans to converge in a single space and time frame via live concerts and fan engagement, but what truly extends the intimate contact are the social media, which transform the live event into life itself.

Digital Phantoms on the Live Stage:
BIGBANG's Made Tour 2015

I looked down from my airplane window on layers of clouds that looked like fluffy popcorn stacked up on shimmery blue paper and only then realized the full meaning of my trip. I was lightheaded with sleep deprivation and unceasing white noise, but I could see that I must be somewhere over the Pacific Ocean, headed for the other shore six thousand miles away from my California home. What had I done? What had motivated me, a middle-aged woman, to leave behind two little children in the care of a husband with a full-time job and a retired mother-in-law who had graciously flown nearly three thousand miles from her East Coast home to stay with them?

BIGBANG's management company YG Entertainment announced on April 1, 2015, that its premier boy band would make a comeback after a hiatus of three full years. It also announced that the band would kick off its second world tour, Made, with a two-day Seoul concert scheduled on April 25 and 26. As with the band's first world tour, officially titled "BIGBANG Alive Galaxy Tour 2012–2013," which had attracted some eight hundred thousand live fans across four continents, the twenty-six thousand tickets for the Made tour were sold out within a few minutes after they were put online for sale. As a result of the commercial success of the tour, BIGBANG's income in 2015 totaled US$150 million, making up 65 percent of YG Entertainment's revenue. Of that amount, approximately US$140 million was generated from the overseas tour, showcasing how K-pop artists' paradigm for generating revenue has shifted dramatically from digital song sales and commercial endorsements to setting out on a yearlong tour.[6]

According to YG's press release, the Made tour was supposed to exceed the band's previous tour record by encompassing a total of seventy tours in fifteen countries, projected to draw 1,400,000 fans throughout the journey.[7] In accordance with this unprecedented global reach, YG Entertainment announced to the mass media that the tour's production quality would be unrivaled in the history of K-pop. To realize such a claim, a global superstar production team was summoned: Beyoncé's videographer Ed Burke; music director Gil Smith II, whose credits included collaboration with Eminem and Britney Spears; and lighting production designer Leroy Bennett, who had worked on world tours of Rihanna, Maroon 5, and Lady Gaga. The renowned American entertainment company Live Nation was once again contracted to manage BIGBANG's overseas tour after its initial collaboration with the band's Alive tour.

In fact, Live Nation was not the only entity to rejoin BIGBANG's second world tour. The success of the Alive tour prompted YG to renew its contract with many other artists and staff members who had been essential participants in the 2012–13 tour: Leroy Bennett and session musicians (keyboardist Gil Smith II, guitarist Justin Lyons, programmer Adrian Porter, keyboardist Dante "Inferno" Jackson bassist Omar Dominick, drummer Bennie "BrIIghtReD" Rodgers II) who were initially recommended by Live Nation gathered forces for the Made tour as seasoned partners of BIGBANG. Although their labor is often overlooked in the face of BIGBANG's enormous stardom, the presence of these live session musicians made a qualitative difference in making possible the claim that the tour was a live music tour.

The star-quality lineup of musicians and staff was not the only factor to enthrall the potential audience in the days leading up to the first Seoul concert on April 25. The visual artists also played a huge role in creating the hype. YG announced that it had spent US$2 million solely for the online tour trailer and the visual clips to be used during the live concert. According to a press report, "The action-packed tour trailer was created with over 100 talented staff members in the U.S., including videographer and concert producer Ed Burke, music video producer Jonathan Lia, *The Fast and the Furious*'s camera operator Onofrio Nino Pansini, and more. The shoot took a total of four days."[8]

Given the tour's glitzy packaging, the press was buzzing with anticipation of the concert throughout the month of April. For fans who had waited three years for the kings of K-pop to set out on another world tour, there simply could not have been enough coverage of the highly anticipated concert. It was also clear to many that the 2015 world tour, with all five band members in appearance, would likely be the last of its kind for some time: although the members were in the prime of their youth, being South Korean citizens meant they were supposed to enlist in the compulsory twenty-month military service in the near future.

So how could one not be in Seoul to witness the history-making tour in the world of K-pop? As the plane neared Incheon International Airport, I reached out for the printout of my Made tour ticket to remind myself of why I was here. The hallucinatory vision of popcorn on shimmery blue paper outside the window had already transformed into a tangible landscape of gray buildings and long bridges—just as my doubt-filled lightheadedness turned into a clear conviction that I was about to witness something significant.

Technology as the Show-Maker

One key issue that emerged in the South Korean press in the days leading up to the concert was the technological triumph that this concert was supposed to embody. Literally every press report I read spoke of the high technological standards that were to differentiate this live concert from the rest—so much so that technology itself came across as the true hero of the show.

All newspaper articles referenced how a bare stage would be adopted for an indoor concert for the first time in Korea with an intention of providing a better view of the stage performance; instead of aluminum truss, which obstructs the visibility of the stage, forty-eight tons of steel truss would be used, allowing optimal visibility for audiences seated anywhere in the venue.[9] Two bridges connecting the proscenium to the runway, which parallels the proscenium and cuts across the middle of the arena, were to glide over the standing area between the proscenium and the runway as a way of highlighting the performance's drama and the high-tech sophistication of its stage machinery. One hundred and six laser lights were deployed, each of them capable of projecting 25,600 shades of chromatic variation. To guarantee a perfect live sound system by eliminating subsonic imbalance caused by frequency interference, the Adamson Energia System was adopted.[10]

In addition, the best cameras were airlifted from Japan, all with the intention of perfectly documenting the live concert. According to a South Korean press report:

> It is the first time that thirty 4K cameras, SK UHD 4000 system by Hitachi, will be deployed in a concert in Korea. Currently there is an increasing interest in 4K broadcasting as the technology of the next generation; there is an anticipation that this concert will present a new horizon for how 4K screens can be applied in the future. 4K UHD has a resolution four times higher than the present Full-HD, promising to present *the vivid pulse of the live stage for those fans who unfortunately could not join the concert*. [emphasis mine][11]

As this article continues with unrestrained praise for the technological triumph and perfection that went into making the concert (an "only the best for BIG-BANG" kind of advertisement), it also draws our attention to the anticipatory recording of a live event, almost as if the live event were only a prerequisite for an immaculate digitization to occur. In light of the overwhelming emphasis placed on the perfect machinery created for the perfect recording of a live event, what is the meaning of live action, which is as imperfect as it is ephemeral? Do real-time human actions have the capacity to measure up to digital technology that is chasing their every move? If so, how?

The more I read the media coverage, the clearer it became that the typical features of live performance, with all the trappings of impulsiveness and imperfection, that attracted me from across the Pacific Ocean were to be minimized by the corrective intervention of perfect visual and sonic technology—for both the live event and its documentation. From my perspective, live performance was trying to do away with signs of liveness with the mediation of what the latest machinery could do to create a flawless embodiment out of deeply flawed human bodies and their limited range of motions.

The Day That Marked the Return of K-pop Kings

As I was reflecting on these questions, the day arrived. The chosen venue for the kickoff concert of BIGBANG's yearlong tour was Olympic Gymnastic Stadium, built for the 1988 Seoul Olympics but nowadays frequently used for large-scale concerts. Having waited three years for this day to arrive, fans congregated from various parts of the globe many hours prior to the scheduled beginning of the concert at 6:00 p.m. In the beautiful sunshine of a late spring afternoon, I spotted many non-Korean fans—black, white, old, and young—who were lined up to get into the venue.

Successful K-pop stars are known to attract global fans, but the dedication of BIGBANG's global fandom is worthy of special note. An entire exterior wall of one entrance was covered with flower bouquets and enthusiastic messages sent from fans across various continents: hailing from Korea, China, Japan, Thailand, Malaysia, Iran, Mexico, Costa Rica, El Salvador, Bolivia, Brazil, Peru, Paraguay, Argentina, Chile, and Venezuela, they sent their gifts, made by these fans in the name of BIGBANG, to be distributed through designated charity organizations in Korea, in an effort to promote a positive public image of their idols (figure 12). These "tributes" made by fans to BIGBANG mounted up to ten tons of rice, 426 boxes of ramen, 198 boxes of diapers, and 2,212 pieces of coal fuel.[12]

K-pop live concerts have become catalysts for rallying community creation and charity work. The shared sense of belonging to an entity that would not have formed if not for the love of these stars was once again defining the atmosphere inside the arena already packed to the gills an hour before the concert's beginning. The sea of people, most of whom were holding BIGBANG's signature yellow light stick in a crown shape, were dancing and screaming to the beat of the band's music videos that were playing on a large central screen on a main stage.

I made my way into the arena in search of my seat at the far end of the third floor, just underneath the ceiling, and found myself surrounded by people from various walks of life—a family of five with three children who did not look older than ten occupied the last row on the third floor of the stadium. Across the aisle I found a college-aged girl wearing a hijab, obviously of non-Korean heritage, excitedly chatting with her Korean friend. In front of me were a young couple who looked like college students, frantically taking pictures of them-

FIGURE 12. BIGBANG fans plaster the wall outside the concert venue with pictures of their favorite stars and enthusiastic comments. Photo by Kim Suk-Young.

selves on their cell phones and posting them on Twitter to evidence their being at this live event. They were not the only ones documenting their presence at this highly anticipated concert: pretty much everyone around me was holding cell-phone cameras and taking as many pictures as possible despite the strict prohibition of staff, who tried to prevent audience members from illegally documenting the event. But their efforts were futile, since they were overmatched by thirteen thousand audience members who compulsively pressed their shutter buttons no matter how severe the warning was—the triumph of an urge to document over the staff's protection of a live event.

The overcrowded standing area adjacent to the center stage was a special hot spot of activities, as the animated fans swayed left and right, back and forth, in search of any trigger to elevate them to the next degree of excitement. In wild and imminent anticipation of seeing their stars live, they could not contain their *heung*. A few large commotions erupted in the area with everyone screaming in excitement and turning their gaze in a certain direction. I could not see anything in particular from my vantage point under the roof far away from the center stage, but after the concert was over I read in the news that the members of IKON, YG's latest boy band, had made an appearance, causing that pandemonium.

In contrast to these excited and enthralled audience members, a girl of high school age was sitting next to me, shoulders stooped, observing the entire sea of fans rather gloomily; she was part of a strange minority of quiet and solitary audience members, to which I myself belonged. The majority was made of a large group of friends, couples, and occasional families, all united by their heated anticipation of BIGBANG's final emergence on stage. If they ever caught a glimpse of me, they must have rolled their eyes: "What is that weirdo *ajumma*[13] doing here—all by herself, frantically taking notes while everyone else is fully enjoying themselves?"

The large screen on center stage started to play the "Fantastic Baby" music video as the lights in the auditorium dimmed. This mega-hit song from 2012 with a strong beat is well known for its phantasmagoric music video, masterfully shot by director Seo Hyeon-seung, in which each BIGBANG member plays a king of some kind created by his own imagination. Featuring breathtaking transformations of BIGBANG members in a dizzying array of futuristic outfits—a crimson-colored velvet coat with elaborate embroidery befitting a Russian tsar, scanty black leather, gold chains, exaggerated high-top sneakers, shining metal plates, and pectoral chains—the music video turned fans into one living organism whose sole purpose of existence at that moment was to respond to every beat of the rhythm they heard as one living body.

Blackout. The screen projected black and white stripes—a visual symbol used for promoting the Made tour. It transitioned into the aforementioned tour trailer, in which each member of the band was introduced via bold close-ups in a highly stylized Tarantino-esque western with intertitles marking the separation between the real-life persona and the stage persona ("Kang Dae-sung [Gang Dae-seong] as Daesung, Dong Young-bae [Dong Yeong-bae] as Taeyang, Choi Seung-hyun [Choe Seung-hyeon] as TOP, Kwon Ji-yong [Gwon Ji-yong] as G-Dragon"). The arena turned into a sea of yellow lights shaking and dancing to the heartbeat of the moment (figure 13). The silent high school girl next to me reached out for the yellow light stick in her backpack and defiantly emerged from her solitary confinement. She was already on her feet, stretching the light stick as if to reach for the stage that was far beyond us. Now the screen, which projected the music video, parted in two and glided to the far left and far right ends of the stage—just like the crimson velvet curtain on the proscenium stage in the *Twinkle* music video or the live stage in EXO's LA performance—to reveal the five members of BIGBANG in dandyish suits standing

FIGURE 13. BIGBANG fans turn the concert arena into a sea of yellow with their BIGBANG light sticks. Photo by Kim Suk-Young.

on center stage to the deafening howls of fans. They started singing "Fantastic Baby" live as if to affirm the idea that the origin of the music video we had just watched before the "curtain" parted was the live delivery of the very same song.

The group remained on the proscenium stage for its second song, "Tonight," but in the next segment the stage theatrics created something that only the live performance audience could appreciate. During the third song, "Stupid Liar," two transparent gangways that connected the proscenium to a parallel runway in the middle of the arena started gliding over the standing area, allowing fans in the standing area to see the performers move over their heads. As the two separate bridges from each end of stage right and left moved over the standing area to converge at the center, they created a vantage point for audience that could not be captured by any recording of the performance. However, this special vantage point was reserved for the thousand special audience members in the standing area surrounded by the proscenium and the runway that cut across arena; the other twelve thousand audience members could only rely on three large screens—one being the large center screen that could split and glide sideways and the other two being smaller fixed screens hanging on both sides of the proscenium ceiling—in order to discern the faces of performers, who appeared in real life as tiny figures far away from the last row of the third floor. The holographic BIGBANG that I saw at Klive was far more real than their living bodies on this live stage.

An arena of this size would not be conducive to a live performance with only five performers if the viewing experience relied exclusively on eyesight unmediated by technology. This is the main reason why three large screens that digitally magnified the performers had to be installed in the arena, together with special lighting effects: to bring better visibility to a large number of spectators who were seated far away from the proscenium stage. In the court theater of Versailles, only Louis XIV's central seat enjoyed perfect visual access to the stage. In today's mega-arena culture, only a few thousand audience members in the standing area are granted such privilege. Screens in live concert venues become means to propagate the best possible view for everyone and thereby democratize the seating hierarchy; and the encroachment of live performance by digital elements, such as amplifiers, screens, and lighting, is in large part due to the unnatural, ever- increasing scale of performance space.

As it transpired, the entire concert was a titillating push and pull between live elements and digitized images and sounds, often seamlessly integrated. If the high-tech stage machinery, such as moving bridges, allows for an optical fantasy that can exist only in live shows for a limited subset of the live audience, then highly seductive video works that are interspersed throughout the live concert, in addition to allowing for stage transitions and costume changes, herald the notion that live concerts nowadays cannot exist without the intervention of the digital if they are to serve audiences of a size to fill domes and arenas.

The inevitable integration of digital materials into a live performance must be one of the reasons why YG Entertainment spent the substantial sum of US$2 million to create five film clips, one focusing on each member of BIGBANG, to be used exclusively during the live concerts; projected on a giant center screen, these videos, which closely resemble cinematic flash projects, give a fairly good view of BIGBANG members to everyone in attendance. Each video has a distinctive visual concept, but when they are put together collectively they merge in a shared mood of violent criminality and psychedelic uncertainty. In the clip that features TOP—the group's main rapper, who also has a successful career as a movie star—a mood of drunken hallucination imbues scenes of mind-blowing parties and glimpses of a silver briefcase submerged in a pool that are wildly strewn together through a series of jump cuts. The most explosive scene for TOP features him staring at the mirror in black-and-white footage that closely resembles scenes from John Cassavetes's *Faces*; in obvious intoxication, he compulsively slaps his face in self-convincing murmur: "Not drunk, not drunk, you bastard!" In a strange concoction of derisive humor and self-inflicted violence, he stares directly at the camera, meeting the gaze of thirteen thousand fans, who, in unison, stare at his eyes on screen in the pitch-dark concert arena. TOP's gaze back at them bears a breathtaking semblance to intimate eye contact. As an extension of this move, when TOP appears on stage in person, he appeals to the audience by saying, "I want to be close to you"—a verbal strategy of establishing intimacy that parallels the visual strategy of making eye contact with the live audience, no matter how far away audience members might be seated.

I confess my heart was electrified by TOP's piercing gaze on screen, but what I found more interesting than the ways of establishing intimacy was how a natural bridge between the recorded footage and the live performance was created. In a fashion similar to TOP's smooth transition from video screen to live stage, G-Dragon's performance presented a fascinating perspective on how reality and illusion, aided by a "screen within a screen," can be inverted. In the footage created for G-Dragon, we find him in a desolate midcentury-style motel room, where he is gazing at a completely outdated CRT TV. That TV, which effectively becomes a screen within a screen for the concert audience, projects a highly seductive woman with all the stereotypical "Oriental" trappings: her flaming red lips, silky black hair, and exaggerated slanted eyes, accomplished by a more than generous application of heavy eyeliner, create an intoxicating atmosphere as her slim, serpentine body sways seductively. But suddenly the screen flickers and buzzes with static as the woman's image disintegrates and re-forms on the screen. Frustrated, G-Dragon bangs the TV and eventually throws it out the window to see it smash into pieces. The footage ends by showing G-Dragon trapped in the flickering screen of the same CRT TV.

While it is possible to make an analogy between G-Dragon in the foot-age and the audience in the concert arena around the notion of impeded vision—just as G-Dragon is infuriated by the flickering screen, audiences who are seated far away from the proscenium are frustrated by the impossibility of seeing their singing idols clearly—this segment also establishes the insepa-rable relationship between images on screen and performances on stage. When G-Dragon emerges on stage and performs live after the footage, the "Oriental" woman's face is projected on a large screen again in the backdrop of the sing-ing G-Dragon, effectively drawing a connection between the world of the live concert and the reality inside the footage where she also appeared on screen.

Equally dramatic staging that connects the live stage and the screen is found in a sequence featuring Daesung, in which he appears as a desperate fugitive running away from something, only to fall into a deep blue pool of water. When the footage is over and Daesung emerges live on stage to sing his solo hit song "Wings," the central screen projects a current of deep blue water, as if Daesung were still immersed in the film footage. Unlike the direct corre-lation we find in the previous videos, the relationship between Taeyang's film footage and live stage performance is a bit more subtle. His video shows him on a dusty road in the middle of a desert, a bleak landscape of ruthless sun and raging lawlessness, where he gets into a deadly car duel with a delirious woman who appears to be possessed by rage, incessantly spewing out incomprehen-sible curses as she accelerates her car. She and Taeyang drive their vehicles at top speed toward an inevitable head-on collision. Both drivers' cars disappear into a large fiery explosion that soars upward to mark the end of the film, and at the end of this unforgettable frozen shot, the concert audience sees Taeyang emerge on stage to sing his solo song "Eyes, Nose, Lips." The backdrop screen to this solo performance no longer projects images of a fiery explosion, and there is no immediate visual bridge between the film and Taeyang's live perfor-mance. But for those who are familiar with the song's music video, which ends with a fire reminiscent of the one in the catastrophic collision, an association is established between the live singing performance and the incendiary digital images found in both the film footage and the music video. The sonic sphere created by the song invites the two visual spheres to merge; in a way, Taeyang's music performance on stage conjures up prerecorded visual images that are so powerful as to define and overwhelm the audience's perception of the live.

These filmic intermissions embedded in a live performance serve as seamless bridges between recorded and live by establishing visual continuity between screen and stage. Whereas "Fantastic Baby" featured a transition from music video to live stage, one of the videos played during the concert showed all five members of BIGBANG wearing the same suits that they were wearing on the opening stage of this live concert. While the persistent entanglement of live and digital was reaffirmed, it is noteworthy that these videos had not previously been seen in full in the tour trailer made available online, thereby adding a dimension of a film premiere to a live music concert. Film clips featuring individual members and the entire group, in their complete form, were seen by a live audience, who had been given the opportunity to see only the significantly shorter version of the trailer online prior to the concert. This, in a way, is similar to how a film is released in a movie theater for a live audience.

In addition to releasing the complete film clips, the group played a brand-new music video for its new title song "Loser" during the concert. I personally felt very excited to be among the first ones to see the full music video and felt that this was a true perk for being at a live concert; this format of release, once again, was akin to a VIP film sneak preview, allowing concert attendees to listen to the new music five days prior to its public release. Hence, it gave a special sense of privilege to all live concert attendees, whether they were in the standing-room area with an optimal view of stage or under the roof, where members of BIGBANG would not have been discernible were it not for close-up camera projection of their faces on stage. Once again, the digital came to rescue the live from its imperfection. And once again, the question arose: Is this a live music concert where digital images function merely as a break for costume changes, or is this a digital show in which live musicians appear on stage to prove that the actors in the footage are real-life people, not holograms or digitally synthesized hollowness?

I may have been the only person in the audience constantly philosophizing about the scene evolving on stage. Sitting alone in an excited crowd who were mesmerizingly holding up BIGBANG yellow light sticks and moving and responding to every gesture and comment by the five performers, I could not stop thinking about the power of ritual. My role was that of a typical participant observer, or fan-scholar, swaying between two different playing fields of emotional rapport and analytical detachment. For these devoted fans, their obstructed natural vision, which could not discern minute details without the help of the cameras that zoomed in on performers' faces, did not in any way compromise their experience or divide them from their idols. Indeed, the rapport between fans and performers was mediated by the camera: during their performance of "Blue," the camera projected the images of individual members against the background of thousands of fans all waving their yellow light sticks. This mirror effect, which allowed the audience to see the projection of themselves on stage as a seamless part of this event, must have been what made them feel that they owned this special moment.

But for a nonparticipating observer, the act of looking away from the screen where one could track the singers' most subtle expressions undermined the hyped notions of glamour that framed this concert, since it meant instead following what looked like five miniature figures prancing across a stage that was too wide for them. Even the head of YG Entertainment, Yang Hyun Suk, who must have occupied a much better vantage point than mine, was known to have said that he could not see any of the BIGBANG members' faces during the concert.[14] Without the intervention of pixel-perfect mediatization of human figures, the real but distant human bodies seemed out of proportion and out of place. Only when the cameras zoomed in on the otherwise indiscernible faces and projected them, to the relief of my eyes, did I return to the usual field of vision where every minute movement of facial muscles could come to life with the help of every single pixel on that digital screen.

This heavy dependence on a screen then raises questions about the ontology of live performance. Why do we still value "live" as more prestigious and desirable than high-definition streaming of recorded live concerts or music videos—a trend that pertains not only to K-pop culture but also to the overall scheme of pop music consumption? The foundational condition for live performance is the temporal-spatial coincidence of performer and spectator. But a more ontological definition of "live" in a live performance would reference a feeling of "aliveness." That feeling of rapport emerges among community members who occupy the same space with a shared purpose; hence the double meaning of *live* as in "live performance" and "feeling alive," which reference spatial and emotional rapport.

"It's the energy of the live audience next to you that makes a live concert a live event. Even for performers like Hatsune Miku, a live concert is still a live concert, due to the energy of the live audience," noted Ian Condry in relation to why people buy tickets to go see this celebrated hologram performer, who is not even a re-mediation of a living performer but an entirely fabricated persona.[15] The significance of the communal energy is heightened when we consider how the production of music has changed with recording technology—the point that has already been established in the introduction to this book. Before the invention of the gramophone, music was a total performance that could only be produced live. But with the advent of recording technology, the aspect of visual performance faded into the background, and music turned into a genre that we listen to. Live performance of music, such as the Made tour, reinforces the notion of music as a synesthetic total performance that stimulates all five senses—not to mention the obvious sensorial coordination of the audial and the visual and the sense of touching the idols' hands, smelling their sweat on stage, and tasting the drops of water that the idols sprinkle on the audience from the stage. For those audience members located far away from the stage, the sensory stimuli could come from inadvertently touching your neighbor while waving your light stick, smelling your neighbor's body odor, and tasting your own tears and sweat that stream down your face in the moment of ecstasy.

What Remains after the Live Concert

That night, when I returned to my Korean family and they asked how the concert was, all I could say was: "It was like a magnificent flower without fragrance. Spectacular sight without real vision." Perhaps I was analyzing too much, but the only presence I viscerally felt was that of the audience, the mighty multitude that instantaneously became one living body. Awe-inspiring spectacle was created by stupendous technology, but what was it trying to show anyway? The triumph of machinery? The way our vision is forever married to technological interventions? The soul of the concert, or the true vision of the event, as I would call it, lay rather with fans who moved and responded with a pulse that made thirteen thousand hearts beat in unison. BIGBANG was only a mediator to trigger that energy in each and every individual to converge in a communal rapport.

What brings them together is the notion that these concerts are, in their essence, a fan meeting. Non-BIGBANG fans are not likely to pay high ticket prices (the lowest admission price for the nosebleed section being approximately US$100) to be there, or to wait in long lines to enter restrooms and subway stations (unless they belong to the odd minority of performance studies scholars, ethnomusicologists, or cultural anthropologists doing their fieldwork). The leader of BIGBANG knew well that they were facing ultraloyal fans and made comments that showed his knowledge of BIGBANG fandom. Toward the end of the concert, G-Dragon confidently turned to the audience in a cocky, yet endearing, manner: "Why do you like us? [Fans respond with loud cheer.] Well, there must be many reasons. [Fans burst out laughing.]" Daesung also joined in addressing the fandom and described their new songs, to be released in pairs every month from May through August, as the presents they offered to their fans: "Instead of releasing all the songs at once, we wanted to release them in a sequential fashion so that we could keep providing presents to our fans for a long time."

In fact, BIGBANG is not the only K-pop group to approach concerts as fan meetings. More often than not, live K-pop concerts not only *double* as fan meetings but also *function* as fan meetings rather than music performances. New formats for concerts emerge out of such attempts to accomplish both goals—for example, SMTOWN Week, an eight-day relay concert hosted at Ilsan Kintex in the city of Goyang from December 21 to 29, 2013. The event was created specifically to enable intimate communication between audience and performers, which is a model differentiated from other performance-oriented concerts featuring SM Entertainment artists. SMTOWN Week featured a star lineup, ranging from veterans such as Super Junior, TVXQ, and Girls' Generation to newer groups, such as SHINee, f(x), and EXO.

Cha U-jin recounted his experience of attending these weeklong events and shared his observation that SHINee paid more attention to pleasing their fans than to performing at their best. They sang songs that most general audiences would not recognize, such as nontitle songs that could be found only on albums:

> When idols release their albums, they basically contain six songs, one of which is a title song—usually dance music—and five associated titles that are predominantly ballad songs. These nontitle songs mostly target fans. They are constructed as some kind of secret code for fans, and only fans understand this. Only those who buy CDs get these songs.

It turned out that SHINee sang songs recognizable only to fans and filled their show with comments that only fans who spent considerable time on fan-club blogs would understand, for example, comments addressing rumors in coded language—all in an effort to converse intimately with their fans.

Taking the notion of music concerts as live fan meetings one step further, YG Entertainment's new boy band, Winner, hosted the World Wide Inner Circle Conference (WWIC) 2015 in mainland China, Korea, and Japan in January and February 2015. The word *conference*, though suggesting an academic meeting, was actually more like a cross between a fans' convention and a traditional music concert. It opened with the group's hit song "Empty" and then moved on to elements that closely resembled conventional fan-meeting activities: Winner held a Q&A with fans, each group member presented his vision for the group's future, and the group invited fans to join in games. Concert time followed, with the group performing ten songs in a row. According to a journalist who attended the conference: "Winner's fan meeting was different from other idols' fan meetings. They presented many songs. It was Winner time that *doubled as both fan meeting and concert* [emphasis mine]."[16] Perhaps it was Winner's senior label mates, BIGBANG, who inspired their juniors to look at live concerts as a unique forum to mobilize their fandom. All in all, live performance in K-pop is not limited to live *music* performance; it also references live dance, live chat, and the live bodily presence of stars, which are often more important than the live performance of music.

A day after the concert, I was flying back to California with jet lag that I had initially accrued on my trip to Korea five days earlier. A few days after my return, I tuned in to BIGBANG's May 3 appearance on SBS's *Ingigayo*—one of the live music shows on terrestrial TV. Just as in the days leading up to a live concert, the media was again busy covering how spectacular BIGBANG's appearance on TV music shows would be: "BIGBANG's Comeback Stage on *Ingigayo* Is Like Nothing You've Seen Before" and "Only BIGBANG Can Perform on the Scale of Stage Never Seen Before" were typical headlines hyping the group's appearance on mass media platforms.[17] Having been exposed to a series of such media warm-ups, I concentrated on how the group would transpose their performance from a ten-thousand-seat arena to a modest-size concert hall inside a TV studio with fewer than one thousand seats.

When BIGBANG performed on TV, what caught my attention more than anything else was the elaborate stage setup: it was indeed quite impressive for an hour-long TV program, which typically features ten or so artists in a live broadcasting show (see chapter 2). The revolving stage with tall mirror panels set up in concentric circles—used during the group's performance of their new song "Loser" in the concert arena—was once again deployed for their *Ingigayo* comeback stage. BIGBANG's performance was obviously prerecorded, since setting up and taking down such an elaborate set would have been impossible during the live broadcasting time. In a similar vein, when they performed another title song, "Bae Bae," on the program, the stage featured a giant statue of a winged angel, which was seen in the song's music video.

The bridges made between live concert and TV music program (in the case of "Loser") and the live concert and the music video (in the case of "Bae Bae") are very much part of the transmedial network that continues to reinforce the central concept of the given song. The continuity is guaranteed by a shared stage set and costumes rather than singers' live performance, which is inevitably too variable. These material remains ironically are what enables memory to endure beyond the caprices of an ephemeral present. They might be the true heroes of liveness, reviving fans' memories each time they are encountered on stage.

Live from KCON:
Affective Labor and Korea's Soft Power

KCON is not just about music. We are here to learn about Korean culture.

Choi Siwon (Choe Si-won), a member of the K-pop boy band Super Junior

at KCON LA, August 1, 2015

When the gates to the Los Angeles Convention Center were flung open at 9:00 a.m. on August 1, 2015, a sizable crowd hailing from all over the United States and beyond flooded into the convention hall where hundreds of booths were already glimmering with spotlights (figure 14). The excited mob, a diverse mix of young and old, Asian and Hispanic, black and white, rapidly dispersed into a mazelike convention-hall floor where bright streaks of halogen lights illuminated a brand new hybrid vehicle, snapbacks with various K-pop group logos, a stand selling spicy instant noodles that was decorated with festive red banners, and dainty cases of facial makeup that promised to make you look at least ten years younger. Delicious-sounding ingredients such as "acai berry" or "apple, lemon, and orange extracts" could mislead consumers into thinking they were looking at various smoothie flavors rather than at facial masks. This was just one edge of the convention hall, and as the visitors turned a corner they found a section called K-ICT Dream Zone exhibiting marvelous technology and products sponsored by the South Korean Ministry of Science, ICT, and Future Planning: virtual dressing rooms and makeup studios operated by 3-D

FIGURE 14. KCON LA 2015 convention hall. Photo by Kim Suk-Young.

imaging and augmented reality; state-of-the-art display panels; and compact robots to provide companionship—that all paraded under the proud banner of the Korean Wave.

Welcome to KCON LA 2015, a three-day celebration of "all things *hallyu*." Both a music concert and a merchandise convention hosted by the South Korean conglomerate CJ Group, KCON was introduced in 2012, the year when K-pop's worldwide fame peaked with the unprecedented success of "Gangnam Style." That year, many South Korean media stations and entertainment companies hastily put together overseas K-pop concerts to meet the demands of K-pop fans around the globe.[18] The organizers of these events were bolstered by the success of the SMTOWN Concert in Paris the year before, an event that demonstrated how Europe could also be taken over by the K-pop craze.[19] The live concert portion of KCON, "M Countdown Concert," was named after the TV music chart show *M Countdown*, which had been airing every Thursday in South Korea since 2005 on the CJ Group–owned music and entertainment cable channel Mnet. KCON's 2012 M Countdown Concert was one of the many to join the overseas K-pop live-concert boom, but what distinguished it from the rest was that KCON was planned not as a one-time music concert but as a more inclusive annual festival-convention celebrating everything that concerned Korean pop culture—K-pop, K-drama, K-dance, K-fashion, K-food, and K-cosmetics—via music concerts, K-pop stars' red carpet events and fan engagements, merchandise exhibits, dance showcases, and makeup workshops.[20] As An Seok-jun, who headed CJ's music department in 2014, categorically stated, "KCON has become an event that sells the Korean lifestyle itself."[21]

KCON indeed attracts not only K-pop fans but consumers of Korean products of all sorts. It has managed to commodify the nation into a transactionable brand that makes human performers almost indistinguishable from material goods. A music concert, a merchandise convention, Korean culture workshops, and fan festival all at once, KCON provides something for everyone: those who are not fans of K-pop heartthrobs but happen to be avid consumers of Korean cosmetics will be tempted by facial masks with unforgettable names such as "pearl essence mask" or "bling bling whitening platinum hydrogel mask," and those who are not into Korean drama but enjoy Korean cuisine will find scrumptious food to munch on throughout the day, from mini wontons to bulgogi rice to deep-fried seaweed wrap, all prepared by CJ's restaurant chain Bibigo.

Since the merchandise booths selling everything Korean were open throughout the three-day event, the crowds there rose and dropped as visitors swarmed to attend events featuring their favorite idols, who engaged in various forms of fan meetings and red carpet events. From sitting in a workshop on how to write K-pop journalism to attending live concerts, fans were busy going back and forth between the convention hall and the concert arena. Being a K-pop fan is not an easy feat. From the second floor I gazed onto the convention hall, where a vivacious stream of people, converging and diverging at different merchandise booths, filled the venue as K-pop stars made surprise appearances for various product-endorsement purposes.[22] Suddenly, a huge crowd congregated at a cosmetic merchandise booth where members of the K-pop girl group Sistar popped up. A few minutes later, a horde of screaming fans flocked and followed the fresh-faced K-pop debutants of Monsta X, who made an appearance at the South Korean Ministry of Science, ICT, and Future Planning booth to test out 3-D display technology. K-pop stars were equally busy, going back and forth between fan engagements, product endorsements, red carpet appearances, and evening concerts. For both stars and fans, being a part of the K-pop scene requires serious physical and mental devotion. It requires, as many would say, a labor of love, or what some might call "affective labor."

By illustrating the corporeal and affective dimensions of labor in tandem with how technology augments the "intimate" nature of such labor, 2015 KCON in LA presents a prime case for exploring the complex layers of affect performed by both fans and stars. The K-pop industry has created an ambiguous emotional realm where intimacy between performers and fans is expressed in terms of an altruistic devotion that is undercut by self-promotion.

The notion of liveness here is twofold, referencing both the temporal and spatial copresence of performers and spectators and repetitive consumption practices in everyday life.[23] Regarding the first definition of liveness as copresence, whether in music performance or merchandise conventions, KCON is inherently a live event brought about by the convergence of live performers and audience, augmenting an affective connection that might not exist solely through the consumption of digital music. However, the unique strength of a live event also comes with a weakness: the strong bonding among live audience and performers can neither sustain itself outside the event time and space nor be reproduced exactly the same way every time it takes place. The temporality of KCON as a live event is one of the main reasons why the corporate hosts hope to perpetuate the convention through constant use of social media to transform the three-day event into everyday practices of consuming the Korean lifestyle. This brings us to the second notion of liveness: for corporate organizers of KCON, extending the live event beyond its ephemeral circumstances means that affect will be commodified in a way that is consumable and that attendees of KCON will not be able to live without Korean music, clothing, food, and cosmetics in their daily lives. In the eyes of the South Korean government, foreign fans and consumers' continuous embodiment of Korean lifestyle outside the three-day convention frame—the process of which involves ongoing dependence on social media for information circulation and exchange—is a dream scenario to enhance its soft power.

Media platforms such as social media need to be included in investigations of liveness and affect largely because K-pop music is predominantly released on digital media forums such as online music stores, TV shows, and YouTube music videos. Consequently M Countdown live concerts at KCON provide a valuable occasion to bring K-pop's producers and consumers into same time and space, although live tours overseas are still rare, albeit increasing, modes of K-pop's global circulation. The purest form of liveness, defined by the copresence of performers and spectators in the same time and space, can be fabricated and extended to everyday life by constant interventions of digitally augmented audiovisual effects, which promote an illusion of intimacy. Ultimately, KCON might be seen as an event where liveness as an expression of the human desire for intimacy masks the neoliberal commodification of affect.

Welcome to All Things Korean

KCON has grown in terms of both event formats and the numbers of attendees. According to the official KCON 2015 promotional video, in 2012 the event was held at the Verizon Wireless Amphitheater in Irvine (now Irvine Meadows Amphitheater, with 16,085 seating capacity). It consisted of a one-day convention and one concert with six artists on stage, and attracted twelve thousand attendees while generating 26 million PR impressions. In 2013, the event expanded to a two-day convention with one concert, where nine K-pop artists and Missy Elliott performed at Los Angeles Memorial Sports Arena (seating capacity roughly 15,000). The event attracted twenty thousand attendees and generated 179 million PR impressions. In 2014, PR impressions more than doubled to 368 million from the previous year, and the event expanded into a two-day convention and two concerts, featuring ten K-pop artists. Forty-three thousand convention attendees and thirty thousand concert attendees flocked to the Los Angeles Memorial Sports Arena, where Mayor Eric Garcetti came to kick off the event. According to the official press release by CJ E&M, the 2017 convention attracted a record-breaking eighty-five thousand attendees and sold out two nights of concerts at the 21,000-seat Staples Center.

Although these numbers establish KCON as an increasingly popular event, KCON did not prove profitable prior to the 2015 convention because, in the entertainment industry, intensive investment is expected in the initial stage of a project to create the momentum for success. It was only in 2015 that the event started generating revenue from the increased number of attendees (seventy-five thousand total attendees for LA and NY KCON combined)[24] and from the paid entry tickets to the convention (in previous years entry had been free). The year 2015 was the first time KCON went to Japan and US tours became bicoastal, with a three-day convention and two concerts in Los Angeles' Staples Center (approximate seating capacity 20,000) and a one-day convention and one concert at the Prudential Center (approximate seating capacity 18,000) in Newark, New Jersey.

According to CJ E&M's own assessment, KCON tends to attract young, loyal, fanatical, and multicultural attendees, with 62 percent of attendees falling into the age group of eighteen to twenty-four, 52 percent having previously attended KCON, and 34 percent having traveled from outside California, and with a diverse spectrum of racial groups (46 percent Asian, 23 percent Hispanic, 19 percent white, and 5 percent African American). Such a demographic breakdown roughly coincides with my impressions of the 2015 LA convention attendees, many of whom had driven or flown from various states or even from outside the country.

The hybrid format of the concert/convention that CJ E&M has devised for KCON has much to do with the company culture of the CJ Group. Although the CJ Group was founded in 1996, its origin goes back to Cheil Jedang (Jeil Jedang), a sub-branch of the Samsung conglomerate, which came to establish itself as the major sugar refinery in South Korea in the post–Korean War era. From its founding in 1953, Cheil Jedang produced not only refined sugar but also all sorts of household products required for daily life: cooking oil, flour, spices, artificial flavorings, snacks, energy drinks, laundry detergents, and even fertilizers. Since its split from the parent company Samsung in 1993, it has established four core business sectors: "Food & Food Service, Bio & Pharma, Home Shopping & Logistics, and Entertainment & Media."[25]

The company's portfolio shows its ability to manufacture and package taste for mass consumption, catering to the literal and figurative palates of Koreans in the postwar era.[26] Two sectors of the CJ Group play a crucial role at KCON: the food division and the entertainment and media division. The food sector, CJ Foodville, includes the bakery chain Tour les Jours, the family restaurant chain VIPS, and the Korean food and restaurant line Bibigo.[27] Another portfolio of the company with growing importance is its media and entertainment sector, under which CJ operates CVG (Korea's first multiplex theater chain), seventeen TV channels, including the aforementioned music channel Mnet, and many other performance/festival events. According to Euny Hong, the author of the widely read book *The Birth of Korean Cool*, "CJ E&M is a quintessential Korean pop culture company in that it is made up of completely integrated units that all feed off each other in a highly efficient, highly profitable ecosystem."[28] To paraphrase Hong's general observation by providing concrete examples, CJ runs a transmedial marketplace where a special recipe featured on CJ cable channel's cooking show eventually makes its way to CJ Foodville's family restaurant menu, while the gift certificate to the CJ-owned multiplex CJV can be purchased on the CJ-owned home-shopping website cjmall.com.

In addition to their prominent role at KCON, CJ Foodville and CJ E&M are linked by the fact that they are service sector businesses that require intensive branding and image making. Their business success is based on the spirit of service, or, to put it more precisely, a performance of affective labor—staged by restaurant servers, cooking-channel hosts, film stars, K-pop singers, and even their passionate fans—that is designed to transform the consumption of a commodity into a satisfactory experience for the body and the mind alike. At a very basic level, food goes into the consumer's body and provides nutrition, but the emotional investment that accompanies the process is an even more significant aspect of food consumption. The experience of consuming media products has an equally powerful impact on the kinesthetic and emotional registers. Both are equally important for the sustenance of everyday life, as they provide food for body, mind, and heart; therefore, the liveness of KCON is embedded in everyday life consumption.

The potentially manipulative nature of affective labor exposes the inevitable nexus between tangible and intangible, internal and external dimensions of the body—a body that becomes a crossroad for material goods and immaterial feelings to collide, wrestle with, and coproduce all sorts of compromises. For instance, Korean stars at KCON never fail to pledge their eternal love for their supporters in front of corporate logos, whereas fans boisterously express their affection for the stars through their consumption of star-related goods, unambiguously marking their bodies' affiliation with certain brands and fan clubs. How has the allegedly pure love between stars and fans come to be so deeply entangled with corporate interests? In the age of heightened neoliberalism, how do the performances of affective labor manipulate fantasies of economic advancement through self-promotion?[29] Finally, how do the dual modes of interaction between stars and fans—live in person and mediated by social media—change the performance of affective labor?

No KCON without Social Media

Affect in many ways works not only through the registers of body and mind but also and more profoundly by the logics of contemporary technology. As Patricia Ticineto Clough noted, affect is theorized not only in terms of the human body but also "in relation to the technologies that are allowing us both to 'see' affect and to produce affective bodily capacities beyond the body's organic-physiological constraints."[30] A closer look at the promotional campaigns of KCON on social media and M Countdown live concerts in tandem provides a way to address this juncture between body and technology in the production and circulation of affect.

KCON LA 2015 officially took place over just three days, but the talk about it and promotion of it started long before the opening date of July 31, 2015. The main channel to ignite excitement among potential attendees and to spread the important announcements about the lineup of artists and guests was the weekly YouTube program *KCONLiveChat*, run by two CJ America staff—Hoon and Vanessa—who, in their capacity as social media marketers, facilitated the communications between would-be attendees and the host CJ Group.

Like Arirang TV's *After School Club* (*ASC*; see chapter 2), *KCONLiveChat* convened weekly (every Thursday at 5:30 p.m.) for online live chats and tweets, with the first episode produced on April 24, 2015, roughly three months prior to the official opening of the convention, and the last episodes airing on July 23, 2015, just one week prior to the opening of KCON. Extending the live feel of the convention with chats taking place between hosts, potential attendees, and special guests regarding what the upcoming convention should and might look like, the chat program convened a virtual KCON before the physical event even took place.[31]

KCONLiveChat did not try to downplay the rough edges that came with live social media interaction, with Hoon openly asking his cohost how many viewers were participating at a given moment—much as *ASC* featured an obsessive live display of the number of viewers and tweets. *KCONLiveChat* closely resembled *ASC* on two additional fronts—its emphasis on the platform's global reach and the frequent use of social media in an attempt to create effective publicity online. Both claim that K-pop is now a global trend that enjoys a prominent place in the virtual world. Practically all episodes of *KCONLiveChat* start with Hoon and Vanessa scrutinizing the callers' location in Google Hangouts in hopes of illustrating the global interest in the upcoming event: "If you are tuning in from outside of the US, do let us know! Wow, someone is from Taiwan, awesome!" or "Oh, Sophia is tuning in from Mexico!" "Somebody's joining us from the Philippines!"[32] Excited comments like these echo those of the *ASC* hosts who proudly announce a long list of countries from which the program's participants hail.

As each episode of *KCONChatLive* organized live chats regarding various aspects of the upcoming convention, such as the lineup of concert performers, panels, and workshop wish lists, or merchandise that visitors wanted to see at the convention, the two hosts actively deployed social media to create and circulate trending of KCON whenever possible. When asking the viewers which guests and panels they wanted to see at KCON 2015, the hosts stated: "The best way to get your guests is to tweet out your favorite,"[33] increasing the Twitter traffic regarding KCON. To augment the live feel of the chat program, the hosts read through responses against the sounds of live tweets transmitted in real time—sonic evidence of fans' voluntary labor. Subsequent episodes also featured many contests using social media, such as Instagram and Snapchat contests, all avidly encouraged by the hosts:[34] "Please give your impression of your favorite member of Super Junior! The lucky winner will get a K-pop product!"

These live chat shows are produced by the affective labor of hosts and callers alike, digitally transmitted through cellular pixel images of computer screens to viewers around the world. In keeping with Eileen Boris and Rhacel Salazar Parreñas's claim that technology is not "the antithesis of intimacy," Hoon and Vanessa's performance showcases how feelings of intimacy can be incited by technologically transmitted messages.[35] But what about instances in which technology produces the semblance of intimacy so pervasively that the notion of intimacy becomes unthinkable without technology to frame the live human-to-human contact?

Not only in preconvention promotions such as *KCONLiveChat* but also during "live" panels and workshops at the convention, social media were used to promote various events and products. Their pervasive use was a threading practice that created a parallel between *KCONLiveChat* and the actual KCON itself. During an MBC-sponsored panel, for instance, the marketing director of MBC America invited the attendees to play various trivia games for prizes but attendees had to "like" MBC America's Facebook page before entering the game. In another popular panel featuring TV drama scenario writer Park Ji-eun (Bak Ji-eun), whose work *My Love from Another Star* (2014) became a megahit not only in Korea but also in large parts of Asia, questions that were submitted via social media and selected prior to the panel were used for the live Q&A session. This event alone generated a flurry of online traffic even before the convention began, extending the live interaction beyond the boundaries of the live convention itself.

In a similar strategy designed to make *KCON* a trending word, CJ Foods' Korean restaurant chain Bibigo distributed attractively designed postcards, on which convention attendees could collect five stamps for a free gift; three stamps involved social media posting, such as "Like Bibigo Facebook page," "Upload photo of you and Bibigo Food Truck on social media (#bibigofoodtruck)," and "Upload photo of you and Bibigo Booth on social media (#bibigobooth)." Attempts like this to use consumers for free online marketing were seen everywhere at conventions. Likewise, during the live music concerts, various measures were taken to encourage fans to increase online traffic regarding KCON. Before the opening of the first concert on August 1, the MC encouraged attendees to download featured artists' music from the online music store Naver, which also happened to be one of the corporate sponsors of 2015 KCON.

To press the "like" or "download" buttons or to upload pictures of oneself with a commercial logo on social media creates a paler version of intimacy than the exchange between the hosts and callers of *KCONLiveChat*, let alone the live interaction between fans and stars at various KCON events. Differing degrees of intimacy between producers and consumers at KCON are mediated through their mutually professed love for K-pop and Korean culture at large, but what brings them together is a profit-driven business called K-pop, which deploys technology to manufacture intimacy. Technology may extend the optical and physiological limitations of the body and temporal-spatial confines of how a live event can be experienced (real-time transmission of televisual information brings distant parties together as in *KCONLiveChat*), but it does not just extend the physiological body's limitations, it also fabricates a new register of intimacy for K-pop fans.

Moreover, it is nearly impossible for affect to be embodied without technology at KCON. Just as there is no such thing as bad publicity in the age of social media—the only bad publicity is having no publicity at all—quantitative overflow of information about KCON, whether it has any qualitative substance or not, becomes the end in itself in signifying affect rather than serving as a means to an end. The hashtag #KCONLA15, which is still circulating online long after KCON 2015's end, is no longer a phantom of a live event from the past but a durational embodiment of that event, sustaining KCON's liveness in our daily digital consumption. The ongoing tweets in cyberspace, creating daily rituals for so many people glued to their smartphones, carve out constant, always "alive" sharing of memories. The new form of "live" emerges from such durational performance of affective labor.

Take, for instance, how CJ E&M promptly released the KCON LA recap video just a day after the 2015 convention concluded. In the four-minute video, various guests of the convention, such as Billboard journalist Jeff Benjamin, K-pop choreographer Aimee Lucas, and YouTube stars the Try Guys, share the excitement they experienced at KCON. Also included in the video is an interview with an enraptured fan, speaking rapidly and breathlessly from excitement at being a part of KCON LA 2015:

> You can just come here and you can just feel the energy wherever you are in the room. And it's a different energy depending: are you looking at merchandise,

are you looking at the dramas, are you looking at the food, are you looking at the music. It's a chance to step into a whole different world, get off your daily routine, come out, just *get alive again* [emphasis mine].³⁶

Here, the interviewee characterizes the feeling of being "alive" as springing from an escape from the mundane ("get off your daily routine, come out, just *get alive again*") and as an ephemeral feeling that will evaporate with the conclusion of a live event. But the fact that this footage started to circulate after the live event was over illustrates that the feeling of being alive is once again confirmed by the recording technology, which makes the excitement a process that lasts beyond the frame of a live event. With the interviewee's raw feelings staged again and again as if for the first time every time the video is played, liveness sustains its affinities with "alive" thanks to the infinitely reproducible nature of this video posting.

Rather than being the static commemoration of the past event, the online postings are sustaining the extended life of an evanescent event. Fan Instagram posts that keep appearing as late as early January 2016, such as the following one, encourage us to consider the beginning and the end of KCON in flexible terms.

Who knew I would have the opportunity to be one of the fan club panelists, share with an audience about one of the things I love to do, and represent the fan base that allowed me to grow as a fan, an individual, and a part of a team. To many more years and achievements with SJWORLD and the lovely people behind it ❤ May 2016 bring more wonderful opportunities. [SJWORLD]³⁷

On Twitter and Instagram, #KCONLA15 was sustained by fans' continued sharing of their KCON photos, short video clips, and comments long after KCON 2015 was over. Without fan labor—or what the corporation would see as free marketers—such extension would not be possible, but we have to pause for a moment and consider whether the fan labor is just an expression of blind love or whether something else lurks behind its altruistic facade.

Self-Promotion as a Neoliberal Virtue

The continuous involvement of attendees' participation, or to put it more astringently, KCON's heavy reliance on attendees' voluntary labor, effectively highlights the codependency of profit-seeking corporations and participatory fandom. In "an age in which labor and leisure are growing ever harder to separate," fan activities, at first glance, might come across more as voluntary participation and leisure activity rather than as hardcore work, designed to promote the stars and their visibility in the public sphere.[38] But the reverse may easily be true: with an endless array of "like," "tweet" and "retweet" buttons to press around the clock, voluntary fan work may very well turn out to be an obsessive full-time job, which promotes not only the stars and the corporations they endorse but also fans themselves.

KCON is a forum where various forms of affective labor facilitate intimacy between stars and fans while masking the profound alienation between them. K-pop stars, created by the notoriously long and painful process of professional training and bodily modification, possess professional qualities that cannot so simply be emulated by fans.[39] K-pop fans, on the other hand, may be seen as amateurs for their lack of performing skills, but the common thread that ties stardom and fandom in a shared fate is that both parties depend on each other in pursuing relentless self-promotion to exist in the actual world and in cyberspace. The K-pop industry—founded on absolute professionalization of stars and institutionalization of fandom—dictates that stars, regardless of their talent and skills, be fully aware of how their success entirely depends on fans' love, whereas fans are aware that not every fan is equally significant in the eyes of stars and their promoters. Therefore, stars do their best to bridge the gap between themselves and fans by performing various gestures of intimacy, including frequent social media postings of how they were moved by fan support, which often include pictures of presents sent by fans. Fans, on the other hand, try to get closer to stars by spending a lot of money on star-related purchases, and thereby gain a chance to become more visible in the hierarchy of fandom.[40]

As Eileen Boris and Rhacel Parreñas have noted, "One of the most striking features of contemporary global capitalism is the heightened commodification of intimacy that pervades social life. We not only seek to buy love, but also express devotion through goods and depend on services to fulfill obligations or display closeness to others."[41] The commodification of love, and the equally important performance of affect through daily consumption, unveil the hidden dimension of fan labor. On the flip side of what often comes across as blind devotion—whether it takes the form of excessive consumption of star-related products or a constant display of knowledge of, and dedication to, the stars on social media—some fans promote themselves though "fame by association" with the stars and position themselves as gatekeepers to other fans, controlling their proximity to stars. K-pop stars and fans are entangled in this network of self-promotion that takes the form of mutual affection and intimacy.

A prime example of the blurred boundary between affective fan labor and neoliberal self-promotion can be found in a CJ staffer's note sent to workshop presenters, who were invited to KCON to share their expertise and experience of Korean culture.

> Special Guests, we can't wait to meet you at KCON 2015! But, before KCON starts, we need to get the word out there about your appearance and your panel. The worst thing that can happen at the convention is that panel rooms are empty, so we would like to prevent that. *We will be promoting you via our website and social media, but we would like to ask you to promote and to bring your fans out to KCON too to see you!* [emphasis mine]. Below are our social media links, logos, and some general information about KCON so that you can encourage your fans to come see you at your KCON 2015 panel.

As one of the special guests invited to KCON LA in 2015 and 2017—and let me honestly confess that I was motivated to appear at KCON by the desire to promote myself as a K-pop expert and to conduct research for this book—I received this message with some bemusement about how special guests were portrayed, as situated somewhere between stars and fans: in the eyes of the organizers, they were cast as some sort of celebrities having fans of their own (*"but we would like to ask you to promote and to bring your fans out to KCON too to see you!"*) while also being faithful followers of the Korean pop cultural scene. Wherever the special guests situated themselves in the spectrum of stars and fans, they were important assets to CJ Corporation in promoting KCON at large in the form of self-promotion. The rhetoric of "We promote you and you promote KCON while promoting yourself" is a typical way of capitalizing on others for self-advancement.

Self-promotional postings on social media by special guests are too numerous to list in their entirety; to start with my own example, I ditched my conventional academic bio and replaced it with a much more humorous and eye-catching self-introduction for KCON in 2015 ("Dr. Ajumma enjoys collecting PhDs, teaching at UCSB, breastfeeding her two future K-pop star babies, and pushing her husband around Korean-style") in hopes that it would attract more attention to myself and my book. Another example comes from Sunny, the host of a YouTube makeup channel, who is well known for K-pop makeover demonstrations. Sunny was seen on her own YouTube channel promoting her appearance at KCON prior to the event: "I have a big announcement. . . . The big announcement is, I am going to KCON, woo hoo!"[42] Behind this exclamation appear KCON logos, and she continues to explain the detailed schedule of her panel appearances while not forgetting to promote the convention itself: "Another easy way to plan your day and schedule your day is to use KCON app, and you can find me there." As if loyally carrying out the win-win directive passed down from the CJ promoter, she links three hashtags, #KCON15LA, #KCON15NY, and #SUNNYSCHANNEL, in support of the convention while promoting herself. After the event, she posted numerous vlogs of her KCON makeup workshops, which featured fans lining up to take photos with her, thereby casting herself as possessing some qualities of a celebrity. The spirit of self-promotion by associating oneself with stars also applied to other attendees who were not necessarily presenters at KCON.[43] Starting in 2017, fans were able to audition during KCON to promote their talent and test out whether they could enter the world of K-pop (figure 15).

These gestures are signs of individuals' self-promotion in the age of neo-liberalism. Michel Foucault saw how "the stake in all neo-liberal analysis is the replacement every time of *homo economicus* as a partner of exchange with

FIGURE 15. Wannabe K-pop stars line up for an audition at KCON LA 2017. Photo by Kim Suk-Young.

homo economicus as entrepreneur of himself, being for himself his own capital, being for himself his own producer, being for himself the source of earnings."[44] What lies at the heart of Foucault's criticism of neoliberalism is the ethos of extolling the power of individuals as grounded in a mercilessly self-serving, seductively entrepreneurial spirit. Gender studies scholar Tom Roach would more freely describe *homo economicus* as "that calculating spawn of neoliberalism who perceives himself and others foremost as human capital."[45] Such calculation directly counters the purist notion of affect, which is often regarded as synonymous with *"forces of encounter."*[46] Rather than seeing affect as meaningful encounters between human beings in the spirit of mutual understanding, neoliberal impulses manipulate it to mask self-interest while staging a spirit of reciprocal exchange. (*"We will be promoting you via our website and social media, but we would like to ask you to promote and to bring your fans out to KCON too to see you!"*)

On the macro level of the state, an understanding of neoliberalism also yields explanatory models that interlace corporate nationalism with individual initiatives. Defined by David Harvey as a view "that proposes that human well-being can best be advanced by liberating individual entrepreneurial freedom and skills within an institutional framework characterized by strong private-property rights, free markets, and free trade," it has nevertheless found many paradoxical applications in the global economy, for instance in "Chile, South Korea, Taiwan, and Singapore," where "the compatibility between authoritarianism and the capitalist market had already been clearly established."[47] As if providing a textbook example of Harvey's definition of neoliberalism, Choe Yang-hui, the South Korean minister of science, ITC, and future planning, commented on his ministry's role in KCON 2015, where for the first time the ministry had sponsored the convention by hosting an ITC booth: "If the private sector is doing a good job [in promoting Korean culture abroad], then the government should not interfere but instead try to provide support in different ways."[48] Minimal government intervention and a maximal guarantee of corporate initiatives foregrounded Minister Choe's statement, reaffirming the foundational spirit of neoliberalism that upholds the freedom of individuals and private sectors.

But in the same interview, Minister Choe was quick to add a uniquely Korean spin to neoliberalism by providing minor criticism—"People working in the cultural industry are still not used to generating profit by integrating technology"—providing a justification for the South Korean government's presence hosting a booth at a pop culture convention like KCON. Hypothetically, a parallel to the South Korean ministry's hosting of a booth at CJ-organized KCON would be the US Department of Commerce's hosting of a booth at an overseas Disney convention.

At the same time, the strong tie between neoliberalism in South Korea and the sentiments of cultural nationalism, according to Harvey, is a widely observed phenomenon in today's world:

> The neoliberal state needs nationalism of a certain sort to survive. Forced to operate as a competitive agent in the world market and seeking to establish the best possible business climate, it mobilizes nationalism in its effort to succeed..
> . . . Nationalist sentiment is equally rife in South Korea and Japan, and in both instances this can be seen as an antidote to the dissolution of former bonds of social solidarity under the impact of neoliberalism.[49]

KCON presents an example of such neoliberal dependency between the market and the nation, which takes the form of branding the nation and nationalizing the brand: the "Korea" that serves as the nationalist underpinning of KCON is less a geopolitical entity than a commercial brand, and CJ E&M positions itself as an ambassador of everything Korean at the convention. To cite CJ E&M's An Seok-jun again, "Through artists and music, it's great that we could promote CJ as well as the brand image of Korea."[50] The nation and the corporation—or Korean pop and korporate pop—work hand in hand to sell everything from food, a necessity as old as mankind itself, to concert tickets to see idol groups that formed just a few months ago.

But the CJ Group's ambition does not seem to stop with promoting just Korea. CJ has its sights set on representing broader Asia. As one representative from CJ E&M commented in an e-mail interview:

> Now KCON is widening its eyes [sic] to more variety sectors of culture rather than focusing only on K-pop. We will make it as a platform where people can enjoy and experience converged Asian culture. At the same time, global companies, entertainment agencies, and start-ups can broaden their perspectives of networking and marketing on our platform of KCON. They will facilitate cooperation and seek ways to encourage mutual growth. In the end, KCON will become a global platform for consolidated Asian culture under the name of K-Culture.[51]

"K" may be a new name for converged Asian culture, even turning the continent and cultural blocs into a brand of their own. After all, if Korea can turn into a merchandise, why not all of Asia? It can all be done in the name of affective labor and reliable technology that enables real-time, live exchange of intimacy.

Afterthoughts

To have ended this chapter with the last sentence would have been quite convenient, with a cohesive vision of KCON as a grand marketplace crowded by calculating corporate organizers, a nation-state that hopes to flex its soft-power muscles, and individual self-promoters who, not always subtly, advance their self-interest under the veil of affection for Korean culture. It is truly difficult not to be critical of the rampant commercialization of culture at a convention like KCON (for instance, during KCON LA 2017, a high-touch event where fans could approach the boy band GOT7 and touch their hands cost $500), but to have ended the story with the last section would have given me an uneasy feeling of having provided only a partial portrayal of this multidimensional event. With all intentions to be fair, I would have been remiss not to note the event's impassioned, not always calculating, affective encounters.

During the first night of the concert, I was seated close to two male fans of K-pop, who were quite recognizable YouTube figures for their prolific production of K-pop news coverage and reaction videos. When the first group, Monsta X, was about to come on stage, I literally felt the ground shaking, as one of them got up on his feet and started bouncing his entire body heavily clad with hip-hop paraphernalia. "It's GOT7, oh my God, it's GOT7!" one of them started shouting at the other while convulsively bopping his head. The jingling sound of his gold chains, heavily draped over a red Chicago Bulls jersey, was matched by the rhythmic howl of the other, who, at the sight of GOT7, also got up and started to jump on the makeshift seating area. At that moment, they were not performing for the camera, which would produce footage of their K-pop coverage on YouTube, but merely caught up in *heung*—an affective mode I have been using throughout the book to capture K-pop's liveness, which is notoriously fluid and amorphous.

When Super Junior, the seasoned K-pop boy band with over ten years of performing under its belt, appeared on stage, the Staples Center was suddenly transformed into a sea of blue light sticks, the color of the group's fandom. The energy of this fairly large venue focused solely on the stage, where spotlights transformed the eight performers of Super Junior into true idols worthy of worship. Hands reached out in the air, as if hoping to touch the aura of presence in the same time and space with the gleaming stars. At least in that moment, they were breathing the same air with their adoring fans—a rare instance of intimacy made tangible in the magical pulse of a live concert.

When I returned to KCON LA again in 2017 in the dual capacity of a panelist and a journalist, I was able to witness an even broader spectrum of fan affection:[52] during an artist engagement with K-pop boy bands VIXX and ASTRO, I was engulfed by a large gathering of fans faithfully waiting for their stars to appear at designated convention booths. With an ethnographer's curiosity, I gave up a comfortable view of idols at a photo line reserved for journalists for a chaotic standing area reserved for fans. There I stood amid sweltering fans of various ethnicities, ages, and genders, many of whom held handmade picket signs and banners showing their favorite idols' names and faces (figure 16). A Hispanic

FIGURE 16. A VIXX fan waits for the band's appearance with a handmade sign displaying the band members' names written in Korean at KCON LA 2017. Photo by Kim Suk-Young.

mother and teenage daughter had driven up from San Diego to see ASTRO with their own eyes; a group of friends had flown in from Maryland and San Francisco for a reunion to cheer for their favorite idol VIXX. They were chatting about how much they loved the group for having such humble attitudes despite their growing fame. Regardless of much delay and the uncomfortable pressure of having to stand in a tightly packed crowd, they were all gleeful with high anticipation. Earlier in the day, when I stepped into a restroom at the convention center, a group of Asian American teenage girls were consoling a friend who was hysterically shaking with tears. When asked if she was all right, she looked up with a smile while her puffy eyes were still welling up: "I just saw Daniel *oppa*,[53] and he smiled at me as he passed by." Obviously, the girl was referencing the front man of the newly formed K-pop band Wanna One, whose sensational popularity motivated many fans, including myself, to attend KCON to see them perform live.

In the broad scheme of things, many of these fans might be involuntary actors in the manipulative workings of affective labor; but many would attest that they were there for the sheer joy of being a part of a large community that endorses and celebrates their passion. How could we describe this other face of KCON—the loving and giving spirit of affect, fully interested in the forces of encounter and bonding—the one that had an equally strong imprint on even a critically minded participant observer like myself? Smiles and tears—and, to tap into the *Game of Thrones* lingo, ice and fire—bookend the opposing forces of this conundrum. It feels strange to witness fiery love born out of the icy machinery to spin profit, but in K-pop parlance, striking sincerity and calculating profitability might have no trouble being synonyms.

CONCLUSION

THE GRAY CLOUDS had settled thickly over the Boulevard de Bercy. Although it was only 1:00 p.m., no natural illumination was to be found in the City of Light. The early summer afternoon in Paris was one of light drizzle and gloom, parsimoniously revealing a nebulous maze of back streets and allies for a dreamy *flâneur*. If it weren't for sudden cheers directed at me, I would have walked straight into Gustave Caillebotte's *Paris Street; Rainy Day*.

"An-nyeong-ha-se-yo!"

A mix of black and white teenage girls waved at me, giggling, dragging me back from my reverie to reality. We did not know each other, but my Korean face was the apparent reason for their excitement, making them perform every "K-gesture" they had mastered by consuming an abundance of Korean dramas and variety shows. From staging *aegyo* to expressing affection by crossing thumbs and index fingers, they tried it all out on me—a random Korean person who they assumed would understand these peculiar body languages generated by the Korean pop culture scene. Tickled by these unexpected greetings from strangers but also feeling uncomfortable with the free-flowing gestures of excessive emotion, I rushed to the Accord Hotels Arena to fulfill my journalistic duty of covering the first KCON to be hosted in Europe.[1] As I waved and turned away from the group, those girls, who by now had been aroused by *heung* in Korean style, offered an even louder proclamation of affection: "Sa-rang-hae-yo!"

Despite the uninviting weather on June 2, 2016, the pyramid-shaped seventeen-thousand-seat arena was already wrapped by a serpentine line of fans who had camped out since before daybreak (figure 17). Passing through the lines of fans would make you wonder if you were attending an EU summit meeting rather than a pop concert: as I walked past, I heard French, British English (the concert preceded the historic Brexit vote by twenty-one days), German, Swedish, Spanish, and many more languages, testifying to the distances these fans must have traveled to see their idols. Consisting predominantly of teenage girls, those fans who noticed my press badge eagerly asked: "Do you know if BTS has arrived in Paris?" and "Have you seen SHINee yet?"

These multiracial, multiethnic fans were elated, fully aware that they were in closer proximity to the stars than ever before. They were on the cusp of viewing 2-D pixels transformed into 3-D human beings, fully flesh and blood. Leaving behind the group of fans united by shared anticipation, I entered the convention in the stadium. The size of the convention hall was only a fraction of that in KCON LA, with only a few private corporations (CJ branches such as Olive Young, MWave, Bibigo, and a couple of cosmetic brands such as John Jacobs and

FIGURE 17. K-pop fans line up for KCON Paris 2016. Many of them camped outside the concert arena the night before in order to secure a place close to the stage. Photo by Kim Suk-Young.

the major sponsor of the KCON "Too Cool for School") promoting their products in a small booth.[2] No merchandise was for sale, and the rest of the convention hall was dedicated to a loud proclamation of soft power by South Korean
government branches—from the Ministry of Culture, Sports, and Tourism, the
Ministry of Education, the Ministry of Agriculture, the Korea Creative Content
Agency, the Korean International Trade Association, and the Korea Tourism
Organization to the 2018 Pyeongchang Winter Olympics Committee—which
turned the nation into "kool" branding machinery under the "K" banner.

This was the first KCON to have taken place in Europe; France was chosen not only for its central location but also for the fact that 2016 marked the
130th anniversary of diplomatic relations between Korea and France. The
South Korean government used the convention to advertise everything about
Korea, but it also made an attempt to tone down blatant commercial nation-
alism by sleekly labeling its products "K-tour" (Ministry of Culture, Sports,
and Tourism), "K-education" (Ministry of Education), "K-food" (Ministry of
Agriculture), "K-content" (Korea Creative Content Agency), "Kmall24.com"
(Korean International Trade Association), and even "K-smile" (Korea Tourism
Organization).[3]

But such a tireless display of the desire to enhance the nation's soft power
was nothing but background noise for the fans in attendance. Most were primarily there to be a part of artist meet-and-greets, which would bring out idols
to a small stage within arm's reach. Instead of looking around the convention
floor, many fans were already congregating around the stage to secure a spot
with a good view of their idols that they normally got to see only on screen.
There they waited patiently, hours ahead of the scheduled meeting, for the
idols to appear.

Part of my assignment as a freelance journalist for the Australia-based online media outlet HelloAsia included posting real-time updates about KCON
Paris on Instagram and Twitter to give K-pop followers a live glimpse of the
event unfolding on the other side of the globe. While my incessant posts featuring the lineup of fans, the convention displays, and the idols themselves might
have accomplished the goal, my sense of being copresent with the idols in an
intimate space where no more than two hundred fans and journalists could
gather was compromised by the mediation of the camera lens. When fan favorite BTS appeared onstage for a meet-and-greet, their lanky limbs all dolled up
in black and white slim suits to face the ecstatic crowd, I was tempted to look
at them directly but could not afford to do so for fear of losing great shots for

HelloAsia readers. I was more concerned with creating lively updates of mediated images for distant followers than with the temporal and spatial copresence that emanated a sense of immediacy for me. But I was far from alone in this; practically everyone surrounding me held up their cell phones and frantically captured BTS, who were standing in front of them, in person, less than ten feet away (figure 18). Never-ending efforts to turn the fleeting present into already documented memories from the past—these are the signs of connectivity in the digital era, which, at times genuinely and at other times illusively, lure us into the fuzzy matrix of liveness.

When BTS disappeared from the stage after their five-minute-or-so fan engagement, I hardly felt that I had really seen them in person. None of their peculiar quirks or traits remained in my mind. So when the next idols, f(x), appeared, I took only a couple of photos, posted them on HelloAsia Instagram and Twitter accounts, and watched their fan engagement with my own eyes. Once a quintet, the group appeared on stage as a trio, featuring only Krystal, Luna, and Amber. Although I have always paid attention to their distinctive music/visual style, I was not particularly fond of this group, but my lukewarm opinion changed when I saw them in person without any mediation of digital screens. The lanky, androgynous Amber was wearing her personality on her

FIGURE 18. BTS appears for an artist meet-and-greet at KCON Paris 2016. Note that many fans hold up their cameras to record the moment. Photo by Kim Suk-Young.

sleeve, making goofy gestures, to the amusement of fans. The ethereal Krystal appeared even more attractive, with a distant, lifeless expression that has become the hallmark of her beauty; Luna's Cleopatra haircut framed her petite face while giving it a charismatic hint (figure 19). Their surreally slender limbs were accentuated by bell-bottom trousers, turning them into embodiments of hardly attainable corporeality.

The visceral beauty of a living human being standing within arm's reach is a force strong enough to convert a random bystander into a worshipper. That aura of intimacy and immediacy emanating from living bodies—mildly disheveled curls on white blouses, shoulders heaving as they take breath, and the minute flutters of their eyelashes—cannot be fully captured by any high-definition camera. But f(x), too, disappeared like an evanescent vision, leaving

FIGURE 19. f(x) appears for an artist meet-and-greet at KCON Paris 2016. Photo by Kim Suk-Young.

fans to sigh and pine for more. When I turned around to exit the convention room, many young girls were inconsolably shedding warm tears, shaking convulsively, and speaking in barely discernable words: "Qui était le meilleur, qui était le meilleur. . . ."

For these distraught fans, the magical three-minute encounter with f(x) was worth a very long wait; between artist meet-and-greets, the organizers of the conference held the fans as involuntary hostages to witness multiple signings of Korea-France treaties to commemorate the 130th anniversary of diplomatic ties between Korea and France.[4] There were also extensive makeup demonstrations and *hanbok* fashion shows, which delayed and shrank the artist meet-and-greet sessions, to the enormous dismay of fans. It was a prime example of how the pursuit and display of Korea's soft power unwittingly needs the presence of a captive audience, who, if it weren't for the promise of seeing more K-pop stars, would have deserted the signing ceremony. The Korean government's staging of national soft power necessitated hijacking K-pop fans for its own audience and free-riding on the K-pop bandwagon.

This episode was mirrored during the evening concert, which followed the convention. While the overheated fans were already howling from the excitement of seeing the MC of the night, Lee Teuk, who is the leader of Super Junior and for whom I once wrote a fan letter on behalf of my non-Korean student, he suddenly announced that the South Korean president, Park Geun-hye, was in the house. The camera rapidly switched from Lee Teuk to zoom in on the smiling face of the president as she waved to the crowd, and the already elated fans who had started cheering for the MC and other stars to appear inadvertently ended up cheering the president. But who really cared about her presence, other than some stuffy government bureaucrats in suits who had to document this moment and capture Korea's creative economy at work? The cheer that greeted the president was meant for Lee Teuk, SHINee, BTS, I.O.I, f(x), FT Island, and BlockB, who were the real magnets for the huge crowd that night. That president now sits in a jail cell after a disastrous corruption scandal carried out under the banner of the creative economy and other causes, but the same K-pop stars from whom she stole thunderous applause are still singing on stage, connecting with their fans, and being loved by them in return.

Two days after KCON 2016, I could still find traces of Korea's soft power attempting to manifest itself throughout various corners of Paris. As I traveled through the city on a metro ride, I quite frequently saw "Visit Korea" campaign advertisements and announcements of a touring modern Korean dance troupe.

The 2016 Korea-France diplomatic celebration was an ongoing event, but the Accord Hotels Arena, which had been the melting pot for the fans of many races and genders who all came to celebrate K-pop, had already moved into another world. The Senegalese music phenomenon Wally Ballago Seck was having a concert on June 4, and the Accord Hotels Arena was flooded with Africans dressed for the party of their lifetime—perfectly coiffed ladies in their long ball gowns and gentlemen in their best colorful tuxedos and pointed dress shoes.

Seeing the vibrant wave of Wally Ballago Seck fans, I could not help asking: Where was the K-pop fever that had packed the arena just two nights before? Where were the motley light sticks, handmade signs, and hysteric cries that captured the pulse of the living moment? The boom is a floating bubble that refuses to ground itself in a particular locale. Just as waves carry sand to the shores and scatter the grains when they retreat, thousands of live fans carried by the heat of the moment dispersed back to their routine lives. The clammy air of the night swallowed the K-pop spark, as it would the tuxes and dresses of Wally Ballago Seck fans.

· · ·

Time will fly and turn this book into an obsolete memory, reducing it to irrelevant dust on the fast-moving tracks of K-pop. Only time will tell whether live concert halls will still echo with the voices of K-pop's brightest stars. As things stand in 2017, live K-pop concerts are growing but are still rare occasions to bring K-pop's producers and consumers, stars and fans, performers and spectators into interactive engagement. The copresence of these agents involved in K-pop's circulation allows for human-to-human connectedness, yet because of the relative scarcity of such events, liveness is often fetishized: if corporations promote live events to maximize profitability, then the Korean nation sees them as a prime platform to advance its soft power.

This book has attempted to capture how the ideological, technological, and affective workings of liveness can make, fake, and break sociality and community. The constant interventions of digitally augmented audiovisual effects at times promote an illusion of intimacy and at other times forge genuine bonding, contributing to the formation as well as the attenuation of community. This dualistic action stems from the complexity of liveness, which is at once a commercial commodity, a mode of ongoing lifestyle consumption, a teleological destination of technological advancement, a means of social connection, and even the affective evidence of life itself. The range of the concept is fluid

and amorphous, but it was precisely the thrilling challenge of chasing this illusive goal that first attracted me to the subject.

Perhaps the most significant feature of liveness lies in the transfiguration of
the abstract noun into adjectives such as *alive* and *living*. While they are imperfect concepts to address the human desire to be connected to others, they also
collectively denote the ephemeral state of human existence and its erasure by
time. To be alive is to be cognizant of our very short lives and the need to brave
the destructive forces of life day by day. The K-pop community has found ways
to do this together through a mutually shared affection for their objects of desire.
This leads at times to true rapport and at other times to exclusionary tribalism.

Nevertheless, even as we confront the undesirable forces of tribalism in the
K-pop world, I remain hopeful and believe that live encounters are always preg-
nant with the possibilities of what Jill Dolan calls the "utopian performative," or
"small but profound moments in which performance calls the attention of the
audience in a way that lifts everyone slightly above the present, into a hopeful
feeling of what the world might be like if every moment of our lives were as
emotionally voluminous, generous, aesthetically striking and intersubjectively
intense."[5] As many moments of this book have shown, K-pop has transformative power to build an affirmative community by making us transcend much
cultural difference, political strife, and racial hatred.

I have often resorted to the Korean notion of *heung* as a way to capture the
magic of liveness, its miraculous confluence of disparate elements that come together as a community via shared enjoyment. As such, *heung* offers a glimpse of
hope for living in the hypercommercialized world: the enchanting rapport created by the lively interaction between the performer and the spectator blurs the
boundary between them, as they are brought together to share the moment as
fully present participants. Unlike the notion of *han* (a word that has no English
counterpart but can be approximately translated as "sorrow," "regret," "resent-
ment," or "suffering"), which has received more critical treatment in studies of
K-pop and Korean culture in general, *heung* has been mentioned only occasionally and in an undertheorized manner.[6] Perhaps this book's small contribu-
tion will be its call to contemplate *heung* more thoughtfully, as a unique Korean
passage to global community.

· · ·

A month back from my trip to Paris, long after my jet lag was gone, I found
myself constantly humming "Reality," a song on the original soundtrack of the

1980 French film *LaBoum*. The film is forever tied to the French actress Sophie Marceau, who became a global star after its release. With her youthful countenance eternally etched in the minds of many, she still potently awakens the blushing feelings of first love.

Thirty-six years after its release and after multiple revivals, "Reality" lived yet another life at KCON Paris when Taemin, a member of SHINee, sang the song to celebrate the cultural ties between Korea and France. A heartbreaker with the soft face of an angel, this androgynous idol appeared on stage solo in a delicately embroidered snow-white blouse and black slacks, which perfectly enfolded his willowy figure (figure 20). His youthful face was shaded by voluminous blond hair, and his eyes were lowered to make his soft features look even softer. Despite the deafening cheers of the crowd, he started singing in a wispy voice, as if there were nobody else in the entire arena other than him and his beloved.

> Met you by surprise, I didn't realize
> that my life would change forever.
> Tell me that it's true, feelings that are new,
> I feel something special about you.
> Dreams of my reality, a wondrous world where I like to be

FIGURE 20. Taemin performs the song "Reality" at KCON Paris 2016. Photo by Kim Suk-Young.

Illusions are a common thing, I try to live in dreams
Although it's only fantasy.
Dreams of my reality, I like to dream of you close to me.
I dream of loving in the night and loving you seems right,
Perhaps it's my reality.

Every listener who nearly filled the seventeen-thousand-seat stadium felt this as an extremely private moment. In the sea of overflowing emotion, it felt as if he were singing to you—and you alone. As one concert attendee remarked about the performance posted on YouTube, "An angel out of nowhere. It's not possible to be so perfect. . . . It is perfect, that's all."[7]

There he was, a luminous phantom and a real human at once, standing in front of you, drawing in the same air that filled your lungs. The splendor of this moment was unreal, yet it was a part of reality. His voice spread and instantly lifted me up from the particularities of that moment, from my jaded skepticism and fatigue, and landed me in the field of memories—memories of lively youth that felt as if it would never come to an end and memories of a strong desire to live a life of dreams.

YOUTH IS THE INCARNATION OF BREVITY and the force that keeps the heart of memories beating. But all too soon it fades away, crippling us with daily impositions and leaving us in a wretched form. Even so, holding on to the fleeting present, its temporality, is what breathes life into our past. Feeling alive at every beat of a song, at every glimpse of beauty—life goes on because of this.

ACKNOWLEDGMENTS

Buried between plump cheeks and frowning eyebrows, the little boy's twinkly eyes become electrified with joy that runs through every inch of his frame. Spewing warm saliva through pouty lips and shrugging his tiny shoulders up and down, his little body is perfectly in sync with the music. A younger version of myself marvels at my four-month-old son as he bursts into an improvised dance in a baby bouncer.

What enormous joy is packed into his tiny body! The faint sound of chiming bells or a fluttering sight of a butterfly is enough for him to respond with his entire presence. He twists his torso, stretching out chubby fingers into open space, trying to grab anything and everything that there is—just for the fun of it. An intense thrill is emitted when the little man explores the highest pitch of his vocal range. By fully embracing the impulse of the moment, he exists, he thrives.

We might become wiser as we grow older, but at the price of losing such primal joy. Something hardens inside, stiffening the agile mind as we learn to suppress ourselves in the face of social pressures. Only occasional sparks can revive the intuitive intensity of play, but even such momentary flames eventually flicker out in the mundane. Now, at age seven, my little boy still beams with mischievous amusement, but he is more reserved, surely having outgrown his infant self—that pure incarnation of celebrating the energy of existence.

This book is about the paradoxical power of Korean popular music. Despite its highly manufactured nature, K-pop has the vigor to ignite hard-edged minds and imbue them with unadulterated forces of primal joy. Its soundscape creates bridges to bygone eras or spaces never visited. K-pop often becomes the solid rock upon which to build a lively global community, yet its high energy is never free from calculation and excessive commercialization. It has the ability to inspire the world to be a better place, yet its backstage reality is often far from idealistic.

Untangling these complicated strands required many helping hands, and I have been fortunate to encounter the generous support of many people and institutions.

I thank Cha U-jin, Sohn Jie-Ae, Kevin Broderick, Bak Hee-ju, Bak Gwang-won, Johnny Au, and anonymous staff members from CJ E&M, SM Entertainment, and

YG Entertainment for their guidance. Global K-pop fans of all walks of life whom I encountered gave me so much inspiration to keep writing. Without fans, there simply is no K-pop.

Choe Youngmin, Ian Condry, Chris Hanscom, David Kang, and those who attended the manuscript review hosted by the University of Southern California's Korean Studies Institute gave valuable feedback on an earlier version of this work. Roald Maliangkay, in particular, read many drafts of this book and gave detailed comments, which were indispensable for completing the project. Friendships I enjoyed with Leo Cabranes-Grant, Michael Emmerich, Leahkim Gannett, Bishnupriya Ghosh, Andrea Goldman, Todd Henry, Daniel Jaffe, Kimberly Jannarone, Eng Beng Lim, Rachel and Everett Lipman, Sean Metzger, Ariel Osterweis, VK Preston, Rho Hyeon-ju, Bhaska Sarkar, Satoko Shimazaki, Elizabeth Son, Shannon Steen, Alex Wang, and Theodore Jun Yoo kept galvanizing this project. The beauty of working with students is that they always expand the limits of my work: Jaime Gray and Grace Jung keep me abreast of the constantly evolving scholarship in digital media; Yassi Jahanmir and Zachary Price have transformed from advisees to colleagues, which brings me great pride; research by Lee So-Rim and Stephanie Choi will broaden the horizon of K-pop scholarship. Michelle Lipinski at Stanford University Press has been a kind and encouraging editor, helping me find a perfect home for this book, Elisabeth Magnus was indispensable in clearing up my often-murky writing style, Carla Neuss assisted me with proofreading the manuscript, and Tommy Tran provided substantial help with romanization of Korean words. As always, I enjoyed working with my editor Leslie Kriesel; this is the fourth book of mine that carries her imprint.

My parents; my sister, Kim Mee-Young; my brother, Kim Young-Eun; my mother-in-law, Beverly St. John; and my dear friend Diana Salvador deserve huge credit for taking over my responsibilities when I indulged in jet-set K-pop adventures. Michael Berry is always a calm, equalizing force to anchor my tumultuous journey of completing this book. My little Naima kept inspiring me to feel the liveness of music with her love for singing and dancing.

This work was supported by the Laboratory Program for Korean Studies through the Ministry of Education of the Republic of Korea and the Korean Studies Promotion Service of the Academy of Korean Studies (AKS-2015-LAB-2250002). Additionally, the 2014–15 ACLS/SSRC/NEH International and Area Studies Fellowship gave me the precious opportunity to devote an entire academic year to research and writing, while the University of California, Santa Barbara Regents Faculty Fellowship allowed me to attend KCON Paris in 2016. The Center for Performance Studies at the University of California, Los Angeles became my new intellectual home to foster this work, and I am grateful for the nurturing spirit and extensive network this community has provided. I hope that the book will turn out to be worthy of the generous support it received.

Various portions of this book have been presented at the University of California, Los Angeles, the University of California, Santa Barbara, the University of Southern

California, the University of Washington, Seattle, Texas A&M University, the University of Maryland College Park, Yonsei University, KCON, the BuzzFeed video series, CNN International, and Radio Lab. Grateful acknowledgment is given to the following publications where portions of this book in their earlier versions were featured: "The Many Faces of K-pop Music Videos: Revues, Motown, and Broadway in 'Twinkle,'" *Journal of Popular Culture 49* (February 2016): 136–54; and "Liveness: Performance of Ideology and Technology in the Changing Media Environment," in *Oxford Research Encyclopedia of Literature,* March 29, 2017, http://literature.oxfordre.com/view/10.1093/acrefore/9780190201098.001.0001/acrefore-9780190201098-e-76.

For a long time, this book has been known to our family as the "Wolf Dance Book," a working title given by my son, who was particularly impressed by EXO's intricate choreography devised for their song "Wolf." He has never been shy in asking why his "Wolf Dance Book" is taking such a long time to complete. Finally, here it is.

This one is for you, Miles. The world is your stage to take.

NOTES

INTRODUCTION

1. The term *multimedia* is used on multiple levels in this book: literally, it references multiple layers of media platforms in order to indicate how the live proscenium stage, television, film, and online media platforms corroborate to produce a network of K-pop content. From the perspective of K-pop performers, the term means versatility in crafting their career path by being not only expert musicians and dancers but also performers on variety shows and even sporting events designed for television consumption. On a phenomenological level, the term designates how K-pop is a performance that appeals to multiple senses—auditory, visual, tactile, olfactory—in order to mobilize fans in a thoroughly synaesthetic way.

2. BIGBANG attracted 590,000 attendees during thirty-four live concerts hosted in Japan in the first half of 2016. Gim Won-gyeom, "Sutjaro bon byeonhameomneun keipap hwangje 'BIGBANG'" [BIGBANG, the unchallenged emperors of K-pop according to statistics], *Dong-A Ilbo*, July 20, 2016, http://sports.donga.com/3/all/20160719/79284955/3.

3. In 2016 alone, the following K-pop bands visited US cities outside the two most prominent tour stops, Los Angeles and New York City: B.A.P. performed in Atlanta on March 16; Teen Top in Dallas on April 8; AOMG in Seattle on April 17; Day6 in Orlando on August 14; and BIGBANG in Honolulu on October 22, to name just a few.

4. The article is based predominantly on an infographic about the K-pop live concert trend from January 2013 to July 2016 provided by the concert Kickstarter website MyMusicTaste.com. Jeff Benjamin, "K-pop Concerts Continue to Grow outside Asia: Exclusive Infographic," *Billboard*, May 3, 2016, http://www.billboard.com/articles/columns/k-town/7350481/international-k-pop-concerts-growth-infographic.

5. The article contrasts the rise of K-pop concerts elsewhere with the fact that East Asia is witnessing a decline in K-pop concerts. Ibid.

6. Europe, North America, and South America combined hosted only 14.26 percent of the concerts during the 2013–16 survey period (as opposed to 77.98 percent in East Asia), but the growing trend of K-pop concerts outside Asia could signal an important tidal shift in K-pop's circulation.

213

7. Another example of the use of the eye-level camera in the K-pop world is female solo artist Lee Hi's music video "Hold My Hand" (https://www.youtube.com/watch?v =cuUEnho33so), released on March 8, 2016, where the viewers enter the illusory world of holding the singer's hands while looking into her eyes.

8. Eve Kosofsky Sedgwick, *Touching Feeling* (Durham, NC: Duke University Press, 2003), 101.

9. Ina Blom, "The Touch through Time: Raoul Hausemann, Nam June Paik and the Transmission Technologies of the Avant-Garde," *Leonardo* 34, no. 3 (June 2001): 211.

10. Media scholar Kay Dickinson uses the term *synaesthesia* to designate "the transposition of sensory images or attributes from one modality into another." Kay Dickinson, "Music Videos and Synesthetic Possibility," in *Medium Cool: Music Videos from Soundies to Cellphones*, ed. Roger Beebe and Jason Middleton (Durham, NC: Duke University Press, 2007), 14. While she uses the term primarily in relation to music videos, I will use it in this book to address a broader spectrum of media platforms and genres that are prone to mixing various senses.

11. Ethnomusicologist Michael Fuhr champions the idea that K-pop is a popular form of cultural practice as well as a multitextual and performative phenomenon. *Globalization and Popular Music in South Korea: Sounding Out K-pop* (London: Routledge, 2016), 13.

12. Slavoj Žižek, *Organs without Bodies* (New York: Routledge, 2004), 2.

13. Quoted in Daniel Sack, *After Live: Possibility, Potentiality, and the Future of Performance* (Ann Arbor: University of Michigan Press, 2015), 164.

14. The term *connectivity* in this book will be used in the way delineated by media studies scholar José van Djick. In her seminal book *The Culture of Connectivity: A Critical History of Social Media* (Oxford: Oxford University Press, 2013), Van Djick distinguishes *connectedness* from *connectivity*; if the former refers to the participatory Internet culture prior to 2007, when social media was yet to be thoroughly corporatized, then the latter refers to the hypercommercialized culture of the Internet, which became prominent with the corporatization of YouTube, Facebook, and other social media networks.

15. Sack, *After Live*, 12.

16. Mark James Russell made a similar observation on the excessive nature of K-pop aesthetics: "There is something distinct and special about K-pop. It's like everything is a little bit louder, the images brighter, the style flashier—it's just *more*." Mark James Russell, *K-pop Now! The Korean Music Revolution* (Singapore: Tuttle, 2014), 18.

17. Joseph L. Flatley, "K-pop Takes America: How South Korea's Music Machine Is Conquering the World," *Verge*, October 18, 2012, http://www.theverge.com/2012/10 /18/3516562/k-pop-invades-america-south-korea-pop-music-factory.

18. Girls' Generation former member Jessica started training with SM Entertainment at the age of ten. Her story is not an exception to the rule but the norm in the world of K-pop.

19. Neil Hannigan, "Interview: Ex-SME Trainee Neil Hannigan on Auditions, Contracts, and Trainee Life," interview by Kpopalypse, June 12, 2015, http://www.asian junkie.com/2015/06/interview-ex-sme-trainee-neil-hannigan-on-auditions-contracts -and-trainee-life. According to *Who Is Next* (aired on Mnet in 2013) and *Mix and Match* (aired on Mnet in 2014), reality survival games that feature YG Entertainment's male trainees, it is quite common for trainees to stay up all night practicing and preparing themselves for impending evaluations and competitions.

20. The term *fan* in the context of performing arts is at times used interchangeably with related terms such as *audience* and *spectator*, but in the age of digital capitalism it sometimes becomes conflated with *netizen* as well as *consumer*. In this book, *fan*, for lack of a better word, will be used to reference these corollary terms. As media studies scholar Choi JungBong (Choe Jeong-bong) noted, the term "falls short of representing the magnitude held by the people involved in the labor of cultural nourishment and refinement. These are deficit concepts, if not outright misnomers, unable to capture the roles and functions of those so labeled in the area of cultural participation." Given the complexity of roles that fans embody in today's mediatized world, Choi advocates the idea that fans deserve the term *cultural curators*. Choi JungBong [Choe Jeong-bong], "Hallyu versus Hallyu-hwa: Cultural Phenomenon versus Institutional Campaign," in *Hallyu 2.0: The Korean Wave in the Age of Social Media*, ed. Lee Sangjoon and Abé Nornes (Ann Arbor: University of Michigan Press, 2015), 42.

21. Recently the K-pop world has witnessed fast-rising popularity in reality survival shows, such as Mnet's *Produce 101* (2016, 2017), which empower voting viewers to determine which contestants will eventually debut as a new K-pop group.

22. Titles such as "Top 3 K-pop Creepy Stories," accessed July 3, 2013, http://www .kpopstarz.com/articles/33316/20130703/top-3-creepy-k-pop-fan-stories.htm, and "13 Extreme Accounts of Sasaeng Fans," accessed July 6, 2015, http://www.allkpop.com/ article/2015/07/13-extreme-accounts-of-sasaeng-fans, provide a sample of the English-language media's sensational coverage of K-pop fan behavior.

23. Quoted in An In-yong, "K-pop, jindani piryohae" [K-pop needs a diagnosis], *Hangyeore* 866, no. 27 (June 2011), http://h21.hani.co.kr/arti/culture/culture_general /29888.html.

24. Fuhr, *Globalization and Popular Music*, 59.

25. Fuhr poses the same question ("What is the K in K-pop?") and uses his book to elaborate on the national, global, and corporate aspects. See *Globalization and Popular Music*, 6–11. I attempt to expand on the semantic range of "K" in "K-pop" by adding the emphasis on newness and disposability ("Kleenex" pop) as well as the digital habitat ("keyboard/keypad" pop).

26. The idea for this term comes from performance studies scholar Shannon Jackson's use of *Kleenex citizens* in reference to young disposable workforces in neoliberal economies. See "Kleenex Citizens and the Performance of Undisposability," in *Perfor-*

mance, Politics and Activism, ed. Peter Lichenfels and John Rouse (London: Palgrave Macmillan, 2013), 237–52. For a detailed account of the disposability of the labor force in the Korean pop culture industry, see Kang Inkyu [Gang In-kyu], "The Political Economy of Idols: South Korea's Neoliberal Restructuring and Its Impact on the Entertainment Labour Force," in *K-pop: The International Rise of the Korean Music Industry*, ed. Choi JungBong and Roald Maliangkay (New York: Routledge, 2015), 51–65.

27. K-pop producers rely heavily on intensive capital investments and therefore cannot simply focus on the domestic market; to generate profit and further develop their products, they must pursue foreign markets aggressively. As Park Jin-young (Bak Jin-yeong), the CEO of JYP Entertainment, stated in an interview: "In Japan there are 100 million consumers, but in Korea we have only 50 million. That's why entertainment companies have no choice but to look at foreign markets if they intend to grow." Park Jin-young [Bak Jin-yeong], interview by Son Seok-hui, *News Room*, JTBC, May 5, 2015.

28. The "K" in "K-pop" stems from various desires to harness the global popularity of Korean pop music. Prominent among them is the Korean government's plan to lay claim to K-pop as a part and parcel of a national branding campaign (see chapters 1 and 5), which has also given rise to similar terms such as *K-drama*, *K-tourism*, and *K-education*. However, the prolific use of "K" has dwindled since the fall of 2016 because of the massive political scandal that launched the impeachment process of the South Korean president Park Geun-hye [Bak Geun-hye], accused of misusing government funds and pressuring business conglomerates to support her confidante Choe Sun-sil's companies—K-Sports Foundation and The Blue K—which many believe to have functioned as illegal fund-raising vehicles. Choe Su-mun, "Munchebu saeopseo 'K'myeongching ppaenda" ["K" is disappearing from project titles supported by the Ministry of Culture, Sports, and Tourism], Daum, December 19, 2016, http://v.media.daum.net/v/20161219175924498.

29. Stephen Epstein and James Turnbull note: "One may well regard Korean popular music artists as general entertainers . . . for with the collapse of recorded music sales success has come to depend not so much on vocal talents as dancing ability, physical attractiveness, and the projection of image through appearance in live performances, television programs, advertisements, and so on." "Girls' Generation? Gender, (Dis) Empowerment and K-pop," in *The Korean Cultural Reader*, ed. Kim Kyung-Hyun [Gim Gyeong-hyeon] and Choe Youngmin [Choe Yeong-min] (Durham, NC: Duke University Press, 2014), 317.

30. Hannigan, "Interview."

31. Edward Kang, interview by author, February 4, 2016, Los Angeles.

32. Hannigan, "Interview."

33. The theoretical discussion of the terms *live* and *liveness* in this section is closely based on Kim Suk-Young [Gim Suk-yeong], "Liveness: Performance of Ideology and Technology in the Changing Media Environment," in *Oxford Research Encyclopedia*

of Literature, March 29, 2017, Oxford University Press, http://literature.oxfordre.com/view/10.1093/acrefore/9780190201098.001.0001/acrefore-9780190201098-e-76.

34. Peggy Phelan, *Unmarked: The Politics of Performance* (London: Routledge, 1993), 146.

35. Jennifer Parker-Starbuck, *Cyborg Theatre: Corporeal/Technological Intersections in Multimedia Performance*, 2nd ed. (New York: Palgrave Macmillan, 2014), 9.

36. Philip Auslander, *Liveness: Performance in a Mediatized Culture* (London: Routledge, 2008).

37. Philip Auslander, "Digital Liveness: A Historic-Philosophical Perspective," *PAJ: A Journal of Performance and Art* 34, no. 3 (September 2012): 3.

38. Shannon Jackson and Marianne Weems, *The Builders Association: Performance and Media in Contemporary Theater* (Cambridge, MA: MIT Press, 2015), 6.

39. More precisely, Couldry defines the term as "the 'liveness' of a mobile group of friends who are in continuous contact via their mobile phones through calls and texting . . . [which] enables individuals and groups to be continuously co-present to each other even as they move independently across space." Nick Couldry, "Liveness, 'Reality' and the Mediated Habitus from Television to the Mobile Phone," *Communications Review* 7, no. 4 (2004): 357.

40. Although "idols for live performance" is a new trend introduced to the K-pop scene in 2016, it closely emulates the way J-pop idols, such as AKB48, operate as idols staging an open-run live performance in their own theater since 2005.

41. Gabriella Giannachi, *Virtual Theatres: An Introduction* (London: Routledge, 2004), 123.

42. Steve Benford and Gabriella Giannachi, *Performing Mixed Reality* (Cambridge, MA: MIT Press, 2011), 1.

43. As Roald Maliangkay pointed out during an informal conversation on April 11, 2016, a DJ presenting a live performance of recorded sound tracks will blur the boundary between not only "live" and "recorded" but also "live" and "digital."

44. John Lie, *K-pop: Popular Music, Cultural Amnesia, and Economic Innovation in South Korea* (Berkeley: University of California Press, 2015), 141.

45. Ibid., 141.

46. Steve Dixon, *Digital Performance: A History of New Media in Theater, Dance, Performance Art, and Installation* (Cambridge, MA: MIT Press, 2007), 132.

47. With a dose of generalization, I perceive a noticeable gap between South Korean fans of K-pop and their overseas counterparts. While overseas fans I encounter at KCON tend to support many bands simultaneously under the banner of K-pop, South Korean fans tend to pledge their loyalty to one group at a time.

48. According to Park E. Chan, *pan* in *pansori* "conjures both mental and physical space for wholehearted participation," whereas *sori* goes beyond "just singing to become narrative expressiveness, a musical metalanguage, or a 'sound language' that is acquired

through method and practice." *Voices from the Straw Mat: Toward an Ethnography of Korean Story Singing* (Honolulu: University of Hawai'i Press, 2003), 1.

49. Michael Fuhr defines the term as "traditional music that comprises various genres of folk (*minsok*), court/ritual (*aak*), and aristocratic music (*jeongak*)." Fuhr, *Globalization and Popular Music*, 244.

50. Yun Yeong-cheol, "Hangugui heung baeunda! Hoju gugak saminbang" [Australian trio to learn Korean *heung* through traditional music], June 22, 2014, http://www.ytn.co.kr/_ln/0104_201406220007351069.

51. Ha Eun-seon, "Hangugui heungi munhwabaljeonui hwallyeokso" [Korea's *heung* vitalizes cultural prosperity], November 17, 2011, http://www.koreatimes.com/article/696517.

52. Yoon Jung-kang [Yun Jeong-gang], *Gugak: Traditional Korean Music Today* (Elizabeth, NJ: Hollym, 2014), 168.

53. Hesselink further emphasizes the importance of the collective spirit in understanding *pungmul*: "Although play exists that is self-sufficient, in that one is able to enjoy oneself alone, play done in the company of many others gives a richer and more joyful satisfaction. The character of a group play is that in which liveness and joy [*hungyoum*] are all the more emphasized." Nathan Hesselink, *P'ungmul: South Korean Drumming and Dance* (Chicago: University of Chicago Press, 2006), 99.

54. Literally translated as "four things at play," *samulnori* refers to the popular urbanized form of *pungmul*. See Hesselink, *P'ungmul*, 267. *Madangnori* literally translates into "play that takes place at *madang*." *Madang* here primarily references "courtyard," but its figurative meaning includes "meeting place" and "movement" as well. Hesselink, *P'ungmul*, 261. Unlike *pansori* performance, which relies on narrative and singing by one performer, *madangnori* involves multiple actors who engage in dramatic acting that is often accompanied by drumming and singing.

55. Heo Yun-hui, "Hanguginui munhwa DNA 3: heung. Pansori myeongchang An Suk-seon, aidol gasu IU" [Korea's cultural DNA (part 3): *Heung*. Pansori singer An Suk-seon and idol singer IU], *Joseon Ilbo*, September 20, 2012, http://pann.news.nate.com/info/254111641.

56. The Pyeongchang Winter Olympics Committee's 2018 site is at http://www.pyeongchang2018.org/language/kor/sub01/sub01_01_02.asp, accessed September 22, 2014.

57. Sohn Jie-Ae [Son Ji-ae], "K-pop Mania: South Korea's Place under the Sun," public lecture, Annenberg School for Communications and Journalism, University of Southern California, November 12, 2014.

58. See Dwight Conquergood, "Performance Studies: Interventions and Radical Research," *Drama Review* 46, no. 2 (Summer 2002): 145–56.

59. Randall Packer and Ken Jordan, introduction to *Multimedia: From Wagner to Virtual Reality*, ed. Randall Packer and Ken Jordan (New York: Norton, 2001), xxxviii.

60. Tom Boellstroff, Bonnie Nardi, Celia Pearce, and T. L. Taylor, *Ethnography and Virtual Worlds: A Handbook of Methods* (Princeton, NJ: Princeton University Press, 2012), 6.

61. Yarimar Bonilla and Jonathan Rosa, "#Ferguson: Digital Protest, Hashtag Ethnography, and the Radical Politics of Social Media in the United States," *American Ethnologist* 42, no. 1 (2015): 6.

62. D. Soyni Madison, *Critical Ethnography: Method, Ethics, and Performance* (Thousand Oaks, CA: Sage Publications, 2005), 32.

CHAPTER 1: HISTORICIZING K-POP

1. Fuhr similarly noted that "music is only one element in the official reading of the Korean Wave that has been used flexibly to embrace other fields of the domestic content industry." Fuhr, *Globalization and Popular Music*, 7.

2. Positing CCTV's airing of *What Is Love* as the origin of *hallyu* is a well-established historiographic position among specialists. For instance, see Baek Won-dam, *Hallyu: East Asia's Cultural Choice* (Seoul: Pentagram, 2005), 34; Jung Sun, *Korean Masculinities and Transnational Consumption: Yonsama, Rain, Old Boy, K-pop Idols* (Hong Kong: Hong Kong University Press, 2011), 1.

3. Many established scholars subscribe to this version of the term's genealogy. For example, see Yun Jae-sik, *Hallyuwa bangsong yeongsang kontencheu maketing* [Hallyu and the marketing of broadcasting media content] (Seoul: Communication Books, 2004), 36–37.

4. Jang Gyu-Su, "Hallyuui eowongwa sayonge gwanhan yeongu" [Study of Korean waves: The origin and the usage [*sic*]], *Hangug-kontencheu-haghoe-nonmunji* 11, no. 9 (November 2011): 169.

5. Ibid.

6. The South Korean government in the 1990s actively conducted a national branding campaign under several presidents who used slogans such as "Dynamic Korea," "Global Korea," and "Creative Korea." While the slogans may differ, they share the goal of conveying the collaborative partnership between government policies and private sectors of the culture industry via multimedia platforms. K-pop grew out of this historic stage when national identity could be clearly articulated only against the backdrop of the country's relations with other global cultures while relying on branding strategies lifted straight from the corporate world.

7. Jang, "Hallyuui eowongwa sayonge gwanhan yeongu," 167–68.

8. In 1997 South Korea was hit by a massive liquidity crisis and had to appeal to international funds, most notably the IMF, for a $58 billion loan to save itself from bankruptcy. In 2001 South Korea completely paid off its debt, declaring that the crisis was officially over. However, this financial crisis, commonly referred to as the IMF crisis, had a lasting impact on many aspects of South Korean life. From massive layoffs that shat-

tered the myth of stable employment for social elites to surging divorce rates stemming from the disintegration of traditional family values, it resulted in a drastic restructuring of conventional social relations.

9. Choi, "Hallyu versus Hallyu-hwa," 42; Lie, *K-pop*.

10. See Lee and Nornes, *Hallyu 2.0*; Jin Dal Yong, *New Korean Wave: Transnational Cultural Power in the Age of Social Media* (Urbana: University of Illinois Press, 2016); Fuhr, *Globalization and Popular Music*.

11. Joseph Nye and Kim Youna, "Soft Power and the Korean Wave," in *The Korean Wave: Korean Media Go Global*, ed. Kim Youna (New York: Routledge, 2013), 41.

12. Lie's book *K-pop* gives a long tour of Korean pop music history by surveying the entirety of Korean history.

13. For instance, see Roald Maliangkay, "Same Look through Different Eyes: Korea's History of Uniform Pop Music Acts," in Choi and Maliangkay, *K-pop*, 19–34.

14. Fuhr, *Globalization and Popular Music*, 133.

15. Jin Dal Yong, *New Korean Wave*, 574.

16. David Kang lays out multiple reasons for the 1997 Asian financial crisis, in which the following three factors made the country vulnerable to financial meltdown: "First an increased demand for political payoffs shifted the advantage to business. Second, Korea's legal and corporate institutions remained underdeveloped even in the 1990s. Finally, given increasingly mobile international capital, the overcapacity and over-diversification of the Korean conglomerates made them vulnerable to international speculative attacks." *Crony Capitalism: Corruption and Development in South Korea and the Philippines* (Cambridge: Cambridge University Press, 2003), 158–59.

17. Because of the historic legacy of Japanese colonization, the South Korean government prohibited Japanese popular culture until 1998, when the Kim Dae-jung administration started to lift the ban gradually. The first stage, in 1998, consisted of allowing Japanese manga and prominent films that had won awards at major international film festivals (Cannes, Berlin, Venice) to be circulated. The second stage (1999) allowed more films and Japanese pop music concerts in venues with less than two thousand seats. The third stage (2000) allowed circulation of animation films that had won major international awards, pop concerts of any scale, game software, and sports and documentary programming. The fourth stage (2004) allowed sales of recorded music and lifted all bans on films.

18. Shin Gi-wook [Sin Gi-uk] and Choi Joon Nak[Choe Jun-nak], *Global Talent: Skilled Labor as Social Talent in South Korea* (Stanford, CA: Stanford University Press, 2015), 34.

19. Song Jesook [Song Je-suk], *South Koreans in the Debt Crisis: The Creation of a Neoliberal Welfare Society* (Durham, NC: Duke University Press, 2009), 208.

20. Ibid., 304.

21. Roald Maliangkay, "The Popularity of Individualism: The Seo Taiji Phenomenon

in the 1990s," in *The Korean Popular Culture Reader*, ed. Kim Kyung Hyun and Choe Youngmin (Durham, NC: Duke University Press, 2014), 304–5.

22. Fuhr notes that Seo Tae-ji and Boys' iconic stature is due not only to their innovative music styles but also to "a substantial shift in the industrial arrangement of pop music production" where the band "had total control over the group's image and songs." Fuhr, *Globalization and Popular Music*, 53.

23. Ibid., 298.

24. The most prominent example of Seo Tae-ji and Boys' eclectic blending of hip-hop, funk, heavy metal, and Korean folk music is the song "Hayeoga" (Anyhow song), which was released on their second album (1993).

25. Maliangkay, "Popularity of Individualism," 309.

26. Timothy Taylor, *The Sounds of Capitalism: Advertising, Music, and the Conquest of Culture* (Chicago: University of Chicago Press, 2012), 207.

27. Ibid.

28. Here I use this term *Teletubbies Generation* not only to indicate the direct shaping influence of the *Teletubbies* program on the viewing culture of the K-pop generation but also to emphasize certain patterns of media consumption in K-pop culture.

29. In the United States, the show was broadcast on the Public Broadcasting Service (PBS) television station from April 6, 1998, until June 19, 2005, and would continue to air in reruns until August 29, 2008. In Korea the show was featured on KBS 2TV from October 5, 1998, to March 25, 2005. In Japan, the program aired from April 1999 to September 2000 and from January to March 2001. The PRC's CCTV introduced the program on February 11, 2002. With some time lapse, the near-simultaneous consumption of *Teletubbies* on a global scale made it possible for an entire generation to be conditioned to receive digital media like K-pop approximately a decade later.

30. Korean audiences' familiarity with *Teletubbies* was deep enough to generate a political satire program titled *Yeouido Teletubbies*, which aired in the latter half of 2012. The program was a special segment on *Saturday Night Live* Korea by tvN, a cable network owned by CJ E&M. Yeouido being the epicenter of South Korean politics, the program lampooned politicians of different party affiliations marked by various color-coded outfits, very similar to the original shape and style of Teletubbies.

31. Sam Anderson, "Watching People Watching People Watching," *New York Times*, November 25, 2011, http://www.nytimes.com/2011/11/27/magazine/reaction-videos.html?pagewanted=all.

32. Cha U-jin, interview by author, April 23, 2015, Seoul, Korea.

33. Nowadays, there is a growing desire for J-pop artists to enter the overseas market. Because the K-pop industry has had more experience attempting to debut its singers in foreign markets, J-pop is trying to tap into that success through Korean-Japanese joint ventures. For example, the South Korean media company CJ E&M established CJ

Victor with partners in Japan, which provides consulting services for Japanese artists trying to reach markets outside Japan. An Seok-jun, lecture, Korean Association of Music Industry Preliminary Forum, July 17, 2014, Mapo Art Center, Seoul, Korea.

34. Of course there are other Weibo accounts related to Justin Bieber, but the fact that there are numerous scattered sites indicates that the singer's promotion team is not managing the Weibo account in the most effective way.

35. "Generation Like," *Frontline*, February 18, 2014, PBS.

36. This clip demonstrates some of the best-known examples of fans creating an ocean in the color symbolizing their idol bands. "Kpop Most Beautiful Oceans and Their Fanchants," YouTube, May 11, 2016, https://www.youtube.com/watch?v=f0bJlmm5qGg.

37. In retaliation for JYJ's breaking the long-term contract, SM Entertainment used their influence to boycott the trio's appearance on Korean TV stations, making it effectively impossible for JYJ to reach a large audience. But the JYJ fandom mobilized to bring changes to the unfair treatment of their idols, and as a result, on November 30, 2015, the Korea Communications Commission proposed an amendment to Korea's Broadcasting Act (known as "the JYJ Law") that prohibits a third party from blackmailing musicians to prevent their appearing on TV. For a more detailed account, see Jung Sun [Jeong Seon], "Fan Activism, Cybervigilantism, and Othering Mechanisms in K-pop Fandom," in "Transformative Works and Fan Activism," ed. Henry Jenkins and Sangita Shresthova, special issue, *Transformative Works and Cultures* 10 (2012), http://journal.transformativeworks.org/index.php/twc/article/view/300/287.

38. See Shin Haerin [Sin Hae-rin], "The Dynamics of K-pop Spectatorship: The Tablo Witch-Hunt and Its Double-Edged Sword of Enjoyment," in Choi and Maliangkay, *K-pop*, 133–45.

39. The following video captures the darkness of the concert venue and antifans shouting, "Get lost" when Girls' Generation performed on stage. "SNSD Black Ocean," YouTube, February 3, 2017, https://www.youtube.com/watch?v=6VWkSgDZ0g4.

40. The interview of the anonymous South Korean fan girl was aired on *Wide Entertainment News*, June 8, 2008, Mnet.

41. Ueno Toshiya, "Techno-Orientalism and Media-Tribalism: On Japanese Animation and Rave Culture," *Third Text* 47 (Summer 1999): 95–96.

42. Ibid., 96.

43. One does not have to join any official K-pop fandom to experience the most conspicuous instances of exclusion. Just visiting online galleries of dcinside.com, dedicated to K-pop idols, will show that without insider knowledge, such as specific lingo and the idols' schedule, there is no way for a random participant to join the online conversation.

44. Ueno, "Techno-Orientalism," 97.

45. Benjamin Barber, *Jihad vs McWorld: Terrorism's Challenge to Democracy* (New York: Times Books, 1995), 4.

46. John Caldwell, "Convergence Television: Aggregating Form and Repurposing Content in the Culture of Conglomeration," in *Television after TV*, ed. Lynn Spigel and Jan Olsson (Durham, NC: Duke University Press, 2004), 40–74.

47. Ibid., 40–74.

48. Henry Jenkins, *Fans, Bloggers, and Gamers: Exploring Participatory Culture* (New York: New York University Press, 2006), 155.

49. Michael Bourdaghs, *Sayonara Amerika, Sayonara Nippon: A Geopolitical Prehistory of J-pop* (New York: Columbia University Press, 2012), 223.

50. Ibid., 224.

51. Ibid.

52. Jeffrey Funk, *Technology Change and the Rise of New Industries* (Stanford, CA: Stanford Business Books, 2013), 5.

53. Ibid., 5.

54. Bourdaughs, *Sayonara Amerika*, 223.

55. Ibid., 225.

56. See Shin Hyun-joon, *Gayo, K-pop geurigo geu neomeo* [Gayo, K-pop and beyond] (Seoul: Dolbaege, 2013).

57. Yan Zheng, "Lighting the Future Takes More Than Just a Few Bright Ideas," *International Year of Light Blog*, May 5, 2015, http://light2015 blog.org/2015/05/05/lighting-the-future-takes-more-than-just-bright-ideas/.

58. Kim Sohee [Gim So-hui], "The 4.7 Billion K-pop Industry Chases Its 'Michael Jackson Moment': YouTube Is Turning South Korea into a Pop Culture Juggernaut," August 22, 2017, https://www.bloomberg.com/news/articles/2017-08-22/the-4-7-billion-k-pop-industry-chases-its-michael-jackson-moment.

59. Edward J. Malecki and Bruno Moriset, *The Digital Economy: Business Organization, Production Processes and Regional Developments* (London: Routledge, 2008), 36.

60. Stephen Witt, *How Music Got Free: The End of an Industry, the Turn of the Century, and the Patient Zero of Piracy* (New York: Viking, 2015), 8.

61. Sam Grobart, "How Samsung Became the World's No. 1 Smartphone Maker," *Bloomberg News*, March 28, 2013, https://www.bloomberg.com/news/articles/2013-03-28/how-samsung-became-the-worlds-no-dot-1-smartphone-maker.

62. Jin Jung-eon, "Li Hyori 'Anymotion'eun gwanggoga anida" [Li Hyori says "Anymotion" is not advertisement], *Chosun*, March 31, 2005, http://www.chosun.com/culture/news/200503/200503310244.html.

63. Yi Su-ji, "Samsung Anycall Anyclub vs. LG Cyon aidieo" [Samsung Anycall Anyclub vs. LG Cyon idea], Korea Advertisers Association, November 12, 2005, 30. "Anyclub" features Lee Hyori and Eric with an appearance by popular actor Kwon Sang-woo. "Anystar" features Lee Hyori, Lee Jungi, and a new face, Park Bom, who was to become a member of the popular girl group 2NE1. "Anyband" is a new band consisting of K-pop icons Tablo, BoA, and Xia Junsu, and jazz musician Jin Bora. "AMOLED" was

produced to advertise Samsung's 2009 release of a new cell phone model, Haptic Amoled; the music video features a collaboration between popular female singer Son Dam-bi and the girl group Afterschool.

64. David Evans, Andrei Hagiu, and Richard Schmalensee, *Invisible Engines: How Software Platforms Drive Innovation and Transform Industries* (Cambridge, MA: MIT Press, 2006).

65. Evans, Hagiu, and Schmalensee offer an example of how smartphones have come to compete with digital devices designed to download and stream digital music. Ibid., 335.

66. Ibid., 43.

67. Seo Yeong-jin, "Twitter, Teheran Valley-e hangukjisa seollip" [Twitter establishes a Korean branch in the Teheran Valley], News1, October 11, 2012, http://news1.kr /articles/?848346.

68. The exact number of viewers as of September 18, 2017, was 2,950,727,660.

69. Malecki and Moriset, *Digital Economy,* 36.

70. Martin Fransman, introduction to *Global Broadband Battles: Why the U.S. and Europe Lag While Asia Leads*, ed. Martin Fransman (Stanford, CA: Stanford Business Books, 2006), 1–57.

71. Chung Inho [Jeong In-ho], "Broadband, the Information Society, and National Systems," in Fransman, *Global Broadband Battles*, 87–108.

72. Ibid., 91.

73. Ibid., 92.

74. Mike Masnick, "Korean Music Industry Embraces the Future While US Counterparts Fight It," *Techdirt*, October 22, 2012, https://www.techdirt.com/articles /20121018/00360120743/korean-music-industry-embraces-future-while-us-counter parts-fight-it.shtml.

75. Organisation for Economic Co-operation and Development, *OECD Communications Outlook 2013* (Paris: OECD Publishing, 2013), 178, doi: http://dx.doi.org /10.1787/comms_outlook-2013-en.

76. Malecki and Moriset, *Digital Economy*, 190.

77. John Howkins coined the term *creative economy* with an emphasis on creativity as a resource for economic production in the postindustrial era: "Economics generally deals with the problem of how individuals and societies satisfy their wants, which are infinite, with resources that are finite; it is thus primarily about the allocation of scarce resources. . . . Ideas are not limited in the same way as tangible goods, and the nature of their economy is different." John Howkins, *The Creative Economy: How People Make Money from Ideas* (New York: Penguin, 2002), 3.

78. Alf Chatell, *Creative Value in the Digital Era: Achieving Success through Insight, Imagination and Innovation* (New York: New York University Press, 1998), 13.

79. Andrew Ross, *Nice Work If You Can Get It* (New York: New York University Press, 2010), 16.

CHAPTER 2: K-POP FROM LIVE TELEVISION TO SOCIAL MEDIA

1. Gang Tae-yeong and Yun Tae-jin, *Hanguk TV yeneung, orak peurogeuraemui byeoncheongwa baljeon* [A history of TV entertainment and variety show programs in Korea] (Seoul: Haneul, 2002), 370–71.

2. Ibid., 75.

3. Jeong Sun-il and Jang Han-seong, *Hanguk TV 40nyeonui baljachwi* [Forty-year history of Korean TV] (Seoul: Haneul Academy, 2000), 209.

4. Ibid., 284.

5. Korean Cable TV Association, *Keibeul TV yeoksa, 1995–2015* [Cable TV history, 1995–2015] (Seoul: Korean Cable TV Association, 2015), 22.

6. Gang and Yun, *Hanguk TV*.

7. Yi Dong-hu, "Transmedia hwangyeonggwa 'Me-TV'-ui uimi" [Transmedia environment and the implications of "Me-TV"], in *TV ihuui television* [Television after TV], ed. Hanguk bangsong hakheo munhwayeonguhoe (Seoul: Hanul Academy, 2012), 62.

8. Auslander, *Liveness*, 14.

9. Lynn Spigel, *Make Room for TV: Television and the Family Ideal in Postwar America* (Chicago: University of Chicago Press, 1992), 138.

10. Korean Cable TV Association, Keibeul TV yeoksa, 37.

11. Korea's first satellite TV service was introduced on July 1, 1996, by KBS. The station used the Korea-made satellite Mugunghwa, with a DBS (direct broadcast satellite) system, as a way of reaching out to a wide global audience that had previously had poor reception.

12. Yi Dong-hu, "Transmedia hwangyeonggwa 'Me-TV'-ui uimi," 62.

13. Gim Gi-beom, "Gim Gi-beom SM Entertainment A&R direkteowa inteobyu" [Interview with Gim Gi-beom, director, artist and repertoire department, SM Entertainment], *Hangyeong News*, January 10, 2013, http://jobnstory.com/news/view.html?section=7609&category=7613&no=1224.

14. *Sseoljeon*, episode 17, JTBC (broadcast June 20, 2013).

15. *Ingigayo* did not air for approximately half a year, from October 18, 1993, to April 23, 1994.

16. Son Nam-won, *YG-neun dareuda* [YG is different] (Seoul: Influential, 2015), 77.

17. *The Show*'s chart system was introduced at the start of its fourth season on October 28, 2014, and was named "the Show Choice."

18. First aired February 14, 2012, on MBC, the show has a charting system that combines digital sales (streaming and downloads), physical sales, online voting by netizens, and rankings by professionals and expert judges.

19. First aired in 2004 on the Mnet cable channel.

20. Auslander, *Liveness*, 61.

21. In the case of Japan, there are long-running music chart shows, such as *Music Station* (1986–present), on Asahi TV, but they cater to all generations rather than focus-

ing on idol music, which appeals to a narrow teenage viewership, as most K-pop music chart shows do.

22. Gwon Seok-jeong, "Seo Tae-ji-wa 'K-Papseuta' geurigo 'Seupeiseu Gonggam'" [Seo Tae-ji, "K-pop Star" and "Space Gong-gam"], *Tenasia*, April 21, 2014, http://tenasia .hankyung.com/archives/244381.

23. According to Nielsen Korea, the major music chart shows on KBS, MBC, SBS, and Mnet in the 2010s all suffered from poor ratings, ranging from 1.4 to 3.0 percent. Nielsen, "Nielsen TV Audience Measurement," n.d., accessed March 23, 2015, http:// www.agbnielsen.co.kr/.

24. *Sseoljeon,* episode 17, JTBC, June 20, 2013.

25. With the rise in global popularity of K-pop, worldwide streaming services such as Spotify, Apple Music, AccuRadio, and China's QQ channel also have created K-pop channels. According to a Bloomberg article, streaming of Korean music doubled in the first half of 2017, "with listeners in the U.S. making up one-quarter of the audience." Kim Sohee, "4.7 Billion K-pop Industry."

26. Gwon Seok-jeong, "Gayopeuro sunwije sihaeng handal . . . aidol wiju bangsong yeojeon" [Music programs still centered on idols since music charts were introduced a month ago], *Tenasia*, May 23, 2013, http://tenasia.hankyung.com/archives/134733.

27. *Sseoljeon,* episode 17, JTBC, June 20, 2013.

28. Korean journalist Bak Chang-u, prior to Kim Gura, pointed out the close partnership between terrestrial television stations and entertainment companies in terms of how they support their mutual interests; while entertainment companies need top-of-the-chart TV shows to promote their new songs, albums, and singers, TV stations need to sustain partnerships with entertainment companies in order to invite popular idols to appear in their variety shows. Bak Chang-u, "Sunwijega jeongdap?" [Is the music chart show the answer?], *OhmyStar*, March 22, 2013, http://star.ohmynews .com/NWS_Web/OhmyStar/at_pg_m.aspx?CNTN_CD=A0001846516&CMPT_CD =TAG_M.

29. Since the trio was promoting two songs simultaneously, their prerecording session for one song began at 8:00 a.m. and for the other at 11:00 a.m. There were still six hours to be spent in the TV studio until the live broadcast of the show at 6:00 p.m. *The TaeTiSeo,* episode 5, Onstyle, September 30, 2014.

30. One of the Korean words that have no exact English counterpart, it roughly translates as "lovely or cute gestures and words." According to *The K-pop Dictionary*, which lists key lingo used in K-pop fandom, the word refers to "a display of affection through various expressions such as making cute gestures or speaking in baby talk. While strongly associated with feminine traits, male KPOP idols often display these affections, but it is not frowned upon." Kang Woosung [Gang U-seong], *The K-pop Dictionary* (New Ampersand, 2016), 10.

31. Bak Su-jeong et al., "Eumakbangsong 24si, ganghaenggun aidol donghaenggi"

[Spending 24 hours on a long march with idols for the music program], January 29, 2015, https://storyfunding.kakao.com/episode/365.

32. *Music Core,* aired live on April 20, 2013, temporarily announced the winner for the given week as K.will, then retracted its announcement with a correction that the boy band Infinite had won first place. This was due to the mixing of live voting results between the two top contenders.

33. My multiple requests to interview the *Music Core* chief producer went unanswered.

34. Exceptions to this pattern exist in some instances when influential artists managed by powerful entertainment companies such as YG make their comeback stage or debut. For instance, G-Dragon's comeback stage for his song "Black" required elaborate props, such as glass panels and shower effects, which could not have been set up and removed during the live broadcasting time. Similarly, the debut for YG's new boy band Winner for the double title songs "Empty" and "Coloring" was prerecorded not because they were rookies but because their performance required intricate spiral staircases that took a long time to set up and remove.

35. Auslander, *Liveness*, 11.

36. Ibid.

37. The definition is from Auslander, who terms this "classic liveness." Ibid., 61.

38. Gim Dong-hwan, "MBC, 'Mudaeeseo imman ppeonggeutaneun aidol toechul'" [MBC will expel idols who lip-sync on stage], *Segye Ilbo,* July 1, 2014, http://www.segye .com/content/html/2014/07/01/20140701002566.html.

39. Auslander, *Liveness*, 61.

40. The ranking system for SBS's *Ingigayo* is quite similar to that of *Music Core*, whereas for KBS's *Music Bank* rank is computed by a combination of digital record sales (65 percent), physical record sales (5 percent), the frequency at which the song was played in the media (20 percent), and a survey of viewers' preference (10 percent).

41. Although the final numerical scores are computed as a combination of the viewers' committee's prevoting, record sales, music video score, and voting in front of a live audience and the performers, nobody gets to know precisely how many votes each contender received in the past hour. This could be in part because revealing the total number of votes could reveal the revenue MBC has generated, since each vote costs fans 100 won, roughly equivalent to ten cents.

42. Lawrence Grossberg, "The Media Economy of Rock Culture: Cinema, Postmodernity and Authenticity," quoted in Auslander, *Liveness*, 90.

43. KBS World is a special channel that airs KBS programs to overseas audiences with subtitles. It has been in operation since 2003.

44. Im Hyeon-wu, "Eumaksijang sunwi bomyeon jeojakgwon seonjingunk boyeoyo" [The rankings of the music market size show which countries have advanced copyrights protection], *Hankyeong News,* February 3, 2017, http://news.hankyung.com/ article/2017020395501.

45. Three members of EXO—Chris, Luhan, and Tao—have left the band since 2014, making it a nine-member band. But during the 2013 recording of ASC, all twelve members of the group were present.

46. Arirang TV, "After School Club: About the Program," n.d., accessed March 2, 2015, http://arirang.co.kr/Tv2/Tv_About_Content.asp?PROG_CODE=TVCR0688& MENU_CODE=101718&code=Po3&sys_lang=Eng.

47. Bak Hui-ju, e-mail interview by author, May 4, 2015.

48. Ibid.

49. Sohn Jie-Ae, "The Worldwide Reach of K-pop," lecture, K-pop and Its Global Reach Symposium, April 18, 2015, University of California, Santa Barbara.

50. Ibid.

51. Bak Hui-ju, e-mail interview by author, May 7, 2015.

52. The Lee Myung-bak (Yi Myeong-bak) administration (2008–13) established the Presidential Council on Nation Branding, which openly claimed to observe the principles of the marketplace. The alignment between national policy and corporate marketing campaigns was in large part supportive of the administration's national branding campaign known as "Global Korea"; to practice this principle successfully, in 2011, Lee's administration announced the Agenda for the Enhancement of Global Competitiveness of Korean Popular Culture (Daejung munhwa saneop geulobeol gyeongjaengnyeok ganghwa bang-an), part of which included mobilizing K-pop as a "centerpiece of the 'New Korean Wave'" that is now "significantly influential to the national image of South Korea." Ministry of Culture, Sports, and Tourism, "Daejungmunhwa saneop geullobeol gyeongjaengnyeok ganghwa bangan" [Agenda for the enhancement of global competitiveness of Korean popular culture], June 23, 2011, 1–3, http://www.mcst.go.kr/web/s_ notice/press/pressView.jsp?pSeq=11436.

53. Sohn Jie-Ae, "Worldwide Reach of K-pop."

54. Charlene Jimenez, e-mail interview by author, March 15, 2015.

55. Lauren Sheng, telephone interview by author, May 18, 2015.

56. Sohn Jie-Ae, "Worldwide Reach of K-pop."

57. Bak Hui-ju, e-mail interview by author, May 7, 2015.

58. Ibid.

59. Sohn Jie-Ae, interview by author, November 12, 2014.

60. Ibid.

61. The precursor to this show was *The M-Wave*, which changed its name to *Simply K-pop* in 2012.

62. Arirang TV, "Simply K-pop: About the Program," n.d., accessed March 20, 2015, http://www.arirang.com/Tv2/Tv_About_Content.asp?PROG_CODE=TVCR0636 &MENU_CODE=101506&code=Po2&sys_lang=Eng.

63. Sohn Jie-Ae, interview by author, November 12, 2014.

64. "About *K-populous* (Past Program)," Arirang TV, n.d., accessed December 30,

2017, http://www.arirang.com/Tv2/Tv_About_Content.asp?PROG_CODE=TVCR0727 &MENU_CODE=101893&code=Po2&sys_lang=Eng. Because of low viewership, perhaps stemming from the lack of popular idol stars who attract large numbers of viewers, the show was discontinued in the summer of 2015.

65. Sohn Jie-Ae, interview by author, November 12, 2014.

CHAPTER 3: SIMULATING LIVENESS IN K-POP MUSIC VIDEOS

1. Consider, for example, Sin Seung-hun's music video "Invisible Love." Aired on *Totojeul* on November 2, 1996, it features a popular actress, Chae Si-ra, as the star but is otherwise low production and low budget, as it mostly consists of close-up shots of her face expressing various emotions that correspond with the mood of the lyrics.

2. Psy's "Gangnam Style" forced YouTube to reconfigure its viewing capability, since according to the *Economist* article, YouTube would have been unable to count any higher than 2,147,483,647 plays. "How 'Gangnam Style' Broke YouTube's Counter," *Economist*, December 10, 2014, http://www.economist.com/blogs/economist-explains/2014/12/economist-explains-6.

3. Fred McConnell, "YouTube Is 10 Years Old: The Evolution of Online Video," *Guardian*, February 13, 2015, http://www.theguardian.com/technology/2015/feb/13/youtube-10-years-old-evolution-of-online-video.

4. Matthew Garrahan, "Google Invests in YouTube Studio in LA," *Financial Times*, July 12, 2013, http://www.ft.com/cms/s/2/3f4c846a-e9c1-11e2-bf03-00144feabdc0.html #slide0.

5. Of course, there are other reasons for YouTube's soaring popularity. For instance, Vernalis points out that "part of what separates YouTube from other media are the clips' brevity and the ways they're often encountered through exchange with other people: a clip's interest derives from its association with colleagues, family, friends, and contexts within communities. Often clips get forwarded because there's an intensity of affect that can't be assimilated." Carol Vernalis, *Unruly Media: YouTube, Music Video, and the New Digital Cinema* (Oxford: Oxford University Press, 2013), 9.

6. Ibid., 181.

7. Brian Robbins, the founder of Awesomeness TV, has already pointed out the parallels between YouTube and MTV in their ability to popularize music videos: "[Online video] is very much like cable TV was 25 years ago." Garrahan, "Google Invests."

8. Beebe and Middleton, *Medium Cool*, 2–3.

9. Dickinson, "Music Video," 13.

10. Ibid., 14.

11. Ibid.

12. Vernalis, *Unruly Media*, 277.

13. Ibid., 15.

14. Epstein with Turnbull, "Girls' Generation?," 317.

15. Releasing teaser images of music videos is a growing trend in K-pop, but the most prominent examples foreshadow the general concept and mood of the album. Those for EXO's *EXODUS* album and Winner's *Exit* are prime examples of how the industry has come to invest heavily in teasers. EXO's ten members all had their twenty-second teasers shot in global locations, such as Colorado, Almaty, London, Lyon, Marseille, Edinburgh, Barcelona, Arizona, Berlin, and Yunnan. The initial letters of these cities and states together spell out the album's title song, "Call Me Baby."

16. The most distinctive examples to showcase the seriality of videos are Super Junior's songs "This is Love" (https://www.youtube.com/watch?v=utmykx9RUEw) and "Evanescence" (https://www.youtube.com/watch?v=dzhOqwF8qHg), released in 2014. Both music videos were shot in the same location with the same idols, but whereas the first shows a pristine urban loft space, the second shows how the same space has been trashed while the characters reminisce about the happy days featured in the first video. Winner also played with the notion of intertextuality with their 2016 release "Baby Baby" (https://www.youtube.com/watch?v=jBBy2p5EQhs) and "I'm Young" (https://www.youtube.com/watch?v=P79G22cJe74). While "Baby Baby" features a clip from "I'm Young," "I'm Young" begins with the song "Baby Baby" as an introduction to the video.

17. As can be gleaned from the 1930 article published in the daily newspaper *Joseon Ilbo*, the Bae Gu-ja Dance Theater Troupe, a pioneer troupe in introducing revue dance to Korea after 1926, led a busy professional life, flying to Japan to shoot a movie after giving a recital in Seoul. "Bonbodokja udaeui Baeguja muyongdan gongyeon" [Deals for readers: Bae Guja dance theater troupe performance], *Joseon Ilbo*, November 4, 1930, 5.

18. Cha U-jin, interview by author, April 23, 2015, Seoul, Korea; An In-yong, "K-pop Needs a Diagnosis," *Hangyeore* 866 (June 27, 2011), http://h21.hani.co.kr/arti/culture/culture_general/29888.html.

19. Gwon Seok-jeong, "Geudeuri bon K-pop 1 DSign Music 'keipap jakgogeneun beopchigi jonjaehaji anneunda'" [K-pop according to outsiders' perspective part 1, DSign Music: there are no set rules in K-pop composition], Tenasia, October 10, 2014, http://tenasia.hankyung.com/archives/339585.

20. It is no wonder that many Hollywood adaptations of Broadway musicals, such as *Oklahoma!* (1955), extol what is perceived as the quintessential American national identity. According to Kathaleen Boche, "Such qualities include rugged individualism, patriotism, expansionism, the provider/protector ideal, and improvisational ingenuity." Kathaleen Boche, "Hatchets and Hairbrushes: Dance, Gender, and Improvisational Ingenuity in Cold War Western Musicals," in *The Oxford Handbook of Dance and the Popular Screen*, ed. Melissa Blanco Borelli (Oxford: Oxford University Press, 2014), 338.

21. Yi Eun-jeong, "Dagukjeok jakgokga SM gok hamkke mandeunda: K-pop jejak jinhwa" [Multinational composers make SM songs together: The evolution of K-pop producing], *Yonhap News*, October 6, 2013, http://www.yonhapnews.co.kr/culture/2013/10/06/0901000000AKR20131006067700005.HTML.

22. "Dokchangjeogin aidieoro gayogyeui heureumeul bakkueonoeun SM ateu direkteo Min Hui-jin" [SM art director Min Hui-jin changes trends in music market with her creative ideas], *Soul Dresser*, accessed December 16, 2014, http://blog.daum.net/_blog/Blog TypeView.do?blogid=03SAW&articleno=3410&categoryId=0&regdt=20140127011701.

23. Jang Seong-eun, "YG Entertainment keurieitibeu direkteo Jang Seong-eun siljangeul mannada" [Meeting YG's creative director Jang Seong-eun], interview, *Hanwha Day's*, October 23, 2013, http://blog.hanwhadays.com/2194.

24. Gim Su-jin, *"Musaekeuro bijeonaeneun osaek imiji miusik bidio gamdok Jang Jae-heok"* [Painting colorful image with no colors: MV director Jang Jae-hyeok], *Scene Playbill*, November 2008, 28.

25. David Savran, "Trafficking in Transnational Brands: The New 'Broadway-Style' Musical," *Theater Survey* 55, no. 3 (September 2014): 320–21.

26. Ibid., 321.

27. Bak Ji-hun, "3000 eokwon miusikeol sijang-ui bitgwa grimja" [Lights and shadows of a 300 billion won musical market], *Luxmen*, March 7, 2013, http://luxmen.mk.co .kr/view.php?sc=51100011&cm=Life&year=2013&no=173086&relatedcode=.

28. Lee Hyun Jung [Yi Hyeon-jeong], "Broadway as the Superior 'Other': Situating South Korean Theater in the Era of Globalization," *Journal of Popular Culture* 45, no. 2 (2012): 337.

29. Ibid., 338.

30. Gim Seong-hui, "Hanguk chochangi miusikeol undong yeongu" [A study of early Korean musicals], *Hanguk Geukyesulhakhoe Hanguk Yesul Yeongu* 14 (2001): 86.

31. Gim Hui-jeong, "Hanguk myujikeorui byeoncheongwa myujikeol uisangui teukseonge gwanhan gochal / A consideration on the change of Korean musical and the characteristic of music costume [*sic*]," [bilingual], *Bogsigmunhwayeongu / Research Journal of the Costume Culture* 18, no. 6 (2010): 1116.

32. Aiwa Ong and Donald Nonini, introduction to *Ungrounded Empires: The Cultural Politics of Modern Chinese Transnationalism*, ed. Aiwa Ong and Donald Nonini (New York: Routledge, 1997), 15.

33. Joo Jeongsuk, "Transnationalization of Korean Popular Culture and the Rise of 'Pop Nationalism' in Korea," *Journal of Popular Culture* 44, no. 3 (2011): 496.

34. Another prominent example of Afro-Asian collaboration stems from K-pop boy band BIGBANG's 2012–13 Alive World Tour, where black musicians performed live musical accompaniment.

35. John Seabrook, "Factory Girls," *New Yorker*, October 8, 2012, http://www.new yorker.com/magazine/2012/10/08/factory-girls-2.

36. Jo Jong-won, "SM Entertainment, myujikeoreseoneun ajik meoreotda" [SM Entertainment, still a long way to go in musicals], *Newsis*, June 17, 2014, http://www.new sis .com/ar_detail/view.html?ar_id=NISX20140616_0012985416&cID=10601&pID=10600.

37. Ibid.

38. The *Folies Bergère*'s multiple reincarnations include two filmic versions of the revue under the title *Folies Bergère de Paris* (1935), *Folies-Bergère* (1956), *Énigme aux Folies Bergère* (1956), and *La Totale!* (1991).

39. "Ziegfield Follies—Trailer 1," YouTube, July 8, 2014, https://www.youtube.com/watch?v=aO_wY10l0Zo.

40. Thomas Hischak, *Through the Screen Door: What Happened to the Broadway Musical When It Went to Hollywood* (Lanham, MD: Scarecrow Press, 2004), 93.

41. Dickinson, "Music Video," 14.

42. Hischak, *Through the Screen Door,* 104.

43. The term is taken from the 1946 film, which introduces individual acts with an image of a turning book page; this close-up shot of the page shows the title of the act and the performers featured in it. It is in the segment called "This Heart of Mine," with Fred Astaire and Lucille Bremmer, that the subtitle "A Dance Story" appears.

44. Gim Yeong-hui, "Ilje gangjeomgi rebyuchum yeongu" [Study of revue dance during the Japanese colonial period], *Gongyeon-gwa Ribyu* 65 (June 2009): 40.

45. Ibid., 42.

46. Mun-meong-ui theqoo, "Tiffany Liked the Concept of 'Twinkle,'" accessed December 15, 2014, http://new.theqoo.net/3648157.

47. *Zradeo,* [Original Korean title not available] "TaeTiSeo's 'Twinkle' Is a Gem, but How Successful Is It?," n.d., accessed November 15, 2014, link no longer available.

48. *The TaeTiSeo*, episode 5, Onstyle (CJ E&M Cable Channel), September 30, 2014.

49. Sheldon Patinkin, *No Legs, No Jokes, No Chance: A History of the American Musical Theater* (Evanston, IL: Northwestern University Press, 2008), 17.

50. YG Family, "G-Dragon 'Niga mwonde' myujikbidio V.I.P chwaryeong yeongsang eomnodeu bangbeop annae" [G Dragon, "Who You?" music video: V.I.P. how to upload footage], October 6, 2013, http://www.ygfamily.com/notice/NList.asp?LANG-DRAGONIV=K&IDX=5263&STYPE=B.

51. Im Se-yeong, "G-Dragon singok 'niga mwonde' myujik bidio chwaryeongh—yeonjang" [Shooting of G-Dragon's new music video "Who You?" takes place], Newsen, October 5, 2013, http://www.newsen.com/news_view.php?uid=201310052312132610.

52. Indeed, when he arrived at the studio for rehearsal, he was wearing a different set of clothes.

53. "Making of 'Who You?' MV," YouTube, January 20, 2014, https://www.youtube.com/watch?v=DU61Cplg57k.

54. Adrian Heathfield and Teching Hsieh, *Out of Now: The Liveworks of Teching Hsieh* (London: Live Art Development Agency; Cambridge, MA: MIT Press, 2009), 17.

55. There are roughly five performance pieces, which can be categorized as one-year performances. From 1978 to 1979, he performed *Cage*; from 1980 to 1981, he performed *Time Clock*; from 1981 to 1982, *Outdoor*, in which he did not go into a man-made structure for an entire year; from 1983 to 1984, *Rope*, in which he lived a whole

year tied by a rope to another artist; finally, from 1985 to 1986, he spent a whole year not performing art, which he dubbed *No Art*.

56. Heathfield and Hsieh, *Out of Now*, 22.

57. O Se-hun, interview by author, July 24, 2014, Seoul, Korea.

58. "Urban Dream Capsule Makes United States Debut at Sears on State Presented by Performing Arts Chicago," PRNewswire, Chicago, March 5, 2001, http://searsholdings.mediaroom.com/index.php?s=16310&item=24816.

59. Yi Jeong-a, "G-Dragon, Niga mwonde myubiseo boyu jadongcha gonggae" [G-Dragon reveals his own car in a new music video "Who You?"], ETV Korea, November 13, 2013, http://etv.sbs.co.kr/news/news_content.jsp?article_id=E10004792930.

60. "G-Dragon ('Who You?') M/V," YouTube, November 13, 2013, https://www.youtube.com/watch?v=doFK7Eanm3I.

61. Ibid.

62. Shannon Winnubst, *Way Too Cool: Selling Out Race and Ethics* (New York: Columbia University Press, 2015), 103.

63. G-Dragon's penchant for visual aesthetics expressed through his fashion statements and music videos like "Who You?" led to collaboration with Korean and international artists that culminated in the exhibition titled "PEACEMINUSONE: Beyond the Stage" at the Seoul Museum of Art from June 9 to August 23, 2015. Among some two hundred items on display were works by SoA, Kwon O-sang (Gwon O-sang), Park Hyung-geun (Bak Hyeong-geun), Bang & Lee, Michael Scoggins, Fabien Verschaere, Universal Everything, Quayola, Sophie Clements, and James Clar.

CHAPTER 4: HOLOGRAM STARS GREET LIVE AUDIENCE

1. "Christie Projectors Make the First Holographic Opera a Reality," Christie, n.d., accessed January 12, 2015, http://www.christiedigital.co.uk/emea/business/visual-solutions-case-studies/visual-solutions-application-stories/Pages/telesio-holographic-opera.aspx.

2. Rex Santus, "Windows Holographic: Microsoft Goes Full Throttle into Virtual Reality," *Mashable*, January 21, 2015, http://mashable.com/2015/01/21/windows-holographic/.

3. Tim Bradshaw, "Apple Hires Leading Virtual Reality Researcher," *Financial Times*, January 21, 2016, http://www.ft.com/intl/cms/s/0/9358ba1e-c07f-11e5-846f-79b0e3d20eaf.html.

4. Todd Haselton and Josh Lipton, "See How Apple Will Erase the Line between Reality and Your iPhone," CNBC.com, August 29, 2017, https://www.cnbc.com/2017/08/29/iphone-8-augmented-reality-apps-from-ikea-food-network-and-more.html.

5. Park's presidency was supposed to last until February 24, 2018, but because of her impeachment it ended prematurely on March 10, 2017.

6. Shannon Steen, "The Creativity Complex," unpublished manuscript, accessed November 1, 2016.

7. The ministry was renamed the Ministry of Science, Technology, Information and Technology on July 20, 2017, as the incumbent Moon Jae-in (Mun Jae-in) administration wished to separate itself from the legacy of Park Geun-hye.

8. In the fall of 2016, South Korea was plagued with a corruption scandal in which President Park Geun-hye and her confidants and aides were implicated in using coercive measures to extract political funds under various pretenses of pursuing creative economy projects. One such scandal involved Cha Eun-taek, a former producer of K-pop music videos and other large-scale performances. Cha squandered government funds to create gymnastics exercises that were supposed to be distributed broadly among South Korean citizens. See Gim Tae-gyu, "Creative Economy Loses Steam," *Korea Times*, December 1, 2016, http://www.koreatimes.co.kr/www/common/vpage-pt.asp?categoryco de=123&newsidx=219313.

9. Only in 2015 did a consortium of sixteen South Korean companies create the "tabletop holographic display" in the form of a floating Rubik's cube. This was arguably the first 360-degree color hologram; up until that point, holograms were a 2-D projection that gave an optical illusion of 3-D. Christina de Looper, "Korean Researchers Say They've Created The World's First True 3D Hologram," *Tech Times*, December 3, 2015, http://www.techtimes.com/articles/113267/20151203/korean-researchers-theyve -create-worlds-first-true-3d-hologram.htm.

10. Yu Jae-hyeok, "SM Lee Su-man hoejang 'SM-i saenggakaneun miraeneun selleobeuriti, roboteu-ui sesang'" [Future as envisioned by SM is one filled with celebrities and robots, says SM CEO Lee Su-man], *Hangyeong News*, October 22, 2015, http://www.hankyung.com/news/app/newsview.php?aid=2015102203541.

11. Bak Su-hyeong, "Jeongbu '2020nyeon hollogeuraem segye choego doegetda'" [Government claims that it will become the world leader in hologram industry by 2020], ZDNetKorea, August 27, 2014, http://www.zdnet.co.kr/news/news_view.asp?art ice_id=20140827140301. Because of the visible ties between the Park Geun-hye administration and YG Entertainment, there is much speculation about how much YG Entertainment owes its success to the protection and favoritism of Park Geun-hye's close confidant Choe Sun-sil, who was at the center of the corruption scandal.

12. The district emerged as a marketplace in the eighteenth century when a hybrid market (*nanjeon*) appeared. In 1905 Gwangjang Company started a much more organized operation in wholesale distribution in the district.

13. The stadium was first built in 1925 during the colonial era as Gyeongseong Stadium; its name was changed to Seoul Stadium in 1945 when Japanese colonial rule ended.

14. Dixon, *Digital Performance*, 215.

15. Ibid.

16. Don Ihde, *Bodies in Technology* (Minneapolis: University of Minnesota Press, 2002), xi.

17. Dixon, *Digital Performance*, 215.

18. Corpos Informaticos Research Group, 1999 "Entrasite" Database Entry, Digital Performance Archive, quoted in Dixon, *Digital Performance*, 236.

19. Emma-Lee Moss, "Robots, Rental Popstars and Spotify Domination: Is This the Future of Music?" *Guardian*, accessed January 28, 2015, http://www.theguardian.com/music/2015/jan/26/emmy-the-great-music-future-predictions.

20. Ji Su-hui, "Jeongbu, hollogeuraem saneobyukseong bakcha" [Korean government plans to stimulate hologram industry], Korean Economy TV, August 27, 2014.

21. Yi Jeong-a, "Psy, BIGBANG, 2NE1 hollogeuraem gongyeon, ilbone cheot seon" [Psy, BIGBANG, 2NE1 hologram debuts in Japan], SBS News, January 22, 2014, http://news.sbs.co.kr/news/endPage.do?news_id=N1002195952.

22. Peter Days, "Korea Change," Global Business, BBC World Service, March 9, 2014, http://www.bbc.co.uk/programmes/p01t4qqc.

23. Yu Kun-ha [Yu Geon-ha], "Korea Can't Just Order Up Creative Economy," *Korea Herald*, May 31, 2013, http://www.koreaherald.com/view.php?ud=20130531000240.

24. As of December 2017, former president Park Geun-hye's corruption trials are still ongoing. The main players in the corruption scandal, Cha Eun-taek (former K-pop music video artist) and Choe Sun-sil (Park Geun-hye's close confidant who acted as the de facto president behind the scenes), were said to have close ties with numerous K-pop artists and entertainment companies, fueling wild speculations about the K-pop industry's direct and indirect involvement in the scandal.

25. For a more detailed account of the appropriation of Psy's global fame by Park Geun-hye, see Keith Howard, "Politics, Parodies, and the Paradox of Psy's 'Gangnam Style,'" *Romanian Journal of Sociological Studies* 1 (2015): 13–29.

26. The Korean government's investment seemed to pay off: in December 2015, a team of sixteen parties consisting of researchers, development groups, and financial backers led by Korea's Electronic and Telecommunication Research Institute (ETRI) triumphantly claimed that they had succeeded in developing "the world's first 360-degree color hologram. The tabletop holographic display can be viewed all the way around in full color, and the view changes from every angle." Using high-powered multicolored lasers, the floating hologram allows visibility from any angle, 360 degrees around, whereas the previous holographic invention out of MIT had a visible radius of 20 degrees. Cloe Olewitz, "Korean Scientists Have Developed a Legitimate 3D Hologram You Can View from Any Angle," *Digital Trends*, December 7, 2015, http://www.digitaltrends.com/cool-tech/researchers-develop-real-floating-3d-hologram/.

27. "President Park Sets the Tone for PP14," ITU News, November 6, 2014, https://itunews.itu.int/En/5547-President-Park-sets-the-tone-for-PP14.note.aspx.

28. David Harvey, "A Brief History of Neoliberalism," in *The Globalization Reader*, ed. Franck J. Lechner and John Boli, 5th ed. (Malden, MA: Wiley, 2015), 72.

29. Diana S, "K-pop Label SM Entertainment to Open 3D Hologram Theater at

Japanese Theme Park Huis Ten Bosch," *KpopStarz*, February 23, 2015, http://www.kpop
starz.com/articles/170894/20150203/sm-hologram-theater-japan.htm.

30. Before SM Entertainment opened SMTOWN at COEX Artium in January
2015, the theater had been rented out to various companies since 2010 for musicals,
special conference events, and other stage plays. Since January 2015, SM Entertainment
has been the only company contracted to use the space. It is used mostly for hologram
shows but occasionally for special events, such as the New Culture Technology 2016
Conference on January 27, 2016, where the company's president, Lee Su-man, made a
presentation about future projects, such as the launching of the new boy band NTC and
the digital music channel STATION.

31. SM Entertainment advertised broadly that *School Oz* was the first hologram
musical in the world to apply floating technology on a transparent screen installed to
forty-five degrees on a stage. Yu Jae-hyeok, "SM Lee Su-man hoejang."

32. Gwon Seok-jeong, "SMTOWN COEX Artium jikjeop gaseo noraboni" [First-
hand experience of SMTOWN COEX Artium], *Hangyeong News*, accessed May 31,
2015, http://news.hankyung.com/article/2015011905894.

33. O Dae-seok, "Lee Su-man Yang Hyun Suk, hollogeuraem gongyeoneseo daebak
kkum kiwo" [Lee Su-man, Yang Hyun Suk dream of big success in hologram business],
Business Post, February 24, 2015, http://www.businesspost.co.kr/news/articleView.html
?idxno=9795.

34. In February 2015 a total of 1,200 people visited SMTOWN, whereas in May
2015 the number of visitors had grown to 1,700. Hong Jeong-pyo, *Kiwoom Jeungkwon
Report*, May 10, 2015, 1. The numbers are for the total number of visitors to SMTOWN
in general, not only to the hologram theater.

35. The lack of the projected audience, mostly in their teens, is partly due to the fact
that the ticket price was set high for teen consumers—approximately seventy US dollars.
If one signed up for SM Passport, a membership card to the SM Entertainment group,
then a discount ticket at the price of twenty US dollars was offered.

36. Max of TVXQ appeared in a proper live musical, *In the Heights*, in November
2015, which followed his act in the hologram musical *School Oz*.

37. Néstor García Canclini, *Hybrid Cultures: Strategies for Entering and Leaving*
(Minneapolis: University of Minnesota Press, 1995), 2–3.

38. Daniel Black, "The Virtual Idol: Producing and Consuming Digital Femininity,"
in *Idols and Celebrity in Japanese Media Culture,* ed. Patrick Galbraith and Jason Karlin
(New York: Palgrave Macmillan, 2012), 209.

39. Suho's character Hans, who transforms into a wolf, conjures up the music video
of EXO's mega-hit song "Wolf." In this video, members of EXO simulate the movement
and the howling of wolves, the performance of which is replicated in *School Oz*.

40. John Seabrook interviewed Tiffany, a member of Girls' Generation, who shared
her views on the importance of proper education provided by SM Entertainment: "I

think we've been brought up to be really careful and to take responsibility in our actions, in order to be in this position." John Seabrook, *The Song Machine: Inside the Hit Factory* (New York: Norton, 2015), 163.

41. Cha, interview by author, April 23, 2015.

42. The general public's perception of SM Entertainment idols as paragons of respectability has been well supported for the most part, especially in comparison to the public's perception of YG Entertainment's idols as troublemakers. However, the image of the SM idols has been tainted by a series of recent scandals, such as SHINee's Onew being accused of sexual harassment in 2017 and Super Junior's Kangin (Gang-in) being repeatedly arrested for drunk driving. But the most tragic event to have disrupted the fantasies of SM idols as perfect role models came when Jonghyun (Jong-hyeon), a member of SM boyband SHINee who battled depression, committed suicide on December 18, 2017.

43. The core idea of cultural technology is that "stars should be made, not born, using a sophisticated system of artistic development." Seabrook, *Song Machine*, 151. According to Lee, the term shares a strong resonance with the world of technology: "SM Entertainment and I see culture as a type of technology. But cultural technology is much more exquisite and complex than information technology" (152).

44. Yu Jae-hyeok, "SM Lee Su-man hoejang."

45. Ibid.

46. As of February 9, 2015, there were fewer than four hundred thousand views of the music video. Given that most of the musical's idols' videos easily garner over a million views in less than twenty-four hours, this is an extremely low number.

CHAPTER 5: LIVE K-POP CONCERTS
AND THEIR DIGITAL DOUBLES

1. Korea Creative Content Agency [KOCCA], "Gungnae eumak saneop hyeonhwang" [The state of the domestic music market], Music Industry White Paper, 2011, 101, published on KOCCA website December 17, 2012, http://www.kocca.kr/cop/bbs/view/B0000146/1779432.do?searchCnd=&searchWrd=&cateTp1=&cateTp2=&useAt=&menuNo=201826&categorys=0&subcate=0&cateCode=&type=&instNo=0&questionTp=&uf_Setting=&recovery=&pageIndex=12.

2. The three 2010 concerts were the Eighth Korean Music Festival at the Hollywood Bowl (May 1, 2010), the Wonder Girls World Tour in various US cities (June 4–July 16, 2010), and the SMTOWN Live World Tour at Staples Center, Los Angeles (September 4, 2010).

3. Stimulated by Super Junior's success in South America, KOCCA closely studied the market and generated a report in 2015, which mentions that South America is the most promising market for its avid consumption of large-scale live concerts, surpassing the European demand by far. The document also noted that South America is mainly divided into two cultural blocs—Spanish speaking and Portuguese speaking—so that it

is easy to move from one Spanish-speaking country to another. KOCCA, "Report on the Current State of the Korean Music Export and Overseas Agencies," June 1, 2015, 113.

4. Ibid.

5. Ibid., 118.

6. "*Pungmuneuro deuleotsso*" [Heard it through the grapevine], episode 15, Channel A, January 26, 2016

7. Half of the audience, seven hundred thousand people, were supposed to be Japanese, but compared to the Alive tour of 2012–13, more Chinese cities were added to the stop: YG's emphasis is on the Chinese market.

8. Grace Danbi Hong, "BIGBANG Drops Blockbuster Trailer for 'Made' World Tour," MWave, April 17, 2015, http://m.mwave.interest.me/en/kpop-news/article-print /91341/.

9. Gim Hyeon-sik, "Daechebulga daseon namja, iraeseo BIGBANG BIGBANG haneunguna" [Irreplaceable five men—BIGBANG is BIGBANG], No Cut News, April 27, 2017, http://www.nocutnews.co.kr/news/4404557.

10. Gim A-reum, "BIGBANG, 3nyeonui gongbaekgien iyuga isseotda" [BIGBANG's three-year absence justified], *Newsway Korea*, April 27, 2015, http://news.newsway.co .kr/view.php?tp=1&ud=2015042619543479601&md=20150427000238_AO.

11. Choe Hyeon-jeong, "BIGBANG, seoulkonseoteue 4Kkamera 30dae tuip cho gohwajil girong namginda" [BIGBANG to use thirty 4K cameras for their Seoul concert in order to leave high-quality documentation], *Donga-A Ilbo*, April 23, 2015, http:// sports.donga.com/3/all/20150423/70864107/2.

12. "BIGBANG dagukjeok paen, BIGBANG konseoteue deurimi ssalhwahwan jonghapseteu eungwon" [BIGBANG's multinational fans cheer the band with charity gifts], Daum, April 27, 2015, http://media.daum.net/press/newsview?newsid=2015 0427142813365.

13. The word generally references a middle-aged woman, usually married with children, while carrying a slightly derogatory connotation. According to *The K-pop Dictionary*, the negative associations include "being pushy, loud, and sometimes selfish." Kang Woosung, *K-pop Dictionary*, 12.

14. According to a South Korean press interview with BIGBANG, TOP mentioned that his band member Seungri disliked strong lighting, so during the first concert Seungri urged the staff to reduce the brightness. Yang Hyun Suk's response came in this context. Choe Jin-sil, "BIGBANG-i 'Loser'reul noraehaneun iyu" [The reason BIGBANG sings "Loser"], *Tenasia*, May 6, 2015, http://tenasia.hankyung.com/ archives/515839.

15. Ian Condry, "J-Rap, AKB48, and Miku: Japan's Musical Creativity in the Age of Free," lecture, University of California, Santa Barbara, May 6, 2015.

16. Seon Mi-gyeong, "Ogeulgeoryeodo gwaenchana, Winner-jana" [Goosebumps are OK, it's Winner!], Osen, January 31, 2015, http://osen.mt.co.kr/article/G1110068273.

17. "Ingigayo BIGBANG, yeokdaegeup keombaekmudae" [BIGBANG's comeback stage on *Ingigayo* is like nothing you've seen before], Kyeongin.com, May 3, 2015, http://www.kyeongin.com/?mod=news&act=articleView&idxno=963919&sc_cod e=&page=; "BIGBANG-ira ganeunghan yeokdaegeup mudae" [Only BIGBANG can perform on the scale of stage never seen before], *Chosun*, May 10, 2015, http://news.chosun.com/site/data/html_dir/2015/05/10/2015051001391.html.

18. Large-scale K-pop concerts staged outside Asia in 2012 included the SMTOWN Live World Tour in Los Angeles, the SBS K-pop Super Concert in Carson, California, the KBS Music Bank World Tour in Paris, and BIGBANG's Alive Galaxy Tour in London, just to name a few.

19. SM Entertainment hosted the SMTOWN Live World Tour in Paris concert at Le Zénith de Paris on June 10–11, 2011, attracting approximately fourteen thousand attendees who hailed from various parts of Europe. This was the first major K-pop concert in Europe, still largely uncharted territory for the K-pop industry, and encouraged other Korean entertainment companies and media stations to host similar events.

20. According to a Harvard Business School case study, the first KCON, with a budget of $1.1 million, did not recoup its investment. However, under the direction of CJ's vice president Miky Lee (Yi Mi-gyeong), the company executives convened a meeting in spring 2013 to decide whether CJ should continue with KCON. In the end, they concluded that the cultural industry in the initial stage needed extensive investment to pave the way for the future and decided to double the budget for 2013 and quadruple it for the 2014 convention. Elie Ofek, Kim Sang-Hoon [Gim Sang-hun], and Michael Norris, "CJ E&M: Creating a K-Culture in the U.S.," Harvard Business School Case 515-015, January 2015, http://www.hbs.edu/faculty/Pages/item.aspx?num=48426.

21. An Seok-jun, lecture, Korean Association of Music Industry Preliminary Forum, July 17, 2014, Mapo Art Center, Seoul, Korea.

22. I was invited to KCON LA 2015 by CJ America as a guest speaker to present on a panel titled "What Is K-pop?" The description of the convention/concert in this chapter is based on my personal experience of the three-day event as a participant observer.

23. As discussed in previous chapters, the permutations of live and mediatized performances in our contemporary media environment have had a profound impact on how the notion of liveness has been transformed in recent years. Philip Auslander has noted that transformation: "The progressive diminution of previous distinctions between the live and the mediatized, in which live events are becoming ever more like mediatized ones, raises for me the question of whether there really are clear-cut ontological distinctions between live forms and mediatized ones." Auslander, *Liveness*, 7.

24. Jeff Benjamin, "KCON Los Angeles and New York Draw 75,000 Total Attendees," *Billboard*, August 10, 2015, http://www.billboard.com/articles/columns/k-town/6656778/kcon-los-angeles-new-york-attendance.

25. CJ Group, *Only One*, brochure, 2013, http://www.cj.net/pr/data/brochure/CJBR _english_2015.pdf.

26. The massive economic reconstruction efforts by the Korean government to fight hunger and to jump-start light industry to supply basic necessities and consumer goods in the post–Korean War era gave Cheil Jedang a foundation for success, as the authoritarian Korean government gave nearly unlimited support to large conglomerates like Samsung, its parent company.

27. Bibigo is a chain of fusion Korean food restaurants with overseas branches in major cultural hubs (London, New York, and Los Angeles), serving in tapas style such hybrid Korean dishes as steamed buns stuffed with grilled spicy pork, pickled radish and cucumber hoisin teriyaki, green tacos with Boston lettuce, bulgogi, and pickled daikon/pepper.

28. Euny Hong, *The Birth of Korean Cool: How One Nation Is Conquering the World through Pop Culture* (New York: Picador, 2014), 127.

29. Chapter 6, "Neoliberalism on Trial," in David Harvey's *A Brief History of Neoliberalism* (Oxford: Oxford University Press, 2005), addresses various setbacks, such as environmental disasters and broadening gaps between the rich and the poor across the global economy.

30. Patricia Ticineto Clough, introduction to *The Affective Turn: Theorizing the Social*, ed. Patricia Ticineto Clough (Durham, NC: Duke University Press, 2007), 2.

31. For the 2017 KCON LA, KCON.TV was launched to livestream convention events and concerts, thereby adding another major platform for viewers to join from a remote location in real time. According to the official CJ E&M release, the KCON.TV livestream hit 180,000 views for both nights' concerts.

32. *KCONLiveChat*, Episode 2, streamed live on May 7, 2015, https://www.youtube .com/watch?v=KAmAmcbzXeY; *KCONLiveChat*, Episode 4, streamed live on May 21, 2015, https://www.youtube.com/watch?v=1ebdzgyFsL0.

33. *KCONLiveChat*, Episode 2.

34. The Instagram contest was publicized on *KCONLiveChat*, Episode 4.

35. Eileen Boris and Rhacel Salazar Parreñas, introduction to *Intimate Labors: Cultures, Technologies, and the Politics of Care*, ed. Eileen Boris and Rhacel Salazar Parreñas (Stanford, CA: Stanford Social Science, 2010), 13.

36. "KCON 2015 LA Recap," August 3, 2015, https://www.youtube.com/watch?v =eTBbBI3Pkhs.

37. pbfv, Instagram posting, accessed September 1, 2015, https://www.instagram .com/p/_9LlOqNclusA_UNpTtwItEhZeAb9BspnSYucI0/.

38. Explaining the rapid rise of reality TV shows, media studies expert Mark Andrejevic commented that this is "symptomatic of an age in which labor and leisure are growing ever harder to separate." Mark Andrejevic, *Reality TV: The Work of Being Watched* (Lanham, MD: Rowman and Littlefield, 2004).

39. SM Entertainment, for instance, has trainees sign a contract with a clause that requires them to have cosmetic surgery if the company deems it necessary.

40. According to KCON LA 2015, platinum tickets sold at $800 guaranteed access to all fan engagements and red carpet events, as well as two guaranteed participations in fan engagement. Holders of the cheapest ticket ($50) would have "a fan engagement audience pass opportunity"; these were in "limited quantities and . . . not guaranteed." For KCON LA 2017, an even higher price of $1,500 was set for a "diamond ticket," which granted unlimited access to artist engagements, red carpet events, a backstage tour, and high-touch events where fans could approach idols and touch their hands.

41. Boris and Parreñas, introduction to *Intimate Labors*, 1.

42. Sunny's Channel, "#KCON15LA #KCON15NY #SUNNYSCHANNEL," July 29, 2015, https://www.youtube.com/watch?v=p71WZwjr5-E.

43. The following vlogger brags about how Bam Bam, one of the members of GOT7, "noticed" her, thereby providing a classical example of how "fame by association" works. heyitsfeiii, "GOT7 BamBam Notices Me (KCON)," August 15, 2015, https://www.youtube.com/watch?v=A6vqTfQwHYI.

44. Michel Foucault, *The Birth of Biopolitics: Lectures at the College de France, 1978–1979* (New York: Palgrave Macmillan, 2008), 226.

45. Tom Roach, "Becoming Fungible: Queer Intimacies in Social Media," *Qui Parle: Critical Humanities and Social Sciences* 23, no. 2 (Spring/Summer 2015): 55.

46. Gregory J. Seigworth and Meissa Gregg, "An Inventory of Shimmers," in *The Affect Theory Reader*, ed. Melissa Gregg and Gregory J. Seigworth (Durham, NC: Duke University Press, 2010), 2.

47. Harvey, *Brief History of Neoliberalism*, 2, 120.

48. Seo Chan-dong, "Choe Yang-hui janggwan hallyumunhwachukje LA KCON hyeonjangchaja" [Minister Choe Yang-hui visits Korean culture festival KCON in LA], *MK News*, August 2, 2015, http://news.mk.co.kr/newsRead.php?year=2015&no=740627.

49. Harvey, *Brief History of Neoliberalism*, 85.

50. CJ E&M Official Blog, accessed June 24, 2015, link no longer available.

51. CJ E&M representative who requested anonymity, e-mail interview by author, July 14, 2015.

52. I was working as an unpaid freelance journalist for an Australia-based Web portal for Asian pop culture called HelloAsia. My duties included updating photos of the KCON LA 2017 convention and concerts on Twitter and Instagram and writing a review for the August 20, 2017, concert.

53. Literally translated as "older brother" of a younger female subject. However, the term carries specific emotional connotations. According to *The K-pop Dictionary*, it "can be used between siblings or anybody who has enough emotional intimacy with the recipient." Kang Woosung, *K-pop Dictionary*, 139.

CONCLUSION

1. I was working as an unpaid freelance journalist for HelloAsia, posting photos of the KCON 2016 convention and concert on Twitter and Instagram and writing a concert review. Kim Suk-Young, "Live Review: KCON France—Accor Hotels Arena, Paris (02.06.16)," HelloAsia, June 5, 2016, http://www.helloasia.com.au/reviews/live/kcon-france-accor-hotels-arena-paris-02-06-16/.

2. A special investigation (December 2016–February 2017), which led to Park Geun-hye's impeachment, revealed that the rather obscure John Jacobs cosmetic brand was owned by Park's confidante. The close ties with the president must have allowed the company the privilege of being featured as the representative Korean cosmetic brand at KCON Paris 2016.

3. This last phrase appeared on the back cover of the *Tourism Korea* brochure, which featured the campaign's official ambassador, Krystal, posing in Bukchon streets. The brochure was handed out by the Korea Tourism Organization during the KCON Paris 2016 convention.

4. There were three separate signing ceremonies, which took place between KOCCA and Paris & Co., Hwarang Art Pyrotechniques and Company Karnavires, and JHC Media Co. and Goden Co. During 2016, many joint projects to celebrate Korea-France cultural ties took place. KCON was arguably the largest-scale event with the loudest media coverage, but it was just one extension of the yearlong celebration.

5. Jill Dolan, *Utopia in Performance: Finding Hope at the Theater* (Ann Arbor: University of Michigan Press, 2005), 5.

6. Korean hip-hop artist Yoon Mirae in an interview with Discovery Channel noted how the shared experience of national pain and the emotional intensity that surrounded it was what drew Korean listeners to music. The December 15, 2012, interview is in the documentary *Korea Next: Finding Hallyuwood*. Likewise, the author of *The Birth of Korean Cool*, one of the recent books riding the K-pop boom in publishing, confirmed the overriding importance of *han*. Euny Hong, *Birth of Korean Cool*, 51–52. Michael Fuhr also dedicates a section in his book to an analysis of *han* as embedded in traditional Korean music as one of the foundational inspirations for Yoon Band. Fuhr, *Globalization and Popular Music*, 174–79.

7. *M Countdown*, episode 438, June 14, 2016, https://www.youtube.com/watch?v=G9Ntmr3YjgY.

WORKS CITED

An, In-yong. "K-pop, jindani piryohae" [K-pop needs a diagnosis]. *Hangyeore* 866 (June 23, 2011). http://h21.hani.co.kr/arti/culture/culture_general/29888.html.

An, Seok-jun. Lecture, Korean Association of Music Industry Preliminary Forum, July 17, 2014, Mapo Art Center, Seoul, Korea.

Anderson, Sam. "Watching People Watching People Watching." *New York Times*, November 25, 2011. http://www.nytimes.com/2011/11/27/magazine/reaction-videos.html ?pagewanted=all.

Andrejevic, Mark. *Reality TV: The Work of Being Watched.* Lanham, MD: Rowman and Littlefield, 2004.

Auslander, Philip. "Digital Liveness: A Historic-Philosophical Perspective." *PAJ: A Journal of Performance and Art* 34, no. 3 (September 2012): 3.

———. *Liveness: Performance in a Mediatized Culture.* London: Routledge, 2008.

Baek, Won-dam. *Hallyu: Dongasiaui munhwaseontaek* [Hallyu: East Asia's cultural choice]. Seoul: Pentagram, 2005.

Bak, Chang-u. "Sunwijega jeongdap?" [Is the music chart show the answer?]. *OhmyStar*, March 22, 2013. http://star.ohmynews.com/NWS_Web/OhmyStar/at_pg_m.aspx ?CNTN_CD=A0001846516&CMPT_CD=TAG_M.

Bak, Ji-hun. "3000 eokwon miusikeol sijang-ui bitgwa grimja" [Lights and shadows of a 300 billion won musical market]. *Luxmen*, March 7, 2013. http://luxmen.mk.co.kr/ view.php?sc=51100011&cm=Life&year=2013&no=173086&relatedcode=.

Bak, Su-hyeong. "Jeongbu '2020nyeon hollogeuraem segye choego doegetda'" [Government claims that it will become the world leader in hologram industry by 2020]. *ZDNetKorea*, August 27, 2014. http://www.zdnet.co.kr/news/news_view.asp?artice_ id=20140827140301.

Bak, Su-jeong, et al. "Eumakbangsong 24si, ganghaenggun aidol donghaenggi" [Spending 24 hours on a long march with idols for the music program]. Kakao, January 29, 2015. https://storyfunding.kakao.com/episode/365.

Barber, Benjamin. *Jihad vs. McWorld: Terrorism's Challenge to Democracy.* New York: Times Books, 1995.

Beebe, Roger, and Jason Middleton, eds. *Medium Cool: Music Videos from Soundies to Cellphones.* Durham, NC: Duke University Press, 2007.

Benford, Steve, and Gabriella Giannachi. *Performing Mixed Reality.* Cambridge, MA: MIT Press, 2011.

Benjamin, Jeff. "KCON Los Angeles and New York Draw 75,000 Total Attendees." *Billboard,* August 10, 2015. http://www.billboard.com/articles/columns/k-town/6656778/kcon-los-angeles-new-york-attendance.

———. "K-pop Concerts Continue to Grow outside Asia: Exclusive Infographic." *Billboard,* May 3, 2016. http://www.billboard.com/articles/columns/k-town/7350481/international-k-pop-concerts-growth-infographic.

"BIGBANG dagukjeok paen, BIGBANG konseoteue deurimi ssalhwahwan jonghapseteu eungwon" [BIGBANG's multinational fans cheer the band with charity gifts]. Daum, April 27, 2015. http://media.daum.net/press/newsview?newsid=20150427142813365.

"BIGBANG-ira ganeunghan yeokdaegeup mudae" [Only BIGBANG can perform on the scale of stage never seen before]. *Chosun,* May 10, 2015. http://news.chosun.com/site/data/html_dir/2015/05/10/2015051001391.html.

Black, Daniel. "The Virtual Idol: Producing and Consuming Digital Femininity." In *Idols and Celebrity in Japanese Media Culture,* ed. Patrick Galbraith and Jason Karlin, 209–28. New York: Palgrave Macmillan, 2012.

Blom, Ina. "The Touch through Time: Raoul Hausemann, Nam June Paik and the Transmission Technologies of the Avant-Garde." *Leonardo* 34, no. 3 (June 2001): 209–15.

Boche, Kathaleen. "Hatchets and Hairbrushes: Dance, Gender, and Improvisational Ingenuity in Cold War Western Musicals." In *The Oxford Handbook of Dance and the Popular Screen,* ed. Melissa Blanco Borelli, 337–50. Oxford: Oxford University Press, 2014.

Boellstroff, Tom, Bonnie Nardi, Celia Pearce, and T. L. Taylor. *Ethnography and Virtual Worlds: A Handbook of Methods.* Princeton, NJ: Princeton University Press, 2012.

"Bonbodokja udaeui: Baeguja muyongdan gongyeon" [Deals for readers: Bae Guja dance theater troupe performance]. *Joseon Ilbo,* November 4, 1930, 5.

Bonilla, Yarimar, and Jonathan Rosa. "#Ferguson: Digital Protest, Hashtag Ethnography, and the Radical Politics of Social Media in the United States." *American Ethnologist* 42, no. 1 (2015): 4–17.

Boris, Eileen, and Rhacel Salazar Parreñas. Introduction to *Intimate Labors: Cultures, Technologies, and the Politics of Care,* ed. Eileen Boris and Rhacel Salazar Parreñas, 1–12. Stanford, CA: Stanford Social Science, 2010.

Bourdaghs, Michael. *Sayonara Amerika, Sayonara Nippon: A Geopolitical Prehistory of J-pop.* New York: Columbia University Press, 2012.

Bradshaw, Tim. "Apple Hires Leading Virtual Reality Researcher." *Financial Times,* January 21, 2016. http://www.ft.com/intl/cms/s/0/9358ba1e-c07f-11e5-846f-79b0e3d20eaf.html.

Caldwell, John. "Convergence Television: Aggregating Form and Repurposing Content in the Culture of Conglomeration." In *Television after TV*, ed. Lynn Spigel and Jan Olsson, 40–74. Durham, NC: Duke University Press, 2004.

Canclini, Néstor García. *Hybrid Cultures: Strategies for Entering and Leaving*. Minneapolis: University of Minnesota Press, 1995.

Chatell, Alf. *Creative Value in the Digital Era: Achieving Success through Insight, Imagination, and Innovation*. New York: New York University Press, 1998.

Choe, Hyeon-jeong. "BIGBANG, seoulkonseoteue 4Kkamera 30dae tuip chogohwajil girong namginda" [BIGBANG to use thirty 4K cameras for their Seoul concert in order to leave high-quality documentation]. *Donga-A Ilbo*, April 23, 2015. http://sports.donga.com/3/all/20150423/70864107/2.

Choe, Jin-sil. "BIGBANG-i 'Loser'reul noraehaneun iyu" [The reason BIGBANG sings "Loser"]. *Tenasia*, May 6, 2015. http://tenasia.hankyung.com/archives/515839.

Choe, Su-mun. "Munchebu saeopseo 'K'myeongching ppaenda" ["K" is disappearing from project titles supported by the Ministry of Culture, Sports, and Tourism]. Daum, December 19, 2016. http://v.media.daum.net/v/20161219175924498.

Choi, JungBong [Choe, Jeong-bong]. "Hallyu versus Hallyu-hwa: Cultural Phenomenon versus Institutional Campaign." In *Hallyu 2.0: The Korean Wave in the Age of Social Media*, ed. Lee Sangjoon and Abé Nornes, 31–52. Ann Arbor: University of Michigan Press, 2015.

Choi, JungBong [Choe, Jeong-bong], and Roald Maliangkay, eds. *K-pop: The International Rise of the Korean Music Industry*. New York: Routledge, 2015.

"Christie Projectors Make the First Holographic Opera a Reality." Christie. N.d. Accessed January 12, 2015. http://www.christiedigital.co.uk/emea/business/visual-solutions -case-studies/visual-solutions-application-stories/Pages/telesio-holographic-opera .aspx.

Chung, Inho [Jeong, In-ho]. "Broadband, the Information Society, and National Systems." In *Global Broadband Battles: Why the U.S. and Europe Lag While Asia Leads*, ed. Martin Fransman, 87–108. Stanford, CA: Stanford Business Books, 2006.

CJ Group. *Only One*. Brochure. 2013. http://www.cj.net/pr/data/brochure/CJBR_english _2015.pdf.

Clough, Patricia Ticineto. Introduction to *The Affective Turn: Theorizing the Social*, ed. Patricia Ticineto Clough, 1–33. Durham, NC: Duke University Press, 2007.

Condry, Ian. "J-Rap, AKB48, and Miku: Japan's Musical Creativity in the Age of Free." Lecture, University of California, Santa Barbara, May 6, 2015.

Conquergood, Dwight. "Performance Studies: Interventions and Radical Research." *Drama Review* 46, no. 2 (Summer 2002): 145–56.

Couldry, Nick. "Liveness, 'Reality' and the Mediated Habitus from Television to the Mobile Phone." *Communications Review* 7, no. 4 (2004): 353–61.

Davis, Lee. *Scandals and Follies: The Rise and Fall of the Great Broadway Revue.* New York: Limelight Editions, 2000.

Days, Peter. "Korea Change." Global Business, BBC World Service, March 9, 2014. http://www.bbc.co.uk/programmes/p01t4qqc.

De Looper, Christina. "Korean Researchers Say They've Created the World's First True 3D Hologram." *Tech Times*, December 3, 2015. http://www.techtimes.com/articles /113267/20151203/korean-researchers-theyve-create-worlds-first-true-3d-hologram .htm.

Dickinson, Kay. "Music Video and Synaesthetic Possibility." In *Medium Cool: Music Videos from Soundies to Cell Phones*, ed. Roger Beebe and Jason Middleton, 13–29. Durham, NC: Duke University Press, 2007.

Dixon, Steve. *Digital Performance: A History of New Media in Theater, Dance, Performance Art, and Installation.* Cambridge, MA: MIT Press, 2007.

"Dokchangjeogin aidieoro gayogyeui heureumeul bakkueonoeun SM ateu direkteo Min Hui-jin" [SM art director Min Hui-jin changes trends in music market with her creative ideas]. *Soul Dresser*, January 27, 2014. http://blog.daum.net/_blog/BlogType View.do?blogid=03SAW&articleno=3410&categoryId=0&regdt=20140127011701.

Dolan, Jill. *Utopia in Performance: Finding Hope at the Theater.* Ann Arbor: University of Michigan Press, 2005.

Epstein, Stephen, with James Turnbull. "Girls' Generation? Gender, (Dis)Empowerment, and K-pop." In *The Korean Cultural Reader,* ed. Kim Kyung-Hyun [Gim Gyeong-hyeon] and Choe Youngmin [Choe Yeong-min], 314–36. Durham, NC: Duke University Press, 2014.

Evans, David, Andrei Hagiu, and Richard Schmalensee. *Invisible Engines: How Software Platforms Drive Innovation and Transform Industries.* Cambridge, MA: MIT Press, 2006.

Flatley, Joseph L. "K-pop Takes America: How South Korea's Music Machine Is Conquering the World." *Verge*, October 18, 2012. http://www.theverge.com/2012/10/18/ 3516562/k-pop-invades-america-south-korea-pop-music-factory.

Foucault, Michel. *The Birth of Biopolitics: Lectures at the College de France, 1978–1979.* New York: Palgrave Macmillan, 2008.

Fransman, Martin. Introduction to *Global Broadband Battles: Why the U.S. and Europe Lag While Asia Leads*, ed. Martin Fransman, 1–57. Stanford, CA: Stanford Business Books, 2006.

Fuhr, Michael. *Globalization and Popular Music in South Korea: Sounding Out K-pop.* London: Routledge, 2016.

Funk, Jeffrey. *Technology Change and the Rise of New Industries.* Stanford, CA: Stanford Business Books, 2013.

Gang, Tae-yeong, and Yun Tae-jin. *Hanguk TV yeneung orak peurogeuraemui byeon-*

cheongwa baljeon [A history of TV entertainment and variety programs in Korea]. Seoul: Haneul, 2002.

Garrahan, Matthew. "Google Invests in YouTube Studio in LA." *Financial Times,* July 12, 2013. http://www.ft.com/cms/s/2/3f4c846a-e9c1-11e2-bf03-00144feabdc0.html#slide0.

G-Dragon. "G-Dragon ('Who You?') M/V." YouTube, November 13, 2013. http://www.youtube.com/watch?V=dofk7Eanm3I.

"Generation Like." *Frontline,* February 18, 2014, PBS.

Giannachi, Gabriella. *Virtual Theatres: An Introduction.* London: Routledge, 2004.

Gim, A-reum. "BIGBANG, 3nyeonui gongbaekgien iyuga isseotda" [BIGBANG's three-year absence justified]. *Newsway Korea,* April 27, 2015. http://news.newsway.co.kr/view.php?tp=1&ud=2015042619543479601&md=20150427000238_AO.

Gim, Dong-hwan. "MBC, 'Mudaeeseo imman ppeonggeutaneun aidol toechul'" [MBC, "We will expel idols who lip-sync on stage]. *Segye Ilbo,* July 1, 2014. http://www.segye.com/content/html/2014/07/01/20140701002566.html.

Gim, Gi-beom. "Gim Gi-beom SM Entertainment A&R direkteowa inteobyu" [Interview with Gim Gi-beom, director, artist and repertoire department, SM Entertainment]. *Hangyeong News,* January 10, 2013. http://jobnstory.com/news/view.html?section=7609&category=7613&no=1224.

Gim, Hui-jeong. "Hanguk myujikeorui byeoncheongwa myujikeol uisangui teukseonge gwanhan gochal / A consideration on the change of Korean musical and the characteristic of music costume [*sic*]]." [Bilingual]. *Bogsigmunhwayeongu / Research Journal of the Costume Culture* 18, no. 6 (2010): 1112–26.

Gim, Hyeon-sik. "Daechebulga daseon namja, iraeseo BIGBANG BIGBANG haneunguna" [Irreplaceable five men—BIGBANG is BIGBANG]. *No Cut News,* April 27, 2017. http://www.nocutnews.co.kr/news/4404557.

Gim, Seong-hui. "Hanguk chochangi miusikeol undong yeongu" [A study of early Korean musicals]. *Hanguk Geukyesulhakhoe Hanguk Yesul Yeongu* 14 (2001): 86.

Gim, Su-jin. "Musaekeuro bijeonaeneun osaek imiji miusik bidio gamdok Jang Jae-heok" [Painting colorful image with no colors: MV director Jang Jae-hyuk]. *Scene Playbill,* November 2008, 28.

Gim, Tae-gyu. "Creative Economy Loses Steam." *Korea Times,* December 1, 2016. http://www.koreatimes.co.kr/www/common/vpage-pt.asp?categorycode=123&newsidx=219313.

Gim, Won-gyeom. "Sutjaro bon byeonhameomneun keipap hwangje 'BIGBANG'" [BIGBANG, the unchallenged emperors of K-pop according to statistics]. *Dong-A Ilbo,* July 20, 2016. http://sports.donga.com/3/all/20160719/79284955/.

Gim, Yeong-hui. "Ilje gangjeomgi rebyuchum yeongu" [Study of revue dance during the Japanese colonial period]. *Gongyeon-gwa Ribyu* 65 (June 2009): 35–51.

Grobart, Sam. "How Samsung Became the World's No. 1 Smartphone Maker." *Bloom-*

berg News, March 28, 2013. https://www.bloomberg.com/ news/articles/2013-03-28/ how-samsung-became-the-worlds-no-dot-1-smartphone-maker.

Gwon, Seok-jeong. "Gayopeuro sunwije sihaeng handal . . . aidol wiju bangsong yeo-jeon" [Music programs still centered on idols since music charts were introduced a month ago]. *Tenasia*, May 23, 2013. http://tenasia.hankyung.com/archives/134733.

———. "Geudeuri bon K-pop 1 DSign Music 'keipap jakgogeneun beopchigi jonjaehaji anneunda'" [K-pop according to outsiders' perspective part 1, DSign Music: There are no set rules in K-pop composition]. *Tenasia*, October 10, 2014. http://tenasia .hankyung.com/archives/339585.

———. "Seo Tae-ji-wa 'K-Papseuta' geurigo 'Seupeiseu Gonggam'" [Seo Tae-ji, "K-pop Star" and "Space Gong-gam"]. *Tenasia*, April 21, 2014. http://tenasia.hankyung.com /archives/244381.

———. "SMTOWN COEX Artium jikjeop gaseo noraboni" [Firsthand experience of SMTOWN COEX Artium]. *Hangyeong News*, January 19, 2015. http://news.hank yung.com/article/2015011905894.

Ha, Eun-seon. "Hangugui heungi munhwabaljeonui hwallyeokso" [Korea's heung vital-izes cultural prosperity]. *Korea Times*, November 17, 2011. http://www.koreatimes .com/article/696517.

Hannigan, Neil. "Interview: Ex-SME Trainee Neil Hannigan on Auditions, Contracts, and Trainee Life." Interview by Kpopalypse. June 12, 2015. http://www.asianjunkie .com/2015/06/interview-ex-sme-trainee-neil-hannigan-on-auditions-contracts -and-trainee-life/.

Harvey, David. *A Brief History of Neoliberalism*. Oxford: Oxford University Press, 2005.

———. "A Brief History of Neoliberalism." In *The Globalization Reader*, ed. Franck J. Lechner and John Boli, 5th ed., 71–76. Malden, MA: Wiley, 2015.

Haselton, Todd, and Josh Lipton. "See How Apple Will Erase the Line between Reality and Your iPhone." CNBC.com, August 29, 2017. https://www.cnbc.com/2017/08/29/ iphone-8-augmented-reality-apps-from-ikea-food-network-and-more.html.

Heathfield, Adrian, and Tehching Hsieh. *Out of Now: The Life Works of Tehching Hsieh*. Cambridge, MA: MIT Press, 2015.

Heo, Yun-hui. "Hanguginui munhwa DNA 3: heung. Pansori myeongchang An Suk-seon, aidol gasu IU" [Korea's cultural DNA (Part 3): Heung. Pansori singer An Suk-seon and idol singer IU]. *Joseon Ilbo*, September 20, 2012. http://pann.news.nate.com/ info/254111641.

Hesselink, Nathan. *P'ungmul: South Korean Drumming and Dance*. Chicago: University of Chicago Press, 2006.

heyitsfeiii. "GOT7 BamBam Notices Me (KCON)." August 15, 2015. https://www.youtube .com/watch?v=A6vqTfQwHYI.

Hischak, Thomas. *Through the Screen Door: What Happened to the Broadway Musical When It Went to Hollywood*. Lanham, MD: Scarecrow Press, 2004.

Hong, Euny. *The Birth of Korean Cool: How One Nation Is Conquering the World through Pop Culture*. New York: Picador, 2014.

Hong, Grace Danbi. "BIGBANG Drops Blockbuster Trailer for 'Made' World Tour." MWave. April 17, 2015. http://m.mwave.interest.me/en/kpop-news/article-print /91341/.

Hong, Jeong-pyo. *Kiwoom Jeungkwon Report*, May 10, 2015.

"How 'Gangnam Style' Broke YouTube's Counter." *Economist,* December 10, 2014. http:// www.economist.com/blogs/economist-explains/2014/12/economist-explains-6.

Howard, Keith. "Politics, Parodies, and the Paradox of Psy's 'Gangnam Style.'" *Romanian Journal of Sociological Studies* 1 (2015): 13–29.

Howkins, John. *The Creative Economy: How People Make Money from Ideas*. New York: Penguin, 2002.

Ihde, Don. *Bodies in Technology*. Minneapolis: University of Minnesota Press, 2002.

Im, Hyeon-wu. "Eumaksijang sunwi bomyeon jeojakgwon seonjingunk boyeoyo" [The rankings of the music market size show which countries have advanced copyrights protection]. *Hankyeong Ne*ws, February 3, 2017. http://news.hankyung.com/article /2017020395501.

Im, Se-yeong. "G-Dragon singok 'niga mwonde' myujik bidio chwaryeonghyeonjang" [Shooting of G-Dragon's new music video "Who You?" takes place]. *Newsen*, October 5, 2013. http://www.newsen.com/news_view.php?uid=201310052312132610.

"Ingigayo BIGBANG, yeokdaegeup keombaekmudae" [BIGBANG's comeback stage on *Ingigayo* is like nothing you've seen before]. Kyeongin.com, May 3, 2015. http://www .kyeongin.com/?mod=news&act=articleView&idxno=963919&sc_cod e=&page=.

Jackson, Shannon. "Kleenex Citizens and the Performance of Undisposability." In *Performance, Politics and Activism*, ed. Peter Lichenfels and John Rouse, 237–52. London: Palgrave Macmillan, 2013.

Jackson, Shannon, and Marianne Weems. *The Builders Association: Performance and Media in Contemporary Theater*. Cambridge, MA: MIT Press, 2015.

Jang, Gyu-Su. "Hallyuui eowongwa sayonge gwanhan yeongu" [Study of Korean waves: The origin and the usage [*sic*]]. *Hangug-kontencheu-haghoe-nonmunji* 11, no. 9 (November 2011): 166–73.

Jang, Seong-eun. "YG Entertainment keurieitibeu direkteo Jang Seong-eun siljangeul mannada" [Meeting YG's creative director Jang Seong-eun]. Interview. *Hanwha Day's*, October 23, 2013. http://blog.hanwhadays.com/2194.

Jenkins, Henry. *Fans, Bloggers, and Gamers: Exploring Participatory Culture*. New York: New York University Press, 2006.

Jeong, Sun-il, and Jang Han-seong. *Hangung TV 40nyeonui baljachwi* [Forty-year history of Korean TV]. Seoul: Hanul Academy, 2000.

Ji, Su-hui. "Jeongbu, hollogeuraem saneobyukseong bakcha" [Korean government plans to stimulate hologram industry]. Korean Economy TV, August 27, 2014.

Jin, Dal Yong. *New Korean Wave: Transnational Cultural Power in the Age of Social Media.* Urbana: University of Illinois Press, 2016.

Jin, Jung-eon. "Li Hyori 'Anymotion' eun gwanggoga anida" [Li Hyori says 'Anymotion' is not advertisement]. *Chosun,* March 31, 2005. http://www.chosun.com/culture/news /200503/200503310244.html.

Jo, Jong-won. "SM Entertainment, myujikeoreseoneun ajik meoreotda" [SM Entertainment, still a long way to go in musicals]. Newsis, June 17, 2014. http://www.news is.com/ar_detail/view.html?ar_id=NISX20140616_0012985416&cID=10601& pID=10600.

Joo, Jeongsuk [Ju, Jeong-suk]. "Transnationalization of Korean Popular Culture and the Rise of 'Pop Nationalism' in Korea." *Journal of Popular Culture* 44, no. 3 (2011): 489–504.

Jung, Sun [Jeong, Seon]. "Fan Activism, Cybervigilantism, and Othering Mechanisms in K-pop Fandom." In "Transformative Works and Fan Activism," ed. Henry Jenkins and Sangita Shresthova, special issue, *Transformative Works and Cultures* 10 (2012). http://journal.transformativeworks.org/index.php/twc/article/view/300/287.

———. *Korean Masculinities and Transnational Consumption: Yonsama, Rain, Old Boy, K-pop Idols.* Hong Kong: Hong Kong University Press, 2011.

Kang, David C. *Crony Capitalism: Corruption and Development in South Korea and the Philippines.* Cambridge: Cambridge University Press, 2003.

Kang, Inkyu [Gang, In-gyu]. "The Political Economy of Idols: South Korea's Neoliberal Restructuring and Its Impact on the Entertainment Labour Force." In *K-pop: The International Rise of the Korean Music Industry,* ed. Choi JungBong [Choe Jeong-bong] and Roald Maliangkay, 51–65. New York: Routledge, 2015.

Kang, Woosung [Gang, U-seong]. *The K-pop Dictionary.* New Ampersand, 2016.

KCONLiveChat. Episode 2. Streamed live May 7, 2015. https://www.youtube.com/watch ?v=KAmAmcbzXeY.

KCONLiveChat. Episode 4. Streamed live May 21, 2015. https://www.youtube.com/ watch?v=1ebdzgyFsL0.

"KCON 2015 LA Recap." August 3, 2015. https://www.youtube.com/watch?v=eTBbBI3 Pkhs.

Kim, Ji-soo [Gim, Ji-su]. "Janice Min Says K-pop Needs Authenticity." *Korea Times,* October 8, 2014. http://www.koreatimes.co.kr/www/news/culture/2015/05/135_165941 .html.

Kim, Sohee [Gim, So-hui]. "The 4.7 Billion K-pop Industry Chases Its 'Michael Jackson Moment': YouTube Is Turning South Korea into a Pop Culture Juggernaut." August 22, 2017. https://www.bloomberg.com/news/articles/2017-08-22/the-4-7-billion-k -pop -industry-chases-its-michael-jackson-moment.

Kim, Suk-Young [Gim, Suk-yeong]. "Live Review: KCON France—Accor Hotels Arena,

Paris." HelloAsia, June 5, 2016. http://www.helloasia.com.au/reviews/live/kcon-france-accor-hotels-arena-paris-02-06-16/.

———. "Liveness: Performance of Ideology and Technology in the Changing Media Environment." In *Oxford Research Encyclopedia of Literature*, March 29, 2017. Oxford University Press. http://literature.oxfordre.com/view/10.1093/acrefore/9780190201098.001.0001/acrefore-9780190201098-e-76.

Korea Creative Content Agency. *Hanguk eumak suchulgwa haeoe eijeonsi hyeonhwang siltaejosa* [Report on the current state of the Korean music export and overseas agencies]. June 3, 2015. Booklet. http://www.kocca.kr/cop/bbs/view/B0000147/1825358.do?menuNo=201825#.Korea Creative Content Agency Library, Naju.

———. "Gungnae eumak saneop hyeonhwang" [The state of the domestic music market]. Music Industry White Paper, 2011. Published on KOCCA website, December 17, 2012. http://www.kocca.kr/cop/bbs/view/B0000146/1779432.do?searchCnd=&searchWrd=&cateTp1=&cateTp2=&useAt=&menuNo=201826&categorys=0&subcate=0&cateCode=&type=&instNo=0&questionTp=&uf_Setting=&recovery=&pageIndex=12.

Korean Cable TV Association. *Keibeul TV yeoksa, 1995–2015* [Cable TV history, 1995–2015]. Seoul: Korean Cable TV Association, 2015.

"Kpop Most Beautiful Oceans and Their Fanchants." May 11, 2016. https://www.youtube.com/watch?v=f0bJlmm5qGg.

Lee, Hi [Yi, Ha-i]. "Hold My Hand." March 8, 2016. https://www.youtube.com/watch?v=cuUEnho33so.

Lee, Hyun Jung [Yi, Hyeon-jeong]. "Broadway as the Superior 'Other': Situating South Korean Theater in the Era of Globalization." *Journal of Popular Culture* 45, no. 2 (2012): 320–39.

Lie, John. *K-pop: Popular Music, Cultural Amnesia, and Economic Innovation in South Korea.* Berkeley: University of California Press, 2015.

Madison, D. Soyni. *Critical Ethnography: Method, Ethics, and Performance.* Thousand Oaks, CA: Sage Publications, 2005.

Maher, Bill. "Bill Maher Reflects on Humor, Politics in Wild 2016 Election." Interview. *Here and Now,* June 6, 2016, NPR.

"Making of 'Who You?' M/V." YouTube, January 20, 2014. https://www.youtube.com/watch?v=DU61Cplg57k.

Malecki, Edward J., and Bruno Moriset. *The Digital Economy: Business Organization, Production Processes and Regional Developments.* London: Routledge, 2008.

Maliangkay, Roald. "The Popularity of Individualism: The Seo Taiji Phenomenon in the 1990s." In *The Korean Popular Culture Reader*, ed. Kim Kyung Hyun [Gim Gyeong-hyeon] and Choe Youngmin [Choe Yeong-min], 296–313. Durham, NC: Duke University Press, 2014.

———. "Same Look through Different Eyes: Korea's History of Uniform Pop Music

Acts." In *K-pop: The International Rise of the Korean Music Industry,* ed. Choi Jung-Bong [Choe Jeong-bong] and Roald Maliangkay, 19–34. New York: Routledge, 2015.

Masnick, Mike. "Korean Music Industry Embraces the Future While US Counterparts Fight It." *Techdirt,* October 22, 2012. https://www.techdirt.com/articles/20121018/00360120743/korean-music-industry-embraces-future-while-us-counterparts-fight-it.shtml.

McConnell, Fred. "YouTube Is 10 Years Old: The Evolution of Online Video." *Guardian,* February 13, 2015. http://www.theguardian.com/technology/2015/feb/13/youtube-10-years-old-evolution-of-online-video.

M Countdown. Episode 438. June 14, 2016. https://www.youtube.com/watch?v=G9Ntmr3YjgY.

Ministry of Culture, Sports, and Tourism. "Daejungmunhwa saneop geullobeol gyeongjaengnyeok ganghwa bangan" [Agenda for the enhancement of global competitiveness of Korean popular culture], June 23, 2011, 1–3. http://www.mcst.go.kr/web/s_notice/press/pressView.jsp?pSeq=11436.

Moss, Emma-Lee. "Robots, Rental Popstars and Spotify Domination: Is This the Future of Music?" *Guardian,* January 26, 2015. http://www.theguardian.com/music/2015/jan/26/emmy-the-great-music-future-predictions.

Mun-meong-ui theqoo. "Tiffany Liked the Concept of 'Twinkle.'" Accessed December 15, 2014. Link no longer available.

Nye, Joseph, and Kim Youna. "Soft Power and the Korean Wave." In *The Korean Wave: Korean Media Go Global,* ed. Kim Youna, 31–42. New York: Routledge, 2013.

O, Dae-seok. "Lee Su-man Yang Hyun Suk, hollogeuraem gongyeoneseo daebak kkum kiwo" [Lee Su-man, Yang Hyun Suk dream of big success in hologram business]. *Business Post,* February 24, 2015. http://www.businesspost.co.kr/news/articleView.html?idxno=9795.

OECD (Organisation for Economic Co-operation and Development). *OECD Communications Outlook 2013.* Paris: OECD Publishing, 2013, 178. doi: http://dx.doi.org/10.1787/comms_outlook-2013-en.

Ofek, Elie, Kim Sang-Hoon [Gim Sang-hun], and Michael Norris. "CJ E&M: Creating a K-culture in the U.S." Harvard Business School Case 515-015, January 2015. http://www.hbs.edu/faculty/Pages/item.aspx?num=48426.

Olewitz, Cloe. "Korean Scientists Have Developed a Legitimate 3D Hologram You Can View from Any Angle." *Digital Trends,* December 7, 2015. http://www.digitaltrends.com/cool-tech/researchers-develop-real-floating-3d-hologram/.

Ong, Aiwa, and Donald Nonini. Introduction to *Ungrounded Empires: The Cultural Politics of Modern Chinese Transnationalism,* ed. Aiwa Ong and Donald Nonini, 3–33. New York: Routledge, 1997.

Packer, Randall, and Ken Jordan, eds. *Multimedia: From Wagner to Virtual Reality.* New York: Norton, 2001.

Park, E. Chan [Bak, Chan-eung]. *Voices from the Straw Mat: Toward an Ethnography of Korean Story Singing*. Honolulu: University of Hawai'i Press, 2003.

Park, Jin-young [Bak, Jin-yeong]. Interview by Son Seok-hui. *News Room*, JTBC, May 5, 2015.

Parker-Starbuck, Jennifer. *Cyborg Theatre: Corporeal/Technological Intersections in Multimedia Performance*. 2nd ed. New York: Palgrave Macmillan, 2014.

Patinkin, Sheldon. *No Legs, No Jokes, No Chance: A History of the American Musical Theater*. Evanston, IL: Northwestern University Press, 2008.

Phelan, Peggy. *Unmarked: The Politics of Performance*. London: Routledge, 1993.

Pred, Allan, and Michael Watts. *Reworking Modernity: Capitalisms and Symbolic Discontent*. New Brunswick, NJ: Rutgers University Press, 1992.

"President Park Sets the Tone for PP14." *ITU News*, November 6, 2014. https://itunews .itu.int/En/5547-President-Park-sets-the-tone-for-PP14.note.aspx.

Pungmuneuro deuleotsso [Heard it through the grapevine]. Episode 15. Channel A. January 26, 2016.

Roach, Tom. "Becoming Fungible: Queer Intimacies in Social Media." *Qui Parle: Critical Humanities and Social Sciences* 23, no. 2 (Spring/Summer 2015): 55–87.

Ross, Andrew. *Nice Work if You Can Get It*. New York: New York University Press, 2010.

Russell, Mark James. *K-pop Now! The Korean Music Revolution*. Singapore: Tuttle, 2014.

S, Diana. "K-pop Label SM Entertainment to Open 3D Hologram Theater at Japanese Theme Park Huis Ten Bosch." *KpopStarz*, February 3, 2015. http://www.kpopstarz .com/articles/170894/20150203/sm-hologram-theater-japan.htm.

Sack, Daniel. *After Live: Possibility, Potentiality, and the Future of Performance*. Ann Arbor: University of Michigan Press, 2015.

Santus, Rex. "Windows Holographic: Microsoft Goes Full Throttle into Virtual Reality." *Mashable*, January 21, 2015. http://mashable.com/2015/01/21/windows-holo graphic/.

Savran, David. "Trafficking in Transnational Brands: The New 'Broadway-Style' Musical." *Theater Survey* 55, no. 3 (September 2014): 318–42.

Seabrook, John. "Factory Girls." *New Yorker*, October 8, 2012. http://www.newyorker .com/magazine/2012/10/08/factory-girls-2.

———. *The Song Machine: Inside the Hit Factory*. New York: Norton.

Sedgwick, Eve Kosofsky. *Touching Feeling*. Durham, NC: Duke University Press, 2003.

Seigworth, Gregory J., and Melissa Gregg. "An Inventory of Shimmers." In *The Affect Theory Reader*, ed. Melissa Gregg and Gregory J. Seigworth, 1–28. Durham, NC: Duke University Press, 2010.

Seo, Chan-dong. "Choe Yang-hui janggwan hallyumunhwachukje LA KCON hyeon-jangchaja" [Minister Choe Yang-hui visits Korean culture festival KCON in LA]. *MK News*, August 2, 2015. http://news.mk.co.kr/newsRead.php?year=2015&no=740627.

Seo, Yeong-jin. "Twitter, Teheran Valley-e hangukjisa seollip" [Twitter establishes a

Korean branch in the Teheran Valley]. News1, October 11, 2012. http://news1.kr/articles/?848346.

Seon, Mi-gyeong. "Ogeulgeoryeodo gwaenchana, Winner-jana [Goosebumps are OK, it's Winner!] Osen, January 31, 2015. http://osen.mt.co.kr/article/G1110068273.

Shin, Gi-wook [Sin, Gi-uk], and Choi Joon Nak [Choe Jun-nak]. *Global Talent: Skilled Labor as Social Talent in South Korea.* Stanford, CA: Stanford University Press, 2015.

Shin, Haerin [Sin, Hae-rin]. "The Dynamics of K-pop Spectatorship: The Tablo Witch-Hunt and Its Double-Edged Sword of Enjoyment." In *K-pop: The International Rise of the Korean Music Industry*, ed. Choi JungBong [Choe Jeong-bong] and Roald Maliangkay, 133–45. New York: Routledge, 2015.

Shin, Hyun-joon [Sin, Hyeon-jun]. *Gayo, K-pop geurigo geu neomeo* [Gayo, K-pop and beyond]. Seoul: Dolbaege, 2013.

"SNSD Black Ocean." YouTube, February 3, 2017. https://www.youtube.com/watch?v=6VWkSgDZ0g4.

Sohn, Jie-Ae [Son, Ji-ae]. "K-pop Mania: South Korea's Place under the Sun." Public lecture at Annenberg School for Communications and Journalism, University of Southern California, November 12, 2014.

———. "The Worldwide Reach of K-pop." Lecture, K-pop and Its Global Reach Symposium, April 18, 2015, University of California, Santa Barbara.

Son, Nam-won. *YG-neun dareuda* [YG is different]. Seoul: Influential, 2015.

Song, Jesook [Song, Je-suk]. *South Koreans in the Debt Crisis: The Creation of a Neoliberal Welfare Society.* Durham, NJ: Duke University Press, 2009.

Spigel, Lynn. *Make Room for TV: Television and the Family Ideal in Postwar America.* Chicago: University of Chicago Press, 1992.

Sseoljeon. Episode 17. JTBC. June 20, 2013.

Steen, Shannon. "The Creativity Complex." Unpublished manuscript. N.d. Accessed November 1, 2016.

Sunny's Channel. "#KCON15LA #KCON15NY #SUNNYSCHANNEL." July 29, 2015. https://www.youtube.com/watch?v=p71WZwjr5-E.

Super Junior. "Evanescence." October 27, 2014. https://www.youtube.com/watch?v=dzhOqwF8qHg.

———. "This Is Love." October 22, 2014. https://www.youtube.com/watch?v=utmykx9RUEw.

The TaeTiSeo. Episode 5. Onstyle (CJ E&M Cable Channel). September 30, 2014.

———. Episode 6. OnStyle (CJ E&M Cable Channel). September 30, 2014.

Taylor, Timothy. *The Sounds of Capitalism: Advertising, Music, and the Conquest of Culture.* Chicago: University of Chicago Press, 2012.

"Top 3 K-pop Creepy Stories." KpopStarz, July 3, 2013. http://www.kpopstarz.com/articles/33316/20130703/top-3-creepy-k-pop-fan-stories.htm.

"13 Extreme Accounts of Sasaeng Fans." Allkpop, July 6, 2015. http://www.allkpop.com/article/2015/07/13-extreme-accounts-of-sasaeng-fans.

Ueno, Toshiya. "Techno-Orientalism and Media-Tribalism: On Japanese Animation and Rave Culture." *Third Text* 47 (Summer 1999): 95–106.

"Urban Dream Capsule Makes United States Debut at Sears on State Presented by Performing Arts Chicago." PRNewswire, Chicago, March 5, 2001. http://searsholdings.mediaroom.com/index.php?s=16310&item=24816.

van Djick, José. *The Culture of Connectivity: A Critical History of Social Media.* Oxford: Oxford University Press, 2013.

Vernalis, Carol. *Unruly Media: YouTube, Music Video, and the New Digital Cinema.* Oxford: Oxford University Press, 2013.

Winner. "Baby Baby." January 31, 2016. https://www.youtube.com/watch?v=jBBy2p5EQhs.

———. "I'm Young." January 31, 2016. https://www.youtube.com/watch?v=P79G22cJe74.

Winnubst, Shannon. *Way Too Cool: Selling Out Race and Ethics.* New York: Columbia University Press, 2015.

Witt, Stephen. *How Music Got Free: The End of an Industry, the Turn of the Century, and the Patient Zero of Piracy.* New York: Viking, 2015.

YG Family. "G-Dragon 'Niga mwonde' myujikbidio V.I.P chwaryeong yeongsang eomnodeu bangbeop annae" [G Dragon, "Who You?" music video: V.I.P. how to upload footage]. October 6, 2013. http://www.ygfamily.com/notice/NList.asp?LANG-DRAGONIV=K&IDX=5263&STYPE=B.

Yi, Dong-hu. "Transmedia hwangyeonggwa 'Me-TV'-ui uimi" [Transmedia environment and the implications of "Me-TV"]. In *TV ihuui television* [Television after TV], ed. Hanguk bangsong hakheo munhwayeonguheo, 51–81. Seoul: Hanul Academy, 2012.

Yi, Eun-jeong. "Dagukjeok jakgokga SM gok hamkke mandeunda: K-pop jejak jinhwa" [Multinational composers make SM songs together: The evolution of K-pop producing]. *Yonhap News*, October 6, 2013. http://www.yonhapnews.co.kr/culture/2013/10/06/0901000000AKR20131006067700005.HTML.

Yi, Jeong-a. "G-Dragon, Niga mwonde myubiseo boyu jadongcha gonggae" [G-Dragon reveals his own car in a new music video, "Who You?"]. ETV Korea, November 13, 2013. http://news.sbs.co.kr/news/endPage.do?news_id=N1002077697.

———. "Psy, BIGBANG, 2NE1 hollogeuraem gongyeon, ilbone cheot seon" [Psy, BIGBANG, 2NE1 hologram debuts in Japan]. *SBS News*, January22, 2014. http://news.sbs.co.kr/news/endPage.do?news_id=N1002195952.

Yi, Su-ji. "Samsung Anycall Anyclub vs. LG Cyon aidieo" [Samsung Anycall Anyclub vs. LG Cyon idea]. *Korea Advertisers Association,* November 12, 2005, 30.

Yoon, Jung-kang [Yun Jeong-gang]. *Gugak: Traditional Korean Music Today.* Elizabeth, NJ: Hollym, 2014.

Yoon, Mirae [Yun Mi-rae]. Interview. In *Finding Hallyuwood: Korea Next*. Discovery Channel, December 15, 2012.

"YouTubers React to K-pop 2." Fine Brothers Entertainment (YouTube channel), August 21, 2014. https://www.youtube.com/watch?v=y2VI1fGKcU8.

Yu, Jae-hyeok. "SM Lee Su-man Hoejang 'SM-i saenggakaneun miraeneun selleobeuriti, roboteu-ui sesang'" [Future as envisioned by SM is one filled with celebrities and robots, says SM CEO Lee Su-man]. *Hangyeong News*, October 22, 2015. http://www.hankyung.com/news/app/newsview.php?aid=2015102203541.

Yu, Kun-ha [Yu Geon-ha]. "Korea Can't Just Order Up Creative Economy." *Korea Herald*, May 31, 2013. http://www.koreaherald.com/view.php?ud=20130531000240.

Yun, Jae-sik. *Hallyuwa bangsong yeongsang kontencheu maketing"* [Hallyu and the marketing of broadcasting media content]. Seoul: Communication Books, 2004.

Yun, Yeong-cheol. "Hangugui heung baeunda! Hoju gugak saminbang" [Australian trio to learn Korean *heung* through traditional music]. YTN, June 22, 2014. http://www.ytn.co.kr/_ln/0104_201406220007351069.

Zheng, Yan. "Lighting the Future Takes More Than Just a Few Bright Ideas." *International Year of Light Blog*, May 5, 2015. http://light2015blog.org/2015/05/05/lighting-the-future-takes-more-than-just-bright-ideas/.

Žižek, Slavoj. *Organs without Bodies*. New York: Routledge, 2004.

Zradeo. [Original Korean title not available] "TaeTiSeo's 'Twinkle' Is a Gem, but How Successful Is It?" N.d. Accessed November 15, 2014. Link no longer available.

INDEX

Page numbers in italics refer to illustrative material.